ASA Essays in Social Anthropology

GENERAL EDITOR: EDWIN ARDENER

VOLUME 3
*Numerical Techniques
in Social Anthropology*

NUMERICAL TECHNIQUES IN SOCIAL ANTHROPOLOGY

edited by J. Clyde Mitchell

A Publication of the
Institute for the Study of Human Issues
Philadelphia

Manufactured in the United States of America

Library of Congress Cataloging in Publication Data:

Main entry under title:

Numerical techniques in social anthropology.

(ASA essays in social anthropology; v. 3)
Papers originally presented at a conference entitled New directions in social
anthropology, held in Oxford, Eng., July 9, 1973.
Includes bibliographies and index.
1. Mathematical anthropology—Congresses. 2. Ethnology—Mathematics—
Congresses. I. Mitchell, James Clyde. II. Series: Association of Social Anthro-
pologists of the Commonwealth. ASA essays in social anthropology; v. 3.
GN34.3.M3N85   306′.01′51   80–11082
ISBN 0–915980–93–2
ISBN 0–89727–013–4 pbk.

This publication was made possible in part by Grant BNS–7915835 from the
Anthropology Program of the National Science Foundation.

For information, write:

Director of Publications
ISHI
3401 Science Center
Philadelphia, Pennsylvania 19104
U.S.A.

General Editor's Note

This is the last of the volumes resulting from the Decennial Conference of the Association of Social Anthropologists of the Commonwealth held at St. John's College, Oxford, 4–11 July 1973. The present volume, edited by Clyde Mitchell, is based on a session convened by him on mathematical approaches in social anthropology.

This is third of the series published by the Institute for the Study of Human Issues (ISHI) under the title ASA Essays in Social Anthropology. The other ISHI volumes are: *Transaction and Meaning,* edited by Bruce Kapferer, and *Text and Context,* edited by Ravindra Jain. Three other volumes were published by Dent under the series title ASA Studies. The Dent volumes are: *Biosocial Anthropology,* edited by Robin Fox; *Marxist Analyses and Social Anthropology,* edited by Maurice Bloch; and *The Interpretation of Symbolism,* edited by Roy Willis. These volumes contain a fuller account of the topics covered by the Decennial Conference and of its organization.

The ASA would like to thank Mr. Douglas Gordon and the staff of ISHI for the meticulous care taken over some difficult texts, and for their excellent cooperation with editors and authors. We should also like to thank the President and Fellows of St. John's College, Oxford, and the Warden of Rhodes House, Oxford, for providing the home for the conference, and the staff of both for their willing assistance. The major convening task was shared with me by Shirley Ardener, and I would like to acknowledge also the help of Nigel Barley, Martin Cantor, Christine Cooper, Robert Heath, Joy Hendry, John Mathias, David Price, Matt Schaffer, and Drid Williams, then mostly graduate students of the Oxford University Institute of Social Anthropology.

As General Editor I warmly acknowledge the role of Professor Meyer Fortes in devising and initiating the Decennial Conference of 1973, and of his successors, Professor Jean La Fontaine and Professor A. L. Epstein, in establishing and continuing this series of publications.

EDWIN ARDENER

Preface

Like all editors I am grateful to the authors whose contributions have made this book possible. I would like to take this opportunity of expressing my gratitude to them collectively. They were forbearing particularly over the long delay between the time their papers were presented in July 1973 and the time when I could assure them that the manuscript had been sent off to the publishers. In mitigation I can only plead that the period between September 1973 and the 15th of August 1976 was extremely distressful to me personally and that it was difficult for me to give my attention to everyday affairs.

I would also like to express my gratitude to an anonymous reader who made some constructive and helpful suggestions; to Douglas Gordon and the staff at ISHI who so carefully read the manuscript and picked up so many vaguenesses, slips, and nonsequiturs; to Phillip Kreager, who helped with some of the bibliographies; and to Sheila Hazelden, Lynne Remnant, and Ann Franklin who at various times have had to carry the burden of extra typing and secretarial assistance in preparing the manuscript for the publishers.

Oxford   J. CLYDE MITCHELL

Contents

Introduction

J. CLYDE MITCHELL

MATHEMATICAL PROCEDURES IN ANTHROPOLOGY

There have recently been several reviews of the uses of mathematical procedures in social anthropology (e.g., Hoffman 1970, Kay 1971, Burton 1973, White 1973). Perhaps the most striking feature of these reviews is how different they are from one another, a fact that indicates how diverse the use of mathematical procedures may be. In one of the most recent of these reviews, White (1973) provides a classification of mathematical procedures covered in reviews and readings on mathematical anthropology. He describes the following categories.

1. *Processual analysis,* which he defines as specifying "the generative relationships between social processes and social forms" (p. 371). Analyses of this type are expressed as models in which, say, the operation of rules of kinship is constrained by economic and demographic factors. These models may be either deterministic in the sense that the model is intended to predict exactly what the outcome of a process will be, given the prior knowledge of a number of preconditions, or probabilistic in the sense that random variations in the preconditions and in the outcome itself lead to a certain range of uncertainty about the exact outcome.
2. *Optimization analysis,* which White explains as "a more precise focus within processual analysis upon the social actor, his conscious goals or plans and his conscious or unconscious values as they enter into the actual contexts of choice" (p. 385). Optimization procedures encompass what has become known as the theory of games, decision theory, and linear programming. There are several good examples in the anthropological literature, and White discusses some of them in detail.
3. *Structural analysis,* which White regards as a form of data reduction, is a procedure that "attempts to identify the nature of ordering relations or structural properties in a body of data," hence "to reduce a complex body of raw data into a finished model that displays these structural properties to a maximal degree" (p. 402). White associates structural analysis particularly with graph theory, about which he

1

comments: "the development of axiomatic systems regarding structural properties of graphs has been one of the most significant innovations in mathematics. The utility of graph theory as a mode of data reduction derives partly from the attempt to provide a formal theory of structural properties of relational systems, quite apart from any specific empirical phenomenon" (p. 402). Graph theory has particularly been used in relation to social networks, but it is obvious that it can be applied to a wide body of material.

4. *Ethnographic decomposition,* which relates to "the identification of the grammatical rules, ordering rules, decision rules, and transformational rules in a cultural system" (p. 415). In effect, this procedure involves using set theory and other forms of modern abstract algebra to express the propositional logic which is deemed to underlie the particular aspect of ethnography being considered. Much of the effort in this field has focused on ways of reflecting the logic of systems of kinship address—an area in which anthropological analysis is well advanced and the underlying logic has been well explored. Once again, however, the procedures could be applied equally well to other fields in which the underlying logic has been described.

5. *Quantification, statistics, and probability.* This aspect of mathematical anthropology is better known than the others so far identified, and for this reason White does not discuss it in his paper. Basically, procedures of this type involve the establishment of associations and patterns in quantitative data and the drawing of inferences about the general situation from samples collected by the ethnographer. Presumably included under this rubric would be the testing of empirical distributions against those generated by known probability processes.

6. *Data reduction via matrix analysis and computer analysis.* This is another branch of mathematical anthropology that White does not discuss in his paper. It relies on a variety of procedures through which the regularities and patterns in complex numerical data relating to the relationships among defined units may be recovered and made apparent. Procedures such as hierarchical linkage analysis and multidimensional scaling (or smallest space analysis) are included here. Because of the intricacy of the operations performed on the data, normally the use of computers is implied.

The chapters in this volume were presented initially as papers at a session of the conference entitled "New Directions in Social Anthropology," held in Oxford on 9 July 1973. As organizer of this session, I had solicited papers from anthropologists who I knew were working with quantitative or mathematical procedures or about whom I was told by colleagues. The only restriction was that each paper should relate to a substantive ethnographic or anthropological problem and should not, therefore, be purely method-ological. The intention was to illustrate a variety of formal procedures that anthropologists had used, or could use, to analyze substantive problems in which they were interested.

The specific procedures reflected in the contributions can in no way be thought of as covering the whole field of mathematical anthropology, which, as we have seen from White's discussion, is very wide and diverse. They represent, rather, procedures that at the time of the conference were probably relatively unfamiliar to the majority of the audience. Even the chapters embodying the more conventional quantitative procedures included features that were likely to be novel to the average anthropologist. In fact, not all of the six categories of mathematical anthropology are equally represented in this volume but most are illustrated. Michael Thompson's article using topological "catastrophe theory" is an example of processual analysis. The papers by Thomas Crump and Kingsley Garbett, which use graph theory, are examples of structural analysis. At the same time Kingsley Garbett's chapter could be thought of as a form of "ethnographic decomposition" reflecting the rules of food exchange. The chapters by Tim Ingold and Paul Spencer involve probability theory and fall into the category of "quantification, statistics, and probability." The paper by Jack Goody and Joan Buckley and that by my late wife and myself also fall into this category, except that insofar as Goody and Buckley make use of hierarchical linkage their chapter overlaps with the next category, data reduction. Kimball Romney's article is an example of data reduction using multidimensional scaling or smallest space analysis. Finally the papers by Ingold and Thompson may also be looked upon as illustrating different types of optimization procedures.

It should be stressed that the particular procedure each author has chosen to analyze the data in question is certainly not the only way that it might have been analyzed and perhaps not even the best way. It is obvious that Romney's intermarriage data, which he treats by means of multidimensional scaling, are of precisely the same sort that Geoghegan analyzes with graph theory (see p. 23 below). The question of which is the "best" procedure to use for any particular set of data hinges on what sort of measurement assumptions may be made about the data and what sort of questions the analyst wants to ask. Implicit in the latter consideration are epistemological issues that may not always be patent. The contributions to this book merely illustrate how certain characteristics inherent in ethnographic data with which the authors were familiar may be thrown into relief through the use of appropriate numerical procedures.

The basic mathematical procedures used in the papers can be considered fairly standard. It is true that some of the techniques—such as hierarchical linkage, multiple regression using dummy variables, multidimensional scaling, the negative binomial distribution, and "catastrophe theory"—are not very widely known. But with the possible exception of Kingsley Garbett's notion of the "graph of inclusion," there is probably little in these chapters that is new to an expert in mathematical anthropology. What is new is the way in which the various procedures have been applied to empirical anthropological problems. The contributions are directed, therefore, not so much to the specialist in mathematical or quantitative anthropology as to the general anthropologist who wishes to learn about possible ways of handling field work material. I had prevailed upon the authors to keep the technicalities down to a minimum and if necessary relegate them to appendices, so as to make their analyses intelligible to anthropological readers who may have only a modicum of mathematical competence. This introduction, in particular, is intended to supply a nonrigorous and nontechnical guide to the contributions.

CONVENTIONAL QUANTITATIVE ANALYSIS

The first two essays in the book rely mainly on well-tried and well-understood statistical procedures to throw light on two rather different types of problem. In the first paper Goody and Buckley use correlation analysis to examine the causal connections among a set of ethnographic variables relating to property, marriage, and descent systems, a topic that Goody has explored before. In this analysis, in collaboration with Joan Buckley, he elaborates a proposition derived from Ester Boserup's work linking the type of agriculture with the type of marriage and the contribution of women to production. Postulating that economy is the starting point in causal change, Goody and Buckley trace a sequence of connections from this initial cause through the intervening variables of the polity, the division of labor, the transmission of property, and marriage, and finally to whether or not sibling kin terms are used.

Their analysis begins with the set of correlations among all the variables they include. Right from the start Goody and Buckley ran into a difficulty that most of those who aim to use ethnographic analysis encounter. This is the problem of isomorphism—to which it will be necessary to return—which concerns the extent to which the mathematical operations performed on anthropological data are strictly consistent with the way in which anthropologists conceptualize those data. The mathematical procedures underlying a number of the most powerful and robust procedures of statistical analysis, for example, assume that the variabilities used in the analyses are measured on some underlying continuous scale. Unfortunately, very few of the variables in which we are interested satisfy this condition.

Sometimes we may be lucky enough to be able to arrange our variables in terms of a set of ordered categories. We may be able to arrange the criteria of prestige, for example, from highest to lowest. But a set of measurement categories of this kind clearly does not meet the requirements underlying usual statistical analysis, since there may not be any reason to assume that the "distance" between any two adjacent categories in an ordered set is the same as that between any other two adjacent categories. Most likely, all we will be able to say is that a phenomenon is a member of a class of that phenomenon or it is not. In terms of the problem with which Goody and Buckley are concerned, a society has a complex polity or it has not. This assumes, of course, that the analyst has a set of rules at his disposal to enable him to make a decision of this kind. But in fact a more complex classification may be called for; descent systems, for example, may be patrilineal, matrilineal, bilateral, or bilineal. In these circumstances, to use statistical procedures which make much stricter measurement assumptions (as, for instance, the existence of an interval scale of measurement) would clearly be inappropriate.[1]

Several strategies are open to an analyst under these conditions. Goody and Buckley have adopted one of them. They have reduced all their variables to dichotomies: the societies that are the elements of their analysis may be classified as belonging to a specified category—ones that "practice polygyny" for example—or not. Under these circumstances the association between any two variables may be gauged by a number of different measures. Because Goody and Buckley wish to make use of path analysis procedures, they opt for the phi (ϕ) coefficient, which is the algebraic equivalent of the product-moment correlation in which the variables take only the values of zero or one.

One of the great advantages of path analysis procedures is that they are derived from a very respectable and well-understood tradition of statistical analysis. The path coefficients in a path diagram are no more than standardized regression coefficients linking the dependent variable, at whatever level of the causal model, with the variables causally prior to it. The computation of path coefficients from raw variables or from correlation coefficients among them is a relatively simple procedure when a digital computer is available. Many standard data analysis packages, such as the *Statistical Package for the Social Sciences* (SPSS), have facilities for doing this.

What path analysis sets out to do is to estimate the direct effect of each variable in the model on each of the variables that succeed it in causal sequence. The relationship between any two variables, as measured by a correlation coefficient, will be affected by the relationships of other variables connected to the two variables in question; the path coefficient takes account of these confounding influences. Goody and Buckley found, for example, that although the existence of "monogamy" and "sibling kin terms" in the societies in their sample correlate to the extent of 0.23, nearly half of this relationship arises from the relationship of other variables to these two: the direct relationship is only 0.11.

The difficult part in path analysis is not the computation of the coefficients but setting up the model. To achieve a numerical solution for the coefficients the analyst must arrange all variables, except those deemed to be given or starter variables, in a strict causal sequence. Reciprocal causal connections or functional relationships cannot be handled. There is a possibility—indeed one might say a probability—that the analyst will be fairly sure of the causal priorities among some of the variables in the model but uncertain about others. Several different models may be feasible, and different solutions for the direct effect of one variable on another are almost bound to emerge. There is no numerical way of validating one of these models against another. The analyst must rely on the plausibility of his model for its validity.

One of the attractive features of Goody and Buckley's procedure is that they set up their model first and then test it. Path analysis procedures lend themselves particularly to "fishing expeditions." It is all too simple to try out a series of orderings of variables, to choose one which has, say, an attractive polarity of path coefficient sizes, and then to find some justification for setting up this particular ordering as the model. I was able to set up the simple table given in note 5 of Goody and Buckley's paper simply because they had derived the model first and tested it subsequently. On the whole the model survives particularly well. The authors have put forward some arguments to discount those inconsistencies that cropped up between the model and the test. I am concerned here not with the substantive aspects of their model but only with the procedures involved. On this score the authors reflect a healthy balance, for they write: "While we would not wish to overvalue the use of such techniques, we do see them as an advance that assists us in getting beyond the much simpler unilineal, single-factor hypotheses that dog so much anthropology, since they reduce the arbitrary element in our assumptions and attempt to replace dispute by argument."

An additional feature of Goody and Buckley's paper that deserves comment is the use of hierarchical linkage procedures as a preliminary to further analysis. Hierarchical linkage procedures are not analytic devices in the same way that regression analysis and correlation analyses are. Instead they are procedures which make manifest the patterns in data that otherwise might remain obscured in a mass of information. Goody and Buckley start off with an 8×8 correlation matrix and ask themselves the question: Are there sets of variables among the eight which are interconnected with one another to a greater extent than they are interconnected with other variables? This is a problem in numerical taxonomy,[2] and there are several different ways of resolving it. Goody and Buckley use an hierarchical linkage analysis in which those variables that correlate with one another more highly than with a third are linked at the initial level. Thus male farming and advanced agriculture, which correlate to the extent of 0.42, and diverging devolution and monogamy, which correlate to the extent of 0.34, are linked together in two "clusters." At the next step "complex polity" becomes linked to "male farming" and "advanced agriculture" to form a cluster of variables in contradistinction to "diverging devolution," "monogamy," and "in-marriage," which had become attracted to "diverging devolution" and "monogamy" at a level of 0.32. At the next step "sibling kin terms" is linked to the cluster centered on "male farming." The procedure, therefore, and the tree diagram based on it, show very clearly how the variables that Goody and Buckley are dealing with may be thought of as two somewhat distinct sets, with "prohibition of premarital sex" linked strongly with neither set. The procedure is, of course, purely mechanical: it only makes apparent relationships that inhere in the data. The analytic task is to explain what lies behind this clustering of variables.

The chapter that my late wife and I prepared for this volume shares with the paper by Goody and Buckley the use of standard statistical procedures to uncover regularities lurking among several interacting variables—in our example, the background social factors that influence the way in which people perceive the causality of disease. Apart from the substantive content of the findings, which may be of interest to those concerned with beliefs about the connection between diseases, witches, and spirits, the paper illustrates two rather well-known procedures which do not, however, seem to be widely used in anthropology. The first is that of reducing a number of indicators to a single index to represent some underlying characteristic which they are deemed to reflect to a lesser or a greater degree. The problem is to weight the individual responses of a subject on each of the component indicators in such a way as to reflect as faithfully as possible the position of that subject along a postulated dimension. We did this with factor analysis, using coefficients derived from the loadings on the factor that seemed to reflect best the characteristic in which we were interested. The method we used was in fact that described by Harman (1967: Chapter 16), which provides a type of "least squares" estimate of the appropriate coefficients. As a gloss on this procedure, we have applied a simple linear transformation to the scores to ensure that the lowest possible score is given a value of zero and the highest possible score a value of 100. The only virtue in this transformation is that it makes it easier for the reader to grasp the value of a score.

The validity of trying to reduce several distinct indicators to a single index purporting to represent the level or intensity of some postulated underlying "factor" has been disputed for some time. Those who oppose the procedure do so partly because they fear that it is not possible to reflect complex sociological notions by a single index or score, or that by doing so the user is throwing away important information (Curtis and Jackson 1962). Those who defend the procedure accept the multidimensionality of social reality but argue that all analysis involves abstractions and that abstracting along one postulated dimension of a complex reality is in no way different from other types of abstract assessment.

Given that an index of some postulated factor is needed, there are several different ways in which a "factor score" may be derived, depending on the sort of qualities the user wants his index to have.[3] The psychometricians have discussed this problem more than most other problems; see, for example, Harris (1967), McDonald and Burr (1967), Tucker (1971), and Susmilch and Johnson (1975). A recent discussion by Alwin (1973) in relation to sociological analysis sets out alternative procedures and the characteristics of the indices they produce. In the chapter by my wife and myself, we used the so-called "regression" method, which produces coefficients (similar in concept to regression coefficients) that may be used as weights for the appropriate items to construct an index.[4]

The main purpose of the paper, however, was not to illustrate the production of scores, but rather to identify factors that were associated with different orientations toward the causation of disease. For this we used multiple regression techniques with dummy variables. The reasons we chose this method are that: (a) the dependent variable by construction was based on an interval scale, and (b) some dependent variables, such as religious affiliation, were at best only nominal variables. In addition, in using dummy variables we were not constrained to assume linear relationships between the dependent variable and the independent variables.[5]

These considerations, in combination with the fact that the techniques are available in many computer packages (once the variables are rescored), seem to make multiple regression with dummy variables particularly appropriate for use in anthropological analyses. A serious disadvantage of the technique, however, is that it proliferates the number of terms in the regression equations—a consideration which, if the sample is small, may turn out to be an embarrassment.

One of the hindrances in using multiple regression techniques with dummy variables is that, strictly speaking, the dependent variable should be measured along a continuous dimension; that is, it ought to be on an interval scale. Unfortunately, as mentioned earlier, anthropological users frequently need to use variables that do not conform to this requirement: what the analyst wants to specify are the conditions under which elements are either members of a class of objects or not. This was the position I found myself in when I wanted to specify the conditions under which Yao headmen were accorded marks of prestige (Mitchell 1962). I resolved the problem by using a logit transformation which converted the proportion of headmen with given profiles of characteristics into a continuous variable. Recent developments stemming from mathematical advances (e.g., Bishop, Feinberg, and Holland 1975) and aided by the extension of computer methods of data analysis have brought about several systematized procedures for handling data which have both discrete dependent and independent variables (Davis 1971, 1974; Goodman 1972, 1973; Coleman 1964; Bishop et al. 1975). Computer programs are beginning to become available to implement procedures of this kind. These procedures are still new and have not yet been tried extensively on empirical data, as have standard multiple regression and analysis of variance procedures, but it looks as if one or another of them will in the future become the standard procedure for the quantitative analysis of the sort of material anthropologists normally collect.

MULTIDIMENSIONAL SCALING

The procedures Romney illustrates in his chapter arose in response to the "measurement problem." Recently a number of similar procedures have been developed to analyze data that rely on rather weak measurement assumptions, such as ordinal or nominal categories rather than interval scales. All of these methods are attempts to make the implicit patterns in data apparent by relaxing the metric connections among the elements sufficiently to allow the relationships to be represented in a fairly simple geometrical form.

The basic procedure is for the interrelationships among a set of elements—in one of Romney's examples, language groups—to be expressed as "distances" of some sort.[6] Romney displays some ingenuity in arriving at a measure of distances among the eight groups involved by considering the intermarriage frequencies among the groups. It would be unlikely that the "distances" derived from procedures such as these would have all the properties of distances in, say, physical space. To assume that they did would be to place a good deal more confidence in the efficacy of our measurement procedures than most of us would feel justified in doing.

For a set of "distances" of this sort to be tractable mathematically, that is, in order for them to constitute a "materic space," they must conform to certain essential conditions or axioms. McFarland and Brown (1973: 218–219) enumerate seven of these. In nontechnical language they are:

1. The distances must relate to specified pairs of elements taken in a particular order from some well-specified underlying set of elements.
2. The distances between the elements cannot be negative.
3. There should be only one possible distance between any two elements.
4. The distance of an element from itself should be zero.
5. The distance from one element to another must be the same in one direction as in the other.

6. The distance directly between any two elements must not be larger than the distance between the two elements via some common third element.
7. If the distance between two elements is zero, then the two elements are indistinguishable.

Unfortunately few formulations of "social distance" can meet these rather demanding conditions, and Romney's analysis of intermarriage among language groups in the Vaupés is no exception. For example, if we are going to use the exchange of spouses among the groups as an indicator of the social distance between them and to postulate that social distance is comparable to physical distance, then we would expect the exchange of spouses between pairs of groups to be balanced: group A would take as many spouses from group B as group B took from group A. This represents the symmetry of distances as set out in condition 5 above. If we examine Romney's Table 2 (p. 75 below), in which he presents the marriage prefer- ences among the eight groups he is studying, having adjusted for the differ- ent numbers of males and females in the groups, we see that most groups do not exchange spouses equally with other groups. The most extreme pair are the Carapana and the Tatuyo. The Tatuyo are nearly twice as likely to take their wives from the Carapana as the latter are from the Tatuyo. Sim- ilar imbalances in exchange of spouses occur between the Tatuyo and Yarutí, the Tuyuka and Tatuyo, and the Yurutí and Bará. But Romney argues that the cultural norm among this set of people is for free spouse exchange and that on the whole this is borne out by the empirical data. In fact, complete balance in exchange of spouses could be achieved by an overall average adjustment of the indices of intermarriage of less than 5%. Romney therefore decides to treat the variations in reciprocal exchange of spouses as variations around the norm of balanced spouse exchange, and so uses the mean of the exchange indices between two groups as an esti- mate of the true intermarriage rate. He employs this mean intermarriage rate in turn as an index of the social distance between the groups.

There are, of course, alternative procedures that Romney might have adopted. For example, he might have used the geometric mean of the two spouse exchange indices instead of the arithmetic mean. This would have depressed the mean rates of those groups showing wide discrepancies toward the lower rate. All those pairs which showed either no wives received or no wives given would automatically have been attributed a zero mean rate. Or he might have taken either the lower or the higher of the two rates as the "true" rate of spouse exchange, reflecting either a conservative or a liberal interpretation of the "true" rate. Any of these procedures would have resulted in a symmetrical set of "distances," but each faces the same difficulty as the procedure that Romney did use: it is not easy to justify any one of them against any other on logical or theoretical grounds.

By imposing symmetry on the "distances," Romney is in fact not using some information contained in the different rates of spouse exchange among the groups. Had he wished to extend the analysis, he could have done so by conducting it from two points of view: first, using the wife-*giving* rates (the lower left half of Table 2) to estimate "distances," he could have constructed one representation of the spatial relationships among the groups; and second, he could have followed the same steps with the wife-*receiving* rates (the upper right half of Table 2). A comparison of these two representations might have revealed features that called for further explanation.[7]

Gower (1966, 1967) has argued that, once a symmetrical set of "distances" has been arrived at, they may be analyzed by standard geometrical procedures; he refers to this method as principal coordinates analysis (see also Torgerson 1958). If, for example, we have a set of "distances" among a set of entities, such as those presented by Romney, we are usually able to establish a set of orthogonal axes to which these points may be related even if the "distances" are not strictly Euclidean. A condition for an analysis of this sort to be feasible is that the space in which the elements are to be located should be "real" in the mathematical sense. In other words, the matrix of interelement distances, when transformed to relate to the centroid of the elements, should be positive semidefinite; there should be no negative roots to the matrix. When I analyzed the data Romney presents by procedures of this kind, I found that, although 86% of the distances among the eight groups could be represented in three dimensions and a configuration of groups very much like that Romney presents could be produced, the matrix of centroid-oriented distances was not strictly positive semidefinite: there was a small negative root accounting for about 2% of the squared distances involved. This violation of the basic assumption is not very severe but it is sufficient, some would argue, to invalidate an analysis based on conventional geometrical assumptions.

We must therefore resort to some other expedient. The expedient adopted in so-called multidimensional scaling procedures is to assume that there is some flexibility in the distances among all the elements—that the distances are in effect approximate. We may thus move the elements around vis-à-vis one another, within limits, so that the distances among them could fit into a relatively simple space. It would seem reasonable to allow ourselves to adjust the *actual* distances among all the elements to the extent that we do not alter too seriously the *relative* distances. A reasonable constraint to impose, therefore, would be to ensure that the elements with the greatest distances from others should remain those with the greatest distances and those with the smallest distances similarly should remain those with the smallest distances, although the actual distances could vary considerably within these constraints. In short, we seek a solution in the smallest number of dimensions consistent with maintaining the same ordinal, not cardinal, distance relationships among all the elements.

In fact, it is often possible to arrive at a solution in two or three dimensions, which means that we can represent the relationships on a surface or a three-dimensional diagram such as Romney's Figures 1, 3, and 4, without violating the order of interelement distances to an unacceptable extent. The degree to which we have been forced to take liberties with the actual interelement distances is expressed by a coefficient of stress or a coefficient of alienation: the smaller the stress, the fewer the liberties we have had to take. In other words, we barter strong measurement assumptions for clearer representations of the pattern of relationships among a set of elements.[8]

There are not yet many straightforward accounts of what is happening in multidimensional scaling or smallest-space analysis, as it is also called. Kendall provides a witty and very readable account of the application of procedures of this kind to problems of seriation in archaeology and to the reconstruction of maps from incomplete medieval historical records (Kendall 1975). More general discussions of the procedures involved tend to be somewhat technical, but there have been attempts to set out the basic ideas in more easily assimilable form (see, for example, Shepard 1972, Coxon n.d., McFarland and Brown 1973, and Bailey 1974b). Romney himself and his associates have been the pioneers in the application of multidimensional scaling or smallest-space analysis to anthropological problems (Romney 1972, D'Andrade et al. 1972, Wexler and Romney 1972, Burton 1972).

Most of these applications are drawn from the field of cognitive anthropology; they deal, in particular, with semantic and lexical problems. This interest is reflected in some of the material in Romney's contribution to this volume. A departure from this dominant theme in smallest-space analysis is reflected in a paper by Bloombaum (1968), who applies the procedure to the favorite arena of quantitative anthropological endeavor: cross-cultural analysis. Romney's material on Bará intermarriage represents another rare application of smallest-space analysis or multidimensional scaling to a "structural problem."

The technique is general, of course, and is particularly appropriate where the analyst would be uneasy about making strong metric assumptions about the indicators being used to reflect regularities in the data. Thus far, however, the method appears to have been utilized more to confirm the assumptions of the analyst than to make apparent features of the data that the analyst may not have suspected. This tardiness in using the procedures analytically instead of illustratively may arise partly from the difficulty anthropologists have in finding appropriate ways to reflect, even if only at an ordinal level, the "distances" among the elements whose interrelationships they wish to explore. But whatever the cause, the procedures are not used in anthropological analysis as much as they perhaps ought to be. There are very efficient computer programs to effect the analysis. We appear to be caught in a "Catch-22" situation: anthropologists do not use the procedures because they are not used in the literature with which the anthropologists are familiar because anthropologists do not use the procedures because they are not used in the literature. . . .

PROBABILITY DISTRIBUTIONS

The contributions of Ingold and Spencer to this volume represent a more conventional mathematical approach to data analysis even though the procedures, like smallest-space analysis, are not widely used in anthropological literature.

Both of these authors examine substantive anthropological problems by relating the data they are seeking to illuminate to an hypothesized distribution of events which they postulate underlies them. Ingold explores the decision-making process of Lapp reindeer husbanders. The particular advantage of presenting an analysis of the strategies open to the husbander is, in Ingold's words, that it "enables us to specify the limits of knowledge, confidence, and rationality within which the husbander of necessity operates."

To do this Ingold makes use of both the binomial and Poisson distributions. Assuming that the number of reindeer a husbander is able to identify in a "separation" is a random event—and there are sound prima facie grounds to argue that it is—he uses these distributions to demonstrate that, with the reduction of the number of animals included in a separation and a general reduction in the extent to which smaller husbanders are able to earmark animals, smaller husbanders are increasingly disadvantaged in the exploitation of the reindeer herds.

It is important to appreciate that Ingold's model is by no means a deterministic one: he does not aim to define the circumstances in which a husbander with a given number of animals must capture a given proportion or be forced off the market. Rather, Ingold uses his ethnographic knowledge to compute the *probabilities* that a husbander will find it profitable to attend a separation and that he will decide to slaughter some or all of his animals that turn up in a separation. The probability distributions themselves are constructs that enable Ingold to put forward a plausible analysis of the dynamics underlying changes in the present-day Lapp reindeer economy. He uses the systematic ethnographic data he has assembled, in conjunction with his understanding of the characteristics of probability distributions, to advance a cogent analysis of the constraints upon and opportunities open to modern Lapp reindeer husbanders.

Note that Ingold uses a probability distribution—the binomial distribution—which is based on a fixed probability of finding a certain proportion of reindeer in a separation and on the independence of the finding proportions in different separations. He infers the actual existence of this distribution from his knowledge of the haphazard movements of the reindeer in relation to the location of the separation. Ingold then uses the known characteristics of the distribution to assess the constraints limiting the economic activities of reindeer husbanders. He does not present data against which the postulated distributions may be tested; they are in fact impossible to assemble.

Spencer's approach is different. He argues that the number of wives that men from different African areas may take beyond the first is a function of both a probability process and a postulated disposition toward polygyny. In other words, he relaxes the assumption underlying the binomial and Poisson distributions by allowing the probability of an event's taking place to vary. He assumes, however, that the variations of the generating probability underlying the curve will follow a skewed type of continuous distribution well known to statisticians as the gamma distribution. For the purposes of his analysis, Spencer does not have to determine the shapes of the gamma distributions that are assumed to underlie the observed distributions of men with one, two, or more wives beyond the first. The parameters that generate the distributions can in fact be estimated directly from the distributions themselves, on the assumption that a distribution is generated by what is known as the negative binomial (see Feller 1957: Chapter 6; Parzen 1960: Chapter 4; Bishop et al. 1975: Chapter 9). Spencer points out that the relatively unfamiliar negative binomial is a general form of probability distribution of which the Poisson distribution is a special case. It has considerable utility when a distribution that is suspected to have arisen from a probability process is not described particularly well by either the binomial or the Poisson distribution.

The attractive feature of this kind of approach is that, if the analyst is prepared to specify what sort of probability process underlies the phenomena he is observing, it is relatively simple to compute what the distribution ought to be. For any of the three probability processes mentioned by Ingold and Spencer, the values that need to be known in order to compute the distributions can normally be estimated without too much difficulty from field data. If the analyst knows what the "success" rate is for the data as a whole and is relatively confident about the underlying probability processes, then the otherwise invisible constraints on the actors may be estimated by, for example, computing the probability that a certain number of reindeer will be found in a separation of a certain size.

Spencer, however, starts off with fifty distributions drawn from black Africa. He postulates that a certain kind of probability process is operating in the taking of additional wives and then asks the question: How well does that probability process reproduce the observed distribution? He proceeds to fit either a binomial, Poisson, or negative binomial distribution to the observed frequencies, depending on the ratio of the variance to the mean of the distribution. On the whole the fit of the negative binomial distribution to the observed frequencies, where it is appropriate, is very close. There are some significant departures from the expected distribution as assessed by chi-square. However, Spencer has probably taken too draconic a measure of fit since with very large samples, as he himself points out, large chi-squares may occur even though the fit is very good. On this point Bishop et al. (1975: 329) suggest that the degree of fit of several distributions with the same number of degrees of freedom might better be compared if the chi-square value is divided by the total number of cases in the sample. If we adopt this procedure, then those instances in which large samples are involved, such as the Basuto, the Hehe, and the Mende, prove to have as good or better a fit than many of the instances with smaller samples in which the fit is accepted as reasonable. The data from the Gonja and from the Nupe of Doko and Kutigi villages show no worse a fit than those from the Otoro of the Sudan; and the Plateau Tonga data show a better fit than the Mokwa village Nupe data, which are accepted by Spencer as having a reasonable fit. Similarly, the 1967 Tallensi sample shows a better fit than the Swazi sample with the same degrees of freedom that was accepted as having a reasonable fit. This leaves only the Ashanti and the Soga which depart appreciably from a theoretical distribution generated by the negative binomial.

As with all formulations of social processes in mathematical terms, the prime difficulty is to ensure that the subtle social processes are adequately reflected in the mathematical operations. With probability models, the assumptions about the relationship of numerical terms to people's decisions and actions can be fairly simple, yet the distributions built up can be complex. This is the strength and elegance of a probability model.

The negative binomial is a more complex distribution than either the binomial or the Poisson; therefore the specification of the fundamental social processes that produce the distribution is more difficult. Spencer argues that in African societies as a whole the ability of a man to take additional wives flows from his prestige, which is indexed by age, wealth, or social standing. He then maintains that it is this skewed distribution of prestige that determines the gamma distribution from which in turn the negative binomial can be generated. In order to accommodate the fact that some of his fifty distributions match the true binomial rather than the negative binomial, Spencer postulates that some societies are basically more egalitarian in according prestige to people. In these societies men are constrained to limit the number of additional wives they take. In other societies, infused by a competitive spirit, prestige is differentially accorded and men demonstrate their prestige by taking additional wives.

I am not concerned here with the plausibility of Spencer's argument. I use his argument only to illustrate the problems inherent in moving from mathematical to sociological concepts and vice versa.

GRAPH THEORY

The contributions of Crump and Garbett represent a very different approach to the analysis of ethnographic data by mathematical techniques. Both of these authors use graph theory, although in rather different ways, to draw out some logical implications of the data they are analyzing.

Graph theory is a branch of mathematics that handles the relationships among points which may or may not be connected by lines. Both Crump and Garbett set out the elementary principles of graph theory, and there is no point in my repeating them here. The essential point, however, as Crump emphasizes in his chapter, is that the mathematics of graph theory is entirely general and abstract, and different analyses may give entirely different connotations to the same pattern of points and lines. For one the points may be towns and the lines roads joining (or not joining) the towns; for another the points may be persons and the lines social relationships of some defined kind. The formal analysis, which starts after the pattern has been established, is conducted through propositions about the extent to which points may be reached directly or indirectly, the extent to which all possible links among the points exist, and whether the links are directional or not.

Perhaps the image of a number of elements connected to one another to a greater or lesser extent is most naturally applied to a social network. The basic textbook setting out graph theoretical propositions of most interest to social scientists, Harary, Norman, and Cartwright (1965), in fact draws mainly on sociometric material for its examples. But as the chapters by Crump and Garbett in this volume demonstrate, the utility of graph theory is not limited to social networks. Per Hage (1973–1974), for example, has used graph theory to reanalyze the alliances and oppositions among sixteen New Guinea Highland groups described initially by Read. The techniques enable him not only to isolate three major alliance sets, but also to pick out those groups that are departures from the pattern and therefore present particular problems of analysis. Subsequently he has applied an aspect of graph theory, structural balance, to the study of kinship relations among a Bushmen group (Hage 1976).

In the preamble to his 1973–1974 analysis, Hage bewails the fact that although "graph theory has frequently been recognized as a potential meta-language for the conceptualization of social networks and network phenomena in general . . . there have been few consistent and extensive applications in the anthropological literature" (p. 280). He attributes this to the difficulty of coordinating graph theoretical concepts with the kind of data ethnographers collect, the relative incompleteness of much data that could otherwise be treated in terms of graph theory, and the fact that many of the applications are indeed trivial and therefore add nothing to the standard kind of ethnographic analysis.

The celebrated problem of intermarriage among Purum sibs has nonetheless been one of the topics analyzed with graph theoretical procedures (Livingstone 1969, White 1973). Here the sibs are represented by points and the wife-giving and wife-taking relationships by directed lines linking the sibs concerned. The relationships among sibs are reduced initially to a zero or a one, depending on whether the sib was predominantly wife-giving or wife-receiving. On the basis of this very much simplified graph theoretical model, Livingstone was able to account for 88% of the observed wife exchanges. Further modifications of the model, also expressed in graph theoretical terms, were able to increase the explanatory power to 98% (see p. 23 below).

Crump's contribution applies graph theory to several different sets of circumstances in Mexico. First he illustrates the use of graph theoretical procedures to analyze the intermarriage relationships among some 100 hamlets. Clearly it would be difficult to present the full set of data. Accordingly Crump shows how graph theory might be used to isolate clusters of exogamous and intermarrying hamlets. He then extends the analysis to the incumbency of politico-religious offices, in which some 150 positions are involved. It was apparently very difficult to gather information about the lending and borrowing of funds that preceded and followed the holding of office, but Crump is able to present illustrative material about a small number of people who were easily identifiable as entrepreneurs and who formed a close-knit central core, although their business and personal contacts radiated into the surrounding villages. He then extends this analysis to a neighboring community in which the holding of office involved the incumbent in extensive long-term credit and debt relationships. This set of circumstances can also be represented as a graph in which the debt and credit relationships are thought of as radiating out from any incumbent through link-men to other incumbents. Although Crump does not in fact present empirical data to support this formulation of the overall relationships, his presentation of his model as a graph enables us to grasp the essentials quickly and to identify exactly where we should look for the appropriate ethnographic evidence.

In his last illustration Crump examines the two communities he has been studying in terms of the system of road links among the component settlements. These roads form, in graph theory language, a "tree" with branches radiating out from the main town. Crump goes on to link the changes in communications among settlements following the opening of a main highway with the changes in the system of office holding in the two communities—both patterns represented by a similar type of graph but involving rather different sets of relationships.

In summarizing his use of graph theoretical ideas to present his data on these Mexican communities, Crump makes some important points. The first is that the use of graph theory was in essence suggested to him by his informants. This is, he says, substantially how *they* analyzed the data for him and often in quite explicit terms. The mathematical model, therefore, had a good deal in common with the folk model. The second point he makes is cautionary: although he has been able to use graph theory to provide a simple and clear representation of the ideas he wanted to communicate, he warns that graph theory, while it may seem sufficiently general and for that reason attractive to the social scientist, cannot yet be thought of as a type of applied mathematics. He writes: "So far the fundamental process of applied mathematics—namely, the constant interaction between the empirical materials of the scientist and the abstract structures of the mathematician, each developing in essential combination with the other, and producing at every stage not only new insights into the character of the already existing corpus, but also signposts for future research—has yet to get under way. This is where to look for significant new developments, but it will be a hard search."

Developing appropriate analytic procedures based on mathematical reasoning is necessarily a slow, crescive process. The sophistication of theory in the physical sciences, it has been argued, is directly related to the feasibility of expressing the relationships among variables in appropriate mathematical terms. But it would be mistaken to imagine that researchers in the physical sciences merely had to call upon existing mathematical thought in order to provide neat and succinct ways of expressing the complex relationships they wished to summarize. Frequently new mathematical ideas emerged in response to the challenge of physical scientists: it is no accident that "applied mathematics" is often synonymous with "mechanics." Many social scientists feel that the procedures developed in the social sciences have been unduly influenced by the applied mathematics of the physical sciences; perhaps somewhat different methods, as suggested by Crump, are called for in social science.

The question of measurement lies very near to the heart of the problem. The physical sciences have, overwhelmingly, been able to operate with very strong measurement assumptions rooted in three-dimensional physical space. Social scientists, as we have seen, must operate frequently with much less rigorous assumptions. But when the measurement simply indicates whether a relationship between two elements exists and whether these elements may be ordered vis-à-vis one another in terms of that relationship, graph theory provides an attractive means of representing social phenomena.

In fact, it is precisely the issue of measurement procedures that provides the springboard for Garbett's analysis of Indian caste relationships. Garbett starts off with data presented by McKim Marriott on the exchange of ritual food and services among a set of caste groups in a village. Marriott had set himself the task of deriving the hierarchy of caste groups merely from the detailed exchanges of food and services among them. He verified the order of caste groups he obtained by asking informants to compare the rank of each caste group with the rank of every other caste group. To derive a single order of caste groups from the entire set of recorded transactions, he established for every group the net balance of food or services received as against food or services given; he did this for each caste group with respect to each element involved in the exchanges. He then aggregated these separate "scores" to arrive at a final set of twelve ranks into which the twenty-four caste groups were arranged. The pragmatic test of this procedure is that it worked, in the sense that the final ranking agreed very well with that arrived at more directly by asking informants to compare caste ranks. Nevertheless, there is always the doubt that the procedure may not work with other data. Garbett's intention was to devise a method relying only on mathematical operations based on set theory and graph theory—with no arithmetic operations involved. The procedure would therefore be independent of measurement assumptions, although, to rank the caste groups, it would require an ordering of the "indicators"—the items of food and services exchanged.

Garbett in fact must purchase generality with complexity. Accepting Marriott's basic reasoning about the way in which exchanges of food and services symbolize the ranks of the caste groups, he uses propositions from graph theory to devise what he calls a "graph of inclusion" for ordering sets of caste groups. The idea is clearly intriguing, but its utility will be tested only when it has been applied to data less robust than Marriott's.

CATASTROPHE THEORY

Thompson's contribution is based on procedures quite unlike the others in this volume—ones which, as far as I am aware, have not been applied before to anthropological data. The substantive problem that Thompson takes up, which he calls "the pig cycle," is well known in New Guinea ethnography. This cycle involves the exchange of pigs, both alive and cooked, and other prestations between partners in a system of neighboring clans. The prestations flow successively in opposite directions among the partners in the system. There are increasing prestations of live pigs in one direction of the cycle until the terminal point of the cycle is reached. The clan at this point can only slaughter the pigs and return cooked pork, a commodity that has limited duration, in the opposite direction. The cycle of pig giving in one direction is temporarily halted. Before long, however, the cycle starts up in the opposite direction. There are several explanations of this gradual accumulation of pigs at the terminal points in the pig-exchange system. Thompson postulates that the actions of local entrepreneurs—the Big Men—who build up extensive credit relationships not only with kinsmen but also with nonkinsmen, are opposed to the ideology of the segmentary lineage system, which puts a constraint upon building up credit relationships with people who are not lineage members. He examines alternative explanations of cyclical phenomena of this sort, in particular the Keynesian explanation of the trade cycle, and suggests that the processes involved may be parsimoniously expressed using topological propositions recently developed by the French mathematician René Thom.

These propositions have become known as "catastrophe theory," a term that in English has unfortunate connotations. Thom's formulation of the relationships among several variables, all of them changing in a smooth and regular fashion, shows how another variable, also operating normally in terms of smooth changes, may under certain designated circumstances reflect "catastrophic" changes in its value. The word "catastrophic" here refers to sudden and violent change rather than to sudden disaster. In many ways "cataclysmic" in its ordinary English usage might have been more appropriate than "catastrophe."

The mathematician Christopher Zeeman has been particularly active in developing Thom's ideas, showing how they may be used to explain sudden changes in physical, biological, economic, political, and sociological variables. For example, Zeeman and his colleague Isnard (1975) illustrate how the simple "cusp" catastrophe may be used to interpret a sudden switch from peace to war or from war to peace, given that the basic preconditions influencing international relationships are not themselves changing with dramatic suddenness. In another example Zeeman and collaborators from the prisons services in England (Zeeman et al. 1976) set up a model based on field data from a particular prison that was beset by disturbances and riots in 1972. Their model provides a rationale for the sudden outbreak of a disturbance, given that alienation and tension among the prisoners were fluctuating smoothly during the period analyzed.

In defending his use of "catastrophe theory," Thompson writes: "The protagonists of catastrophe theory place great emphasis on the way in which, with a single simple picture, one can describe something that would require pages and pages of verbal description. The claim goes even further, for with the appropriate picture one can describe clearly, concisely, and without contradiction something that either cannot be adequately described in words at all or else requires a verbal description that is full of seeming contradictions and tautologies." Thompson goes on to develop the point about contradictions and tautologies. I wish, however, to make the distinction between the heuristic role of "catastrophe theory" that Thompson describes in the passage quoted and its analytical role.

For catastrophe theory to be more than a suggestive heuristic device—if it is to become instead a model testable against field data—then clearly we need to define the basic expression from which the fold surface can be generated. Thompson admits that he does not have sufficient data to set up an equation of this sort, and he uses catastrophe theory, admittedly in a most stimulating way, primarily as an heuristic device. The paper by Zeeman and his colleagues on the prison disturbances (1976) is one of the few studies in the social sciences in which some attempt is made to set up the basic equations through which the area of uncertainty may be defined and hence the likelihood of sudden changes predicted. Although the study is a retrospective one and the measurement procedures are crude, a convincing case is made for interpreting the course of events in terms of catastrophe theory. The authors of the paper, however, find it necessary to take account of appreciable departures from the model, a fact that re-emphasizes that the model is not yet, and possibly can never be, a deterministic one.

The notion of the catastrophe surface clearly has considerable intuitive appeal for anthropologists who are concerned essentially with change, often with sudden and dramatic change. Such phenomena as lineage fission, peasant revolutions, warfare, village splits, and similar events lend themselves particularly to statement in terms of catastrophe theory. The difficulty is, however, that while the model may help us to decide on the basic factors underlying the changes and encourage us to construe these factors in a way that leads naturally to the generation of the catastrophe fold, a vigorous testing of the notion can come only when we have sufficiently detailed information to set up the mathematical expressions that describe the surface. We will not know whether it is feasible until we have tried.

ISOMORPHISM

In the concluding section of his paper Garbett raises what, as we have already seen, appears to be the crucial problem in the application of numerical procedures to substantive anthropological issues. This is the problem of what has been called isomorphism, that is, the extent to which the operations performed in mathematical procedures are consonant with the logical relationships among the components of the anthropological theory to which the numerical operations refer. Cicourel (1964: 9) provides a good definition of isomorphism, though it relates to stricter mathematical manipulations than the ones I have referred to as "numerical":

> If the axioms of a mathematical system have the same structure as the laws of
> an explicit theory, such that (1) the axioms of the mathematical system can be

"translated" into the laws of the explicit theory so that (2) there is a one-to-one correspondence between the terms of the two systems and their statements; and (3) logical connections between the axioms and the laws, respectively, are preserved. the two systems are *isomorphic*. The relevant question here is how are such isomorphisms presupposed by sociologists using "mathematical models" and "measurement models" with implicit theories, and what are the consequences for theory and method that follow?

Garbett provides a simple example in which the question of isomorphism is raised: a person represented by one point in a graph of a social network may not be able to "reach" another person, represented by a second point, even though the two points in the graph are in a technical sense "reachable." There may be many reasons why a person may not be able to communicate with someone else with whom he is in indirect contact. There may be barriers to the communication of highly personal and confidential information about a person through an intermediary to a third person. A graph representing close friendship may show that point A is linked to point C through point B and therefore that point C is reachable from A, but that does not mean that information *necessarily* flows from A to C.

This is, of course, a very simple illustration of a recondite difficulty. The same problem was also raised in connection with levels of measurement, to which I have referred in passing. It is clear, however, that the issue of isomorphism may be raised at somewhat different levels of analysis. Garbett identifies three stages or levels in the analytical process. At the lowest level there are the empirical data collected in terms of some set of concepts. Then, making use of the procedures Willer (1967) describes, and using what Willer refers to as nominal definitions, one may construct an *iconic* model. The word "iconic" here refers to the representational nature of the model. The relevant features of the empirical data are placed in juxtaposition to one another in such a way as to make their connections apparent. Some analysis must be carried out on the data to construct the iconic model: those data's features must be defined nominally in terms of a conceptual scheme, and the analyst must spell out some postulated necessary conditions. The isomorphism between the iconic model and the data exists to the extent to which the analyst finds relationships among the features of his data that the analytical scheme predicates. An adjacency matrix reflecting the links among a set of actors, so manipulated as to reveal the clusters of actors linked to one another more strongly than to others, would be a simple iconic model of this kind. Willer remarks that nearly all models in sociology are iconic, and this is probably true of anthropology as well.

The weakness of iconic models is that they lack what Garbett, following Willer, refers to as a "mechanism," but which I would prefer to call a "dynamic" if that term were not likely to be misunderstood. A mechanism, for Willer, is a statement of the relationships among the defined features of an analytical scheme that allows us to understand why some of the features take the form or value they do under certain circumstances. Models that can specify how features change, given other changes either within the scheme or exogenous to it, Willer refers to as *symbolic* models. If the model is stated in mathematical terms, then the isomorphism we are concerned with is that between the mathematical operations carried out on the features of the analytical scheme and the *logic* of the analytical scheme itself. The isomorphism is between logics rather than between procedures.

A possible example of a symbolic model is that which Geoghegan has developed on the basis of Harrison White's pioneering exploration of the algebra of kinship (see D. White 1973: 402–409). Geoghegan's analysis takes the original material prescribed by Das relating to Purum marriages. Earlier, Harrison White had reduced the rules of exogamy among the component sibs to a simple digraph which accounted for nearly three-quarters of the observed marriages reported. At this stage there is an isomorphism between the cultural rules and the model, but the model is iconic and furthermore does not fit the data particularly well. Geoghegan noted that the relative size of the sibs would impose constraints on the operation of the rules of intermarriage, since it is obvious that for some sibs it would be impossible for some of their members to find mates in the designated sibs. He then postulated contingency rules which would come into action only if unfavorable demographic circumstances prevented choices from being made in terms of the formal rules of intermarriage. By including in the model parameters for the de facto size of the sibs and subsidiary rules for the choice of a spouse when the demographic circumstances nullified the conventional rules, Geoghegan was able to account for 98% of the observed marriages. My uncertainty in attributing full symbolic status to this model turns on whether there is ethnographic evidence for the contingency rules that Geoghegan postulates. I simply do not know the literature well enough to answer this question.

Much of the discussion of the problem of isomorphism has been in terms of levels of measurement. If some analytical method ascribes a *numeral* to a feature as if it were a *number,* for example, the assumptions underlying the measurement procedure may be violated. If an analyst assigns the numerals 4 and 6 to features in his analysis, he may simply have chosen these labels in order to produce a distribution table. In this case they are merely substitutes for whatever other names the features may be given. Alternatively the analyst may wish to indicate that the feature labeled "6" is larger or more important in some way than that labeled "4." The fact that 6 is distanced by a value of 2 from 4 is irrelevant except that it provides for the existence of some other feature larger than that labeled "4" and smaller than that labeled "6." Obviously, to carry out mathematical operations on the labels other than those consonant with their nominal or ordinal level of measurement would be erroneous because of the lack of isomorphism between the operations performed and what the numerals really stand for. In exactly the same way, to assume that the numerals represent points on some interval scale, without verifying that the method of measurement ensured it, is to commit an error arising out of the lack of isomorphism between the numerical operations and the level of measurement.

This is very elementary. It is unlikely that any anthropologist but the most ignorant of numerical procedures will fall into this trap. But when more complex mathematical procedures are being used, it may be quite difficult to demonstrate the lack of consistency between an analytical model and the mathematical procedures that purport to follow the logic of the analysis. The challenge of using numerical and mathematical procedures is precisely that of documenting the isomorphism between analytical models and the mathematical procedures used to represent them.

This challenge is more easily presented than met. In general, while it may be feasible to demonstrate that a mathematical or numerical procedure is *not* isomorphic with some analytical scheme, it is much more difficult to demonstrate that an isomorphism *does* exist. The pragmatic test is, of course, whether given certain conditions the model based on these procedures reflects accurately the disposition of specified features in the empirical data. Geoghegan's model, for example, fits the Purum data very well. But we all know that it is possible for rather different models to explain the same data equally well. It is not surprising that the desert of mathematical anthropology is littered with half-buried, Ozymandias-like visages of procedures once deemed to be isomorphic with analytical schemes.

Again we face the question of which mathematical procedures are most trustworthy for the social sciences. Abell (1968, 1969) is among those who have argued that mathematical methods inherited from the natural sciences are patently inappropriate for social science. His observations, while addressed to sociologists, are also germane to anthropologists. In essence he maintains that the relationships anthropologists and sociologists are concerned with are most faithfully represented by ordinal graphs—that is, by points, representing clans, castes, groups, villages, persons, or any other theoretically significant feature of analysis, and a set of lines representing relationships linking those points. The analyst accords each line a numeral, which represents the ordinal value of the particular interpoint relationship—not necessarily unique—among all the interpoint relationships. Abell believes that actors in social situations operate mostly in terms of ordinal rather than cardinal evaluations, to the extent that they sometimes even reduce differentiation based on continuous metric properties to broad equivalence classes—just as people reduce the enormously fine gradations of wealth to a relatively small number of socioeconomic classes. To analyze data of this ordinal kind, we should use procedures that can encompass several different types of relationships simultaneously—relationships that are ordinally expressed in terms of a set of relevant analytical characteristics. The answer, Abell feels, lies in algebraic topology, particularly in algebraic simplexes and complexes which, he argues, have the distinct advantage that no metric notions need be built into them (Abell 1969: 404). Basically, the procedure is to represent the concatenation of links among elements in the analysis as algebraic structures: those links involved in only one relationship as points, those with two as lines, those with three as triangles, and those with four as three-dimensional polyhedra. Empirical examples will be located at the vertices, along the lines, on the surface of the triangles, or in the bodies of the polyhedra according to the number of relationships that are involved. Just where they are placed along the lines, on the surface of the triangles, or within the interior of the polyhedra will depend on the ordinal valuations of the relationships defining these forms.

Abell argues that empirical social systems may be analyzed using simplexes like these points, lines, triangles, and polyhedra, which may be looked upon as component elements of the set of data that may be fitted together to give a total picture. The social system, then, is represented by simplicial complexes. Given the nature of social phenomena, Abell argues that "this is much more realistic than mapping the phenomena into the real number system and adding numbers together" (1969: 406).

Apart from the obvious advantage of maintaining isomorphism between the data and the analytical scheme, these procedures have three further advantages. The first is that, in Abell's words, "The really interesting feature of any algebraic treatment is associated with the search for so-called topological invariants. These are in some sense global properties of a complex that show that those complexes (structures) which might on the face of it seem different are indeed very much alike" (1969: 406). "Superficial" differences may thus be distinguished from "real" differences, and regular forms of structure may be established in data sets which at first sight seem very dissimilar.

The second advantage, in Abell's own words, is that "the simplicial treatment lends itself naturally to algebraic analysis in terms of group theory. Such algebraic analysis may lay the foundations for the analysis of law-like regularity in these structures." The third advantage, finally, is that "the simplexes can be embedded in a suitable space so that we can attach meaning to the positions within them" (Abell 1969: 405).

Algebraic group theory manipulation of simplicial complexes may remove the suspicion that the structures determined on the basis of algebraic topology are nothing more than exceedingly elegant iconic models. So far I have not seen any analysis of anthropological data using these procedures, nor can I visualize precisely how the dynamic in a social system may be represented by group theory. Until someone is proficient enough in both anthropological and mathematical analysis to develop the idea, we will not know.

NOTES

1. See Burton (1973) for a discussion of levels of measurement and their implications for data analysis.

2. The standard work on numerical taxonomy is Sokal and Sneath (1963). Bailey (1974a) provides a useful critique of the procedures. A less technical account related to the social sciences is available in Everitt (1974). The topic is discussed briefly in relation to ethnographic analysis by Majone and Sanday (1971) and by Burton (1973).

3. Methods of deriving factor scores are discussed in textbooks on factor analysis, such as Harman (1967) or Lawley and Maxwell (1971).

4. In view of the points raised by Heise and Bohrnstedt (1970), Alwin (1973), and Allen (1974), who are concerned with the reliability of factor scores derived from different methods of factor analysis, if I were repeating the exercise I would use either maximum likelihood factor analysis or canonical factor analysis.

5. For a concise discussion of the advantages and use of dummy regression analysis see Miller and Erickson (1974).

6. McFarland and Brown (1973) provide a very useful discussion of the notion of social distance and how it may relate mathematically to physical distance.

7. This assumes, of course, that the ordering of groups is determinate. Alternatively, the data Romney presents in Table 2 could be looked upon as the basis for a conditional proximity matrix and could be analyzed by one of the methods proposed by Coombs (1964: Chapters 17 and 22). Multidimensional scaling procedures exist to perform analyses of this sort, e.g., SSA-II (see Lingoes 1973: 80 et seq.). Lingoes suggests, incidentally, that the results from an analysis of this kind may be used to symmetrize an asymmetrical matrix according to what he calls "rational" procedures as against "the common practice of averaging cell *ij* with *ji* prior to a symmetrical analysis" (Lingoes 1973: 87), as Romney in fact does.

There is, of course, a third alternative: to eschew the analogy with distances entirely and to treat the matrix as a contingency table. It has been known for about forty years that it is possible to extract what Hope calls "the contingency hierarchies" from a contingency table (see Hope 1972: 108) by a process of canonical analysis. Each "hierarchy" is a matrix of values which when aggregated over all "hierarchies" reproduce the original frequencies in the table. Each "hierarchy" may be regarded as reflecting an interaction effect of the rows and columns at the particular level of extraction, thus providing a possible basis of substantive analysis. Using this method, Hope (1972) provides an instructive analysis of the marriage of people drawn from different "social classes" in Scotland. The procedure has been called conjoint measurement by Lingoes (1973) and is described clearly by Davis (1977), but without the sophistication Hope exhibits

8. There have recently been some interesting attempts to set up transformations of initial estimates of distances such that the derived distances will satisfy all the axioms of metric spaces but need not necessarily imply a dimensional structure. See, for example, Cunningham and Shepard (1974), who adopt a procedure that maximizes the variance of the set of distances among a set of elements by stretching the larger distances and squeezing the smaller. This method aims to retain the ordinal relationships among all the distances as in multidimensional scaling, while at the same time meeting the conditions for metric spaces. The object is to try to recover the characteristics of the distance function which gave rise to the set of interelement distances in the first instance. Since the function need not imply a spatial structure,

distance functions such as those generated by graphs, for example, could be recovered by this procedure. I do not know of any application of this device to social anthropological data.

REFERENCES

Abell, P. 1968. Measurement in sociology: measurement systems. *Sociology,* 2: 1–20.

———. 1969. Measurement in sociology: measurement structure and sociological theory. *Sociology,* 3: 397–411.

Allen, M. P. 1974. Construction of composite measures by the canonical-factor-regression method. In H. L. Costner, ed., *Sociological Methodology, 1973-1974,* pp. 51–78. London: Jossey-Bass Ltd.

Alwin, D. F. 1973. The use of factor analysis in the construction of linear composites in social research. *Sociological Methods and Research,* 2: 191–214.

Bailey, K. D. 1974a. Cluster analysis. In D. R. Heise, ed., *Sociological Methodology, 1975,* pp. 59–128. London: Jossey-Bass Ltd.

———. 1974b. Interpreting smallest space analysis. *Sociological Methods and Research,* 3: 3–29.

Bishop, Y. M. M., S. E. Feinberg, and P. W. Holland. 1975. *Discrete Multivariate Analysis: Theory and Practice.* London: MIT Press.

Bloombaum, M. 1968. Tribes and traits: a smallest space analysis of cross-cultural data. *American Anthropologist,* 70: 328–330.

Burton, M. 1972. Semantic dimensions of occupational names. In R. N. Shepard, A. K. Romney, and S. B. Nerlove, eds., *Multidimensional Scaling: Theory and Applications in the Behavioral Sciences,* Vol 2, pp. 55–72. New York: Seminar Press.

———. 1973. Mathematical anthropology. In B. J. Seigel, ed., *Annual Review of Anthropology,* pp. 189–197. Palo Alto: Annual Review Inc.

Cicourel, A. 1964. *Method and Measurement in Sociology.* London: Collier-Macmillan Ltd.

Coleman, J. S. 1964. *Introduction to Mathematical Sociology.* New York: Basic Books.

Coombs, C. H. 1964. *A Theory of Data.* New York: John Wiley and Sons.

Coxon, A. P. M. n.d. *Multidimensional Scaling ECPR Course Notes.* Monograph on Social Science Data Analysis. Colchester: University of Essex.

Cunningham, J. P., and R. N. Shepard. 1974. Monotone mapping of similarities into a general metric space. *Journal of Mathematical Psychology,* 11: 335–363.

Curtis, R. F., and E. F. Jackson. 1962. Multiple indicators in survey research. *American Journal of Sociology,* 67: 195–204.

D'Andrade, R. G., N. R. Quinn, S. B. Nerlove, and A. K. Romney. 1972. Categories of disease in American-English and Mexican-Spanish. In R. N. Shepard, A. K. Romney, and S. B. Nerlove, eds., *Multidimensional Scaling: Theory and Applications in the Behavioral Sciences,* Vol. 2, pp. 11–54. New York: Seminar Press.

Davis, J. A. 1971. *Elementary Survey Analysis.* Englewood Cliffs, N.J.: Prentice-Hall.

———. 1974. Hierarchical models for significance tests in multivariate contingency tables: an exegesis of Goodman's recent papers. In H. L. Costner, ed., *Sociological Methodology, 1973–1974,* pp. 189–231. London: Jossey-Bass Ltd.

Davis, P. B. 1977. Conjoint measurement and the canonical analysis of contingency tables. *Sociological Methods and Research*, 5: 347–365.

Everitt, B. 1974. *Cluster Analysis*. London: Heinemann Educational Books Ltd.

Feller, W. 1957. *An Introduction to Probability Theory and Its Applications*, Vol 1. London: John Wiley and Sons.

Goodman, L. A. 1972. A general model for the analysis of surveys. *American Journal of Sociology*, 77: 1035–1086.

———. 1973. Causal analysis of data from panel studies and other kinds of surveys. *American Journal of Sociology*, 78: 1135–1191.

Gower, J. C. 1966. Some distance properties of latent root and vector methods used in multivariate analysis. *Biometrika*, 53: 325–338.

———. 1967. Multivariate analysis and multidimensional geometry. *The Statistician*, 17: 13–28.

Hage, P. 1973–1974. A graph theoretic approach to the analysis of alliance structure and local grouping in Highland New Guinea. *Anthropological Forum*, 3: 280–294.

———. 1976. Structural balance and clustering in Bushmen kinship relations. *Behavioural Science*, 21: 36–47.

Harary, F., R. Z. Norman, and D. Cartwright. 1965. *Structural Models: An Introduction to the Theory of Directed Graphs*. New York: John Wiley and Sons.

Harman, H. H. 1967. *Modern Factor Analysis*. London: University of Chicago Press.

Harris, C. W. 1967. On factors and factor scores. *Psychometrika*, 32: 363–379.

Heise, D. R., and G. W. Bohrnstedt. 1970. Validity, invalidity and reliability of a composite score. In E. F. Borgatta and G. W. Bohrnstedt, eds., *Sociological Methodology, 1970*, pp. 104–129. London: Jossey-Bass Ltd.

Hoffman, H. 1970. Mathematical anthropology. In B. J. Siegel, ed., *Biennial Review of Anthropology, 1969*, pp. 41–79. Stanford: Stanford University Press.

Hope, K. 1972. Marriage markets in the stratification system. In K. Hope, ed., *The Analysis of Social Mobility: Methods and Approaches*, pp. 105–120. Oxford: Clarendon Press.

Isnard, C. A., and E. C. Zeeman. 1975. Some models from catastrophe theory in the social sciences. In L. Collins, ed., *Use of Models in the Social Sciences*, pp. 44–100. London: Tavistock.

Kay, P., ed. 1971. *Explorations in Mathematical Anthropology*. London: MIT Press.

Kendall, D. G. 1975. The recovery of structure from fragmentary information. *Philosophical Transactions of the Royal Society of London*, 279(1291): 547–582.

Lawley, D. N., and A. E. Maxwell. 1971. *Factor Analysis as a Statistical Method*, 2nd ed. London: Butterworth.

Lingoes, J. C. 1973. *The Guttman-Lingoes Nonmetric Program Series*, pp. 277–338. Ann Arbor, Mich.: Mathesis Press.

Livingstone, F. B. 1969. The applicability of structural models to marriage systems in anthropology. In I. Buckler and H. Nutini, eds., *Game Theory in the Behavioral Sciences*, pp. 235–252. Pittsburgh: University of Pittsburgh Press.

McDonald, R. P., and E. J. Burr. 1967. A comparison of four methods of constructing factor scores. *Psychometrika*, 32: 381–401.

McFarland, D. D., and D. J. Brown. 1973. Social distance as a metric: a systematic introduction to smallest space analysis. In E. O. Laumann, ed., *The Bonds of Pluralism: The Form and Substance of Urban Social Networks*, Appendix A, pp. 213–253. New York: John Wiley and Sons.

Majone, G., and P. R. Sanday. 1971. On the numerical classifications of nominal data. In P. Kay, ed., *Explorations in Mathematical Anthropology,* pp. 226–241. London: MIT Press.

Miller, J. L. L., and M. L. Erickson. 1974. On dummy variable regression analysis: a description and illustration of the method. *Sociological Methods and Research,* 2: 409–430.

Mitchell, J. C. 1962. *The Yao Village,* 2nd ed. Manchester: Manchester University Press.

Parzen, E. 1960. *Modern Probability Theory and Its Applications.* London: John Wiley and Sons.

Romney, A. K. 1972. Multidimensional scaling and semantic domains. *The Study of Man,* 1: 1–19.

Shepard, R. N. 1972. Introduction to Volume 1. In R. N. Shepard, A. K. Romney, and S. B. Nerlove, eds., *Multidimensional Scaling: Theory and Applications in the Behavioral Sciences,* pp. 1–20. New York: Seminar Press.

Shepard, R. N., A. K. Romney, and S. B. Nerlove, eds. 1972. *Multidimensional Scaling: Theory and Applications in the Behavioral Sciences,* Vols. 1 and 2. New York: Seminar Press.

Sokal, R. R., and P. H. A. Sneath. 1963. *Principles of Numerical Taxonomy.* London: Freeman.

Susmilch, C. E., and W. T. Johnson. 1975. Factor scores for constructing linear composites: do different techniques make a difference? *Sociological Methods and Research,* 4: 166–188.

Torgerson, W. S. 1958. *Theory and Method of Scaling.* New York: John Wiley and Sons.

Tucker, L. R. 1971. Relations of factor score estimates to their use. *Psychometrika,* 36: 427–436.

Wexler, K. N., and A. K. Romney. 1972. Individual variations in cognitive structures. In R. N. Shepard, A. K. Romney, and S. B. Nerlove, eds., *Multidimensional Scaling: Theory and Applications in the Behavioral Sciences,* Vol. 2, pp. 73–92. New York: Seminar Press.

White, D. R. 1973. Mathematical anthropology. In J. J. Honigmann, ed., *Handbook of Social and Cultural Anthropology,* pp. 369–446. Chicago: Rand McNally.

Willer, D. E. 1967. *Scientific Sociology: Theory and Method.* Englewood Cliffs, N.J.: Prentice-Hall.

Zeeman, E. C., C. S. Hall, P. J. Harrison, G. H. Marriage, and P. H. Shapland. 1976. A model for institutional disturbances. *British Journal of Mathematical and Statistical Psychology,* 29 (Part 1): 66–80.

Part One

QUANTITATIVE ANALYSIS

Implications of the Sexual Division of Labor in Agriculture

JACK GOODY AND JOAN BUCKLEY

THE PROBLEM

In looking at the background to the role of women in development, Ester Boserup (1970) distinguishes between "male and female farming systems," which she then tries to relate to population density, technology, and type of cultivation. Her thesis is summarized in the following words: "In very sparsely populated regions where shifting cultivation is used, men do little farm work, the women doing most. In somewhat more densely populated regions where the agricultural system is that of extensive plough cultivation, women do little farm work and men do much more. Finally, in the regions of intensive cultivation of irrigated land, both men and women must put hard work into agriculture in order to earn enough to support a family on a small piece of land" (p. 35). She associates the sexual division of labor with differences in the position of women in rural communities, which fall into two broad groups:

> The first type is found in regions where shifting cultivation predominates and the major part of agricultural work is done by women. In such communities, we can expect to find a high incidence of polygamy [polygyny], and bride wealth being paid by the future husband or his family. The women are hard working and have only a limited right of support from their husbands, but they often enjoy considerable freedom of movement and some economic independence from the sale of their own crops.
>
> The second group is found where plough cultivation predominates and where women do less agricultural work than men. In such communities we may expect to find that only a tiny minority of marriages, if any, are polygamous; that a dowry is usually paid by the girl's family; that a wife is entirely dependent upon her husband for economic support; and that the husband has an obligation to support his wife and children, at least as long as the marriage is in force [p. 50].

This thesis has much in common with that developed in connection with a series of studies of the relationship between types of production and aspects of kinship and marriage. In these papers the main concern has been

33

to relate patterns of transmitting property to forms of polity and agriculture ("shifting" versus "advanced") as the independent variables, and forms of marriage, kinship terminologies, etc., as the "dependent" variables. The investigation has been carried out by searching the relevant (or available) ethnographic literature, as in the work on adoption (Goody 1969a), or, more systematically, more extensively, but less intensively, by means of the material that has been arranged for us in coded form in the "Ethnographic Atlas" (Murdock 1967, with subsequent corrections).[1] It is the second of these two procedures that we wish to employ here. Our intention is to use the "Ethnographic Atlas" in order to explore the relationship between the sexual division of labor and the other variables with which we were earlier concerned, as well as those that enter into Boserup's analysis. The aim is to create a model that incorporates the division of labor by sex. For this purpose we employ the techniques of hierarchical linkage analysis and path analysis, as in our earlier attempt to set up a causal model (Goody, Irving, and Tahany 1971).[2]

THE MODEL INCORPORATING THE DIVISION OF LABOR BY SEX

We have made certain changes in the variables used in our earlier study. In three cases, two closely linked variables have been combined: "plough agriculture" and "intensive agriculture" have been combined to form "advanced agriculture"; "endogamy" and "father's brother's daughter marriage" have been combined to form "in-marriage"; "large states" and "stratification" have been combined to form "complex polities."

In Table 1 we show the roles of the sexes in farming in relation to the prevailing type of agriculture for the 863 societies studied. Aside from the cases of equal participation, the difference between male and female farming is marked: male farming is associated with the more advanced agriculture ($\chi^2 = 83.7$, $p < 0.001$), while female farming is found mainly with simple agriculture ($\chi^2 = 77.5$, $p < 0.001$). As predicted by Boserup, the association is strong.

Another variable discussed by Boserup (1970) is that of population density. We cannot test this directly, since the information is not included in the "Atlas." The nearest indicator, not a very satisfactory one, is the size of the population of the local community (Table 2). Here we find that societies with male farming tend to have larger communities than societies in which female labor predominates. Fifty-nine percent of those with male farming fall into the category of 400+ persons, and most of these have over 10,000 members; in contrast, only 22% of those with female farming have communities of 400 or more, and few of these have more than 10,000 people. Thus some support is given to the idea of greater population density in societies with male farming as opposed to those with female farming. On the other hand, according to Boserup's argument, equal participation ought to be more closely associated with intensive agriculture and with communities of the largest size. But the equal division of labor between the sexes seems to be found in a wide range of societies, not only those with a high degree of intensive agriculture (as she suggests) but also those in which agriculture no longer plays the dominant role in the economy.

TABLE 1   *Sex Roles in Agriculture and the Presence of Advanced Agriculture*[a]

| Sex Participation | Advanced Agriculture | | Total |
	Present	Absent	
Female farming	42 (25.8%)	191 (69.7%)	233
Male farming	121 (74.2%)	83 (30.3%)	204
Total	163	274	437[b]

Note: Data are from the "Ethnographic Atlas" (Murdock 1967). Sex roles in agriculture are coded from Col. 62: G, F = present; M, N = absent; D, E = equal participation; no entry, P, O, I = insufficient information, no agriculture, or unspecified. Advanced agriculture is coded from Cols. 28 and 39: Col. 28 O, C, E or Col. 39 no entry = absent; Col. 28 H, I, J or Col. 39 Q, P = present; Col. 28 no entry or Col. 39 O = insufficient information.

[a]$\chi^2 = 77.5$, $p < 0.001$.

[b]Total of table = 437. Total of societies with equal participation or no agriculture, where sex participation is irrelevant or where there is no information = 426. Total number of societies is therefore 863.

TABLE 2   *Sex Roles in Agriculture and Community Size*[a]

Population of Community	Female Farming	Male Farming	Equal Participation	Total
0–99	35 } (77.8%)	17 } (40.8%)	33 } (63.3%)	85
100–399	56	32	36	124
400–1000	19 } (22.2%)	16 } (59.2%)	15 } (36.7%)	50
1000+	7	55	25	87
Total	117	120	109	346[b]

Note: Data from the "Ethnographic Atlas" (Murdock 1967). Sex roles in agriculture are coded as in Table 1. Community size is coded in Col. 31: 1 + 2 = 0–99; 3 + 4 = 100–399; 5 = 400–1000; 6 + 7 + 8 = 1000+; 0 or no entry = no information. (Communities in which agriculture is absent are mainly of small size.)

[a]Taking the figures for male and female farming in relation to large and small sizes of local communities gives $\chi^2 = 33.4$ (df = 1), $p < 0.001$.

[b]Total of table = 346; no agriculture = 188; no information on agriculture = 33; no information on community size = 296; total = 863.

Boserup argues that the contrast between female farming (with shifting cultivation) and male farming (where women are either secluded in the home or occupied almost wholly in the domestic sphere) is also related to "the difference in the pattern of social hierarchy between regions of tribal organization and regions of settled farmers with individual ownership of land" (1970: 27). Plough agriculture is found in areas where there is private land ownership and a landless class whose labor is available for hire. "As hired labourers are called in, so are the women of cultivator families released from agricultural work. On the other hand, women always seem to bear a large part of the work burden in the more egalitarian communities" (p. 31). We can test the association suggested here between the sexual division of labor and complex polity; the association between female agriculture and simple polities is strong ($\phi = 0.26$).[3]

Again the role of women in agriculture is seen as connected with the type of marriage. In regions of female farming, Boserup writes, women are valued both as workers and as child bearers; in "such communities, we can expect to find a high incidence of polygamy, and bride wealth being paid by the future husband or his family" (p. 50). Where women do little agricultural work, they are valued as mothers only and the status of a barren woman is particularly vulnerable; in such communities "we may expect to find that only a tiny minority of marriages, if any, are polygamous; that a dowry is usually paid by the girl's family" (p. 50). Table 3 shows the distribution of sex roles in agriculture in relation to the plurality of marriage.

TABLE 3   *Sex Roles in Agriculture and Plurality of Marriage*[a]

Type of Marriage	No Agriculture	Female Farming	Male Farming	Equal Participation	Total
Monogamy	16 (8.6%)	19 (8.2%)	57 (28.4%)	38 (18.5%)	130
Limited polygyny	98 (52.7%)	65 (28.0%)	82 (40.8%)	82 (40.0%)	327
General polygyny	72 (38.7%)	148 (63.8%)	62 (30.8%)	85 (41.5%)	367
Total	186	232	201	205	824[b]

Note: Data are from the "Ethnographic Atlas" (Murdock 1967). Sex roles in agriculture are coded in Col. 62: zero = no agriculture; F, G = female farming; M, N = male farming; D, E = equal participation; no entry, I, P = no information. Plurality of marriage is coded in Cols. 14 and 15: M = monogamy; N = limited polygyny; O, G, F, E in Col. 14 and R, S, Q, P in either column = general polygyny; no entry in Col. 14 and Col. 15 = no information.

[a]$\chi^2 = 81.3$ (df = 6), $p < 0.001$.

[b]Total of table = 824; no information on agriculture = 33; no information on plurality of marriage = 6; total = 863.

Monogamy is most likely to be found with male farming and general polygyny least likely (although limited polygyny is common); the reverse occurs with female farming. If we simply test the association of male (compared to female) farming with monogamy (as opposed to polygyny), the ϕ result is 0.26. With type of marriage transaction, the position is less clear (Table 4); male farming is somewhat less strongly associated with bridewealth than is female farming (or equal participation) and slightly more with dowry, but the latter type is rare even with male farming. However, dowry (transmission of property to women at marriage) is only part of a wider system of intergenerational transmission we have called "diverging devolution," which includes inheritance by women (transmission of property to women at death). If we test the association of male farming with diverging devolution, we find this to be strong ($\phi = 0.40$). Here again the tests we are able to carry out lend support to the hypotheses.

Boserup's thesis is similar in several respects to that we proposed in an earlier paper, where we tried to test for the concomitants of methods of transmitting property by using data available in the "Ethnographic Atlas" (Goody 1969b). A hypothesis was put forward linking a number of features

TABLE 4 *Sex Roles in Agriculture and Marriage Transactions*[a]

Marriage Transaction	No Agriculture	Female Farming	Male Farming	Equal Participation	Total
Bridewealth	51 (27.1%)	135 (58.4%)	85 (41.7%)	116 (56.6%)	387
Bride service	30 (16.0%)	27 (11.7%)	16 (7.8%)	19 (9.3%)	92
Gift exchange and sister exchange	33 (17.6%)	20 (8.7%)	10 (4.9%)	15 (7.3%)	78
Dowry	2 (1.1%)	0 (0.0%)	15 (7.4%)	7 (3.4%)	24
No payment taken	72 (38.3%)	49 (21.2%)	78 (38.2%)	48 (23.4%)	247
Total	188	231	204	205	828[b]

Note: Data are from the "Ethnographic Atlas" (Murdock 1967). Sex roles in agriculture are coded as in Table 3. Marriage transactions are coded in Col. 12: B = brideprice; S = bride service; G, X = gift or sister exchange; D = dowry; T, O = no payment taken; no entry = insufficient information.

[a]$\chi^2 = 93.9$ (df = 12), $p < 0.001$.

[b]Total of table = 828; no information on agriculture = 33; no information on marriage transaction = 2; total = 863.

of domestic organization with specific ways of transmitting property to women as well as men (diverging devolution). These methods of inheriting property were in turn seen as associated with the development of an elaborate social stratification based on increased production through use of the plough, irrigation, or other forms of advanced agriculture.

Boserup (1970) is concerned mainly with the division of labor by sex and specifically with the part played by women in the development of the economy and with the effect of "traditional" systems on the modern scene. She also links shifting cultivation with polygyny and bridewealth, and advanced agriculture with monogamy and dowry. However, she introduces an added dimension into the analysis by emphasizing the variable of the division of labor by sex. Table 5 sets out to compare the correlation coefficients (ϕ) of the set of "Atlas" variables with the sexual division of labor in agriculture on the one hand and with diverging devolution on the other, in order to discover the strength of the respective degrees of association. These two "explanatory" variables are themselves highly correlated with one another (0.40). Both are closely linked with the other variables; in two cases diverging devolution produces the best results, in four cases the division of labor does. However, (and this is the third point), when we examine the individual results, we find that the division of labor behaves better in relation to the two "independent" variables, namely "advanced agriculture" and "complex polity."

This is to be expected. The sexual division of labor in farming is bound to be closely linked to the type of agriculture, specifically in the case of advanced agriculture. The plough, in particular, is a male instrument employed almost entirely by men; indeed large livestock, whether horses, cattle, or camels, are almost exclusively in male hands. Their use in agri-

TABLE 5   *Diverging Devolution and Division of Labor,*
φ Coeffcients Compared

Variable	Diverging Devolution	Division of Labor[a]
Diverging devolution	—	0.40
Division of labor	0.40	—
Prohibition of premarital sex	0.21	0.19
Sibling kin terms	0.28	0.29
Advanced agriculture	0.22	0.42
Complex polity	0.25	0.26
In-marriage	0.32	0.33
Monogamy	0.34	0.26

[a]That is, the relative predominance of women or men.

cultural production means that the male role becomes equal, if not dominant.

When we add the sexual division of labor to the original variables and attempt a hierarchical linkage analysis, we find that two main clusters emerge (Figure 1). The first is made up of diverging devolution, monogamy, and in-marriage. The second consists of male farming and advanced agriculture, closely linked to complex polity; these three variables in turn are linked more loosely to sibling kin terms. Prohibited premarital sex is linked directly to neither of the two main clusters; rather, the two clusters themselves link together at a median correlation of 0.26 before both are linked to prohibited premarital sex at a median correlation of 0.14. The resulting hierarchical structure differs from the one published earlier (Goody et al. 1971), because of the combining of the two pairs of variables mentioned earlier and the introduction of the "sexual division of labor." The previous results were based on the McQuitty procedure, which averages the correlation coefficients. The present procedures, for which we are indebted to Dr. J. C. Mitchell, avoid this problem. There are indeed three alternative procedures: the Median method, the Minimum method (also known as the "nearest neighbor" method), which links clusters by the highest correlation between them, and finally the Maximum method, which links clusters by the lowest correlation between them and hence imposes more stringent conditions. Figure 1 is based on the Median method and is similar in shape to that produced by applying the McQuitty method, except that the values are a little different. The most rigorous of the alternatives, the Maximum method, gives a slightly different picture in that "diverging devolution" joins in-marriage at the first level before attaching itself to the other variables at the third level. In these hierarchies, the sexual division of labor is closer to the political and economic variables (as one might expect) than diverging devolution, which lies closer to the "kinship" variables, with the one exception of the kin terminology. In other words, we have a politico-economic cluster and a kinship cluster, with the division of labor being associated with the former and inheritance with the latter. Division of labor and inheritance are, in turn, closely linked to each other (as shown in Table 5).

CAUSAL RELATIONSHIPS

In order to test a possible causal sequence, we attempted to apply the method of path analysis, as described in the earlier paper (Goody et al. 1971). The type of model we thought might account for our data is shown in Figure 2. Inevitably this model is an oversimplification of reality; in order to apply path analysis it is necessary to assume a one-way flow, and a separation of variables, relative to one another, into dependent and inde-

FIGURE 1

Hierarchical Clustering by Median Method

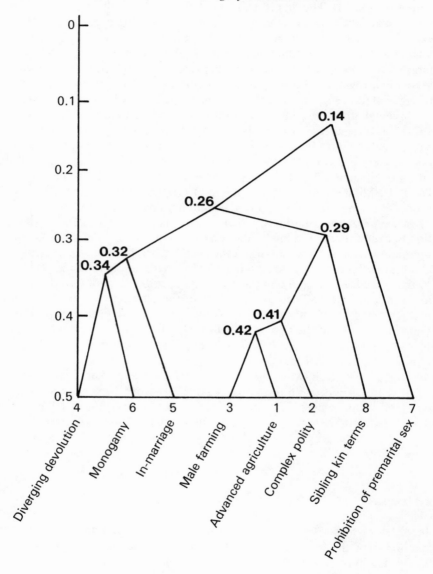

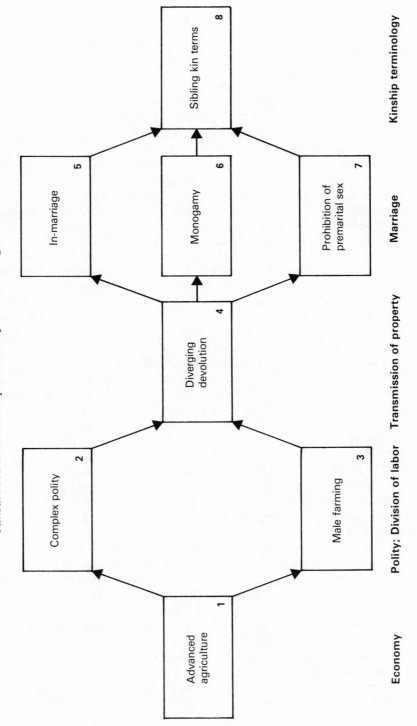

FIGURE 2

Causal Model: Social Implications of Advanced Agriculture

Economy   Polity; Division of labor   Transmission of property   Marriage   Kinship terminology

pendent.[4] Moreover, in this particular instance it was also necessary to impose a strict order on the variables, as indicated by the numbers in Figure 2. Figure 3 shows the model as it emerges from the test. The testing was again carried out by Dr. Mitchell, who comments, "From this model you will see that a great deal of your paradigm survives quite well. I have arbitrarily omitted all paths of less than 0.1. The difficulties at the moment are the relatively strong paths between Complex Polity and Prohibited Premarital Sex and Sibling Kin Terms."[5]

Comparing the hypothetical model with the results of the path analysis, we note that account has to be taken of the independent influence of complex polity on in-marriage (the path coefficient being 0.20) as well as on the prohibition of premarital sex. In addition, account has to be taken of the independent influence of the sexual division of labor in agriculture on in-marriage and to a lesser extent on the plurality of marriage and on the prohibition on premarital sex. While these paths were not predicted in the tentative causal model we suggested, the results are not antithetical to our general argument. One element, however, does run contrary to our hypothesis, namely the absence of the predicted path between monogamy and sibling kin terms, despite the correlation between them ($\phi = 0.23$). In other words, the latter relationship would appear to be accounted for by the effects of antecedent causal variables. This is perhaps not altogether surprising, since the cluster analysis places sibling terms apart from the major groupings of variables, and it would appear from other ethnological evidence that there is considerable latitude in the adaptation of kin terms to systems of kinship and marriage in the wider sense. A change in the latter certainly does not entail an immediate change in the terminologies employed; indeed similar terminologies are found in a wide range of social systems.

While we would not wish to overvalue the use of such techniques, we do see them as an advance that assists us in getting beyond the much simpler unilineal, single-factor hypotheses that dog so much of anthropology, since they reduce the arbitrary element in our assumptions and attempt to replace dispute by argument.

There are many aspects of Boserup's thesis that we could pursue. The connection between female farming and matriliny has been the subject of much discussion, from Hahn (1896) and Baumann (1928) to Aberle (1961).[6] There is the associated problem of the house-property complex, which we have discussed in an earlier paper (Goody and Buckley 1972). Boserup's argument raises the question of polygyny and agriculture and of purdah and the withdrawal of women from "economic" life. Indeed it raises in acute form the whole problem of defining the woman's contribution to the economy. But here we have had a more limited objective: to test Boserup's thesis by means of the "Ethnographic Atlas" and to relate her thesis concerning the role of women in agricultural economies to the analysis of

FIGURE 3

Causal Model Tested by Path Analysis

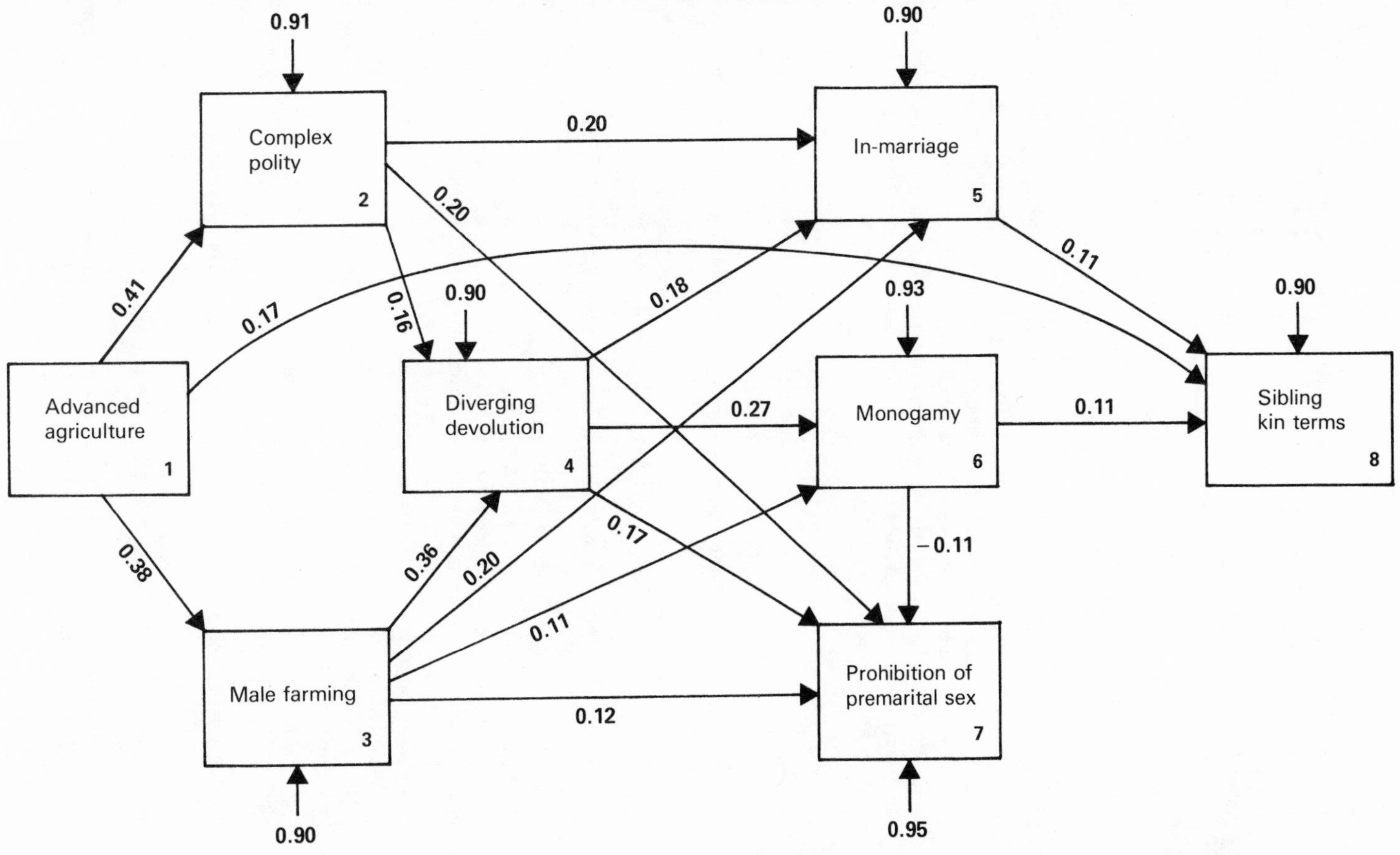

This figure omits paths with coefficients less than 0.1, which is taken as an arbitrary cutoff point since estimates of standard deviation are not possible.

modes of transmitting property. We find support for certain of the associations suggested by Boserup; her stress on the role of women in shifting
agriculture adds an important dimension to the study of the social implications of productive systems. Finally we tentatively suggest a model that
reconciles her thesis with the devolution hypothesis.

APPENDIX

The "Ethnographic Atlas" (Murdock 1967) also enables us to look at the broad
continental distribution of male and female farming (Table 6). Plough agriculture
with male farming is largely confined to Eurasia; in Africa, hoe farming with female
farming predominates; in North America, although most societies have hunting
economies, female farming is associated with extensive, male farming with intensive
agriculture. In the Pacific, the predominant horticulture is not exclusively associated with any type of division of labor by sex, although equal participation is only
slightly less frequent than in Eurasia.

NOTES

1. Our data are from Murdock's 1967 article in *Ethnology* and from subsequent
corrections printed in the same journal. The data file is available on punched cards
from the Department of Social Anthropology, Downing Street, Cambridge, where
it is known as the "Ethnographic Atlas File (Cambridge, 1974)." Any small differences in the figures from earlier papers are due to corrections that have been published since 1967. For our own analysis, see Goody (1969b) and Goody, Irving, and
Tahany (1971). Murdock's material was published in book form as *Ethnographic
Atlas* (University of Pittsburgh Press, 1967).

2. We are grateful to Dr. J. C. Mitchell for his valuable suggestions and for help
with programs. We would have wished to submit this data to analysis by means of
the AID program developed by Survey Research Center, Michigan, but have been
unable to do so in the time available. We also wish to thank Ian Beeson, Dyanne
Grant, and Colin Duly for their help at various stages.

3. We have run the variable "sex roles in agriculture" by the same variables used
in our previous study (1969b); the summary results (but not the tables themselves)
are given in Table 5.

4. Another problem that is encountered when path analysis handles sociological
data is the requirement that interval scales be assumed, although Boyle (1970) suggests that this problem is not a reason for abandoning the technique when only
"ordinal data" are available. Both Boyle (1970) and Lyons (1971) offer procedures
for recalibrating ordinal scales to make them more nominal. The present paper,
however, has used dichotomized or "dummy" variables, and although some sub-
tlety of interaction has been lost, the model has gained in parsimony and has overcome the problem of the ordinality of the scales used. More sophisticated techniques are now available or are being developed; some of these—e.g., Goodman
log odds ratio procedures—are summarized by Leik (1975). But for the moment we

TABLE 6 *Sex Participation in Agriculture by Continent*[a]

Sex Participation	Africa	Circum-Med.	East Eurasia	Insular Pacific	North America	South America	Total
Female farming	125 (53.9%)	4 (4.7%)	7 (7.6%)	36 (29.8%)	29 (13.6%)	32 (37.6%)	233
Male farming	39 (16.8%)	56 (65.1%)	32 (34.8%)	28 (23.1%)	28 (13.1%)	21 (24.7%)	204
Equal participation	60 (25.9%)	22 (25.6%)	41 (44.6%)	48 (39.7%)	12 (5.6%)	22 (25.9%)	205
No agriculture	8 (3.4%)	4 (4.7%)	12 (13.0%)	9 (7.4%)	145 (67.8%)	10 (11.8%)	188
Total	232	86	92	121	214	85	830[b]

Note: Data are from the "Ethnographic Atlas" (Murdock 1967). Sex participation in agriculture is coded from Col. 62: F, G = female farming; M, N = male farming; D, E = equal participation; 0 = no agriculture; no entry = no information.

[a] $\chi^2 = 505$ (df = 15), $p < 0.001$.

[b] Total of table = 830; no information on agriculture = 33; total = 863.

have presented a simple model using dichotomous variables, which is intended to be exploratory rather than exhaustive.

5. Letter from Dr. J. C. Mitchell dated November 4, 1974. In a subsequent letter Dr. Mitchell suggests testing the model by comparing the postulated presence or absence of a path against the observed value of the path coefficient (absence being arbitrarily defined as being less than 0.1).

Model	Analysis		Total
	Larger than 0.1	Smaller than 0.1	
Path predicted	9	1	10
No path predicted	6	12	18
Total	15	13	28

This test gives a χ^2 value of 7.42 and a ϕ coefficient of 0.51, a fit that he describes as "not bad." Clearly one could improve the fit by allowing for some independent effect of the polity and the division of labor on subsequent variables. Indeed the fit might also be improved by a reordering of the variables for input purposes.

6. For a review of the earlier discussions, see Lowie (1937).

Aberle, D. 1961. Matrilineal descent in cross-cultural perspective. In D. Schneider and K. Gough, eds., *Matrilineal Kinship*. Berkeley: University of California Press.

Baumann, H. 1928. The division of work according to sex in African hoe culture. *Africa*, 1: 289–319.

Boserup, E. 1970. *Women's Role in Economic Development*. London: Allen and Unwin.

Boyle, R. P. 1970. Path analysis and ordinal data. *American Journal of Sociology*, 75: 461–480.

Goody, J. 1969a. Adoption in cross-cultural perspective. *Comparative Studies in Society and History*, 11: 55–78.

———. 1969b. Inheritance, property and marriage in Africa and Eurasia. *Sociology*, 3: 55–76.

Goody, J., and J. Buckley. 1972. Inheritance and women's labour in Africa. *Africa*, 43: 108–121.

Goody, J., B. Irving, and N. Tahany. 1971. Causal inferences concerning inheritance and property. *Human Relations*, 24: 295–314.

Hahn, E. 1896. *Die Haustiere und ihre Beziehungen zur Wirtschaft des Menschen*. Leipzig.

Leik, R. K. 1975. Causal models with nominal and ordinal data: retrospective. In D. R. Heise, ed., *Sociological Methodology, 1976*, pp. 271–275. London: Jossey-Bass Ltd.

Lowie, R. H. 1937. *The History of Ethnological Theory*. London: Harrap.
Lyons, M. 1971. Techniques for using ordinal measures in regression and path analysis. In H. L. Costner, ed., *Sociological Methodology, 1971,* pp. 147–171. London: Jossey-Bass Ltd.
Murdock, G. P. 1967. Ethnographic atlas: a summary. *Ethnology,* 6: 109–236.

Social Factors in the Perception of the Causes of Disease

HILARY FLEGG MITCHELL AND J. CLYDE MITCHELL

ORIENTATIONS TOWARD ILLNESS AND DISEASE

Illness and disease are personal misfortunes which people may explain in various ways. Among the African peoples of Central Africa, in particular the Shona-speaking and the Ndebele-speaking peoples of Rhodesia, disease and illness were explained traditionally in terms of several different causal categories, including the following:

1. Some illnesses and diseases were considered to be "natural" or the result of processes that were not thought of as problematical. The diseases of very young children or the infirmities of the aged, for example, might be seen as requiring no further explanation than the natural condition of the sufferer.
2. Some illnesses and diseases were seen to be the natural consequences of the actions of those who suffered from them. For example, some of the diseases of young children who were considered to be "ritually cold" were seen to be the consequence of their having been exposed to "ritually hot" circumstances. In adults some chest conditions were thought to be the consequence of adultery.
3. Some illnesses were considered to be the consequences of the actions of wraiths or spirits and frequently followed some violation on the part of the patient, or one of his close kinsmen, of custom or kinship obligations.
4. Some illnesses and diseases were considered to result from the actions of sorcerers or witches.
5. Some illnesses, particularly fits, were considered to be due to the action of spirits, usually of kinsmen but not necessarily so, who had selected the patient as a medium through which they could speak.

These causal categories are essentially collective representations to which people may appeal in order to provide rationales for the misfortunes that assail them. As such, the categories influence the action people feel would be appropriate. Like all causal explanations, they are essentially constructions of reality which are open to reconstructions in the light of the different interests of the actors in any social drama (J. C. Mitchell 1964).

Modern scientific causal categories provide yet another way of explaining the same objective phenomena, and we would expect them to be used in the same way as traditional categories to provide a rationale for appropriate action.

Most observers have devoted more attention to the traditional categories of thinking than to the ways in which categories derived from Western thought have been used in the variety of social situations in which non-Western people find themselves.

It is common knowledge, and has been documented extensively, that so-called "traditional" or "folk" explanations of disease and those explanations that are called "Western" or "scientific" (or "modern") are not mutually exclusive bases for action. In Rhodesia several observers have noted how patients made simultaneous use of "traditional" and of "Western" healing agencies.[1] There are thus many individual case histories reflecting the behavior of individuals and even of groups who oscillate between medical practitioners and traditional healers, but we do not yet have data to show how most people are likely to behave or whether there is a trend one way or the other. We know that traditional healers flourish while at the same time hospitals are overcrowded, but we do not know how the patients themselves interpret the condition they suffer from when they seek treatment. This study does not purport to throw light directly on these questions, but it may suggest factors likely to influence change in the present situation.

The data in fact refer to the responses of a relatively large number of young Africans in Rhodesia to a set of items in a standard type of attitude questionnaire designed for a somewhat different purpose. Clearly data of this sort are heavily influenced by the situation in which they are generated. In this respect they are no different from data assembled by other procedures such as observation or interviewing. What is essential is that the constraints of the particular way in which the data were created in the first instance should explicitly condition the way in which the data are subsequently interpreted. Frequently attitude studies are pilloried by critics who unjustifiably attribute qualities to the data which they cannot possess simply because of the way in which they were generated. One of the simplest and crudest confusions of this sort arises when it is expected that people in day-to-day situations will in fact behave in accordance with their responses to items in an attitude questionnaire. The way in which a respondent "constructs the reality" of his attitude in a test situation is, of course, likely to be entirely different from the way in which he "constructs the reality" of an everyday situation. To equate the two is to commit an elementary blunder.

In this study our aim is not to examine the disparity between these different "constructions of reality." Our more limited aim is to argue that we are able to arrange respondents along a continuum according to the way in which they answered certain selected questions. At one extreme would be the respondents who reacted to the questions in such a way as to lead us to suppose that they were operating predominantly within a "traditional" orientation; at the other extreme would be those who were operating within a "nontraditional" framework. Note that from the material available to us we cannot argue that the orientations we adduce have validity outside the specific test situation in which the questions were posed. This is something that other investigators, possibly using other research procedures, could settle. In this sense our analysis raises rather than answers questions. What we can do with this material, however, is to pose the following question: Given that the respondents were operating within a predominantly "traditional" or predominantly "nontraditional" framework in answering the questions, do those with a particular set of personal characteristics tend to respond one way or the other, and if so can we postulate any relationship between these characteristics and the way in which the respondents answered the questions?

THE DATA

The data were collected in a study with a different purpose from the analysis presented here. One of us (H. F. M.) was engaged in a study of the incidence of cancer among Africans in Rhodesia, and in the course of this study had become aware of the extent to which cancer rates computed from the evidence collected for migrant populations in a large urban area may be seriously distorted because of the extent to which some patients important in cancer rates (as, for example, the old) might escape the diagnositic net of the survey (cf. H. F. Mitchell 1967). It seemed essential, consequently, to understand something about the use of medical services by the African population, and a part of this study was to assess the attitudes toward these services of the "rising" generation of educated young people.

For this purpose a survey was conducted among secondary school students and teachers in training in the larger African educational institutions in the southwestern part of Rhodesia. A population of this sort was able to participate in a study requiring a fair degree of literacy in English and could be conveniently organized at centers and in suitable groups to facilitate testing. It could in no way be thought of as representative of the whole African population of Rhodesia or even of the population of the southwest of Rhodesia since it was naturally both younger and better educated than the total population.

Elementary social characteristics of 2663 respondents whose returns were usable are given in Table 6. The loss rate by refusals and unusable returns was negligible: one respondent refused to cooperate on religious grounds and six returns were rejected because they were not completed satisfactorily. In all, fourteen schools and institutions of further education were included in the study. Two were situated in town and the rest in the rural areas, but the latter were boarding schools with students and trainees drawn from town and country. Some of the institutions were secular but the majority were mission controlled and run. The data were collected in February and March 1964.[2]

By arrangements with the principals of the institutions,[3] the scholars and students were assembled and seated at desks in a central hall. One of us (H. F. M.) then explained the purpose of the study and elicited the cooperation of those involved. She was accompanied and assisted by two African social workers throughout the fieldwork. The schedules, mimeographed on two sheets of paper of double foolscap size, were then distributed to the group and completed by them in silence and without reference to one another. At the conclusion of this session, usually after about half an hour, the research worker collected the schedules and then engaged in a general discussion with the group about medical topics.

The schedules, printed in English, covered two sets of data. The first related to a number of "background variables" or social characteristics of the respondents which we thought might have some bearing on their attitudes toward the use of medical services. The names of respondents were specifically excluded. The second set consisted of a number of statements about medical services and the treatment of disease to which the respondents were asked to react in terms of five categories of intensity of agreement or disagreement.

Among the items in the second part of the schedule were ten that could be construed as reflecting the attitudes respondents might have toward the basic causes of illness. These items and the distribution of responses to them in terms of agreement and disagreement are presented in Table 1.

The crude distributions for these items are interesting in themselves. A common criticism of responses to formal questions of this sort is that they tend to reflect what the respondents think the investigators want them to say. In this case the study was conducted under the auspices of the African Studies Department of the University College of Rhodesia and Nyasaland, and those who supervised the completion of the schedules were associated with the largest African hospital in the region. Whether or not the respondents wanted to please the Department of African Studies at the university or the representatives of the medical services would be difficult to say, but it certainly did not prevent some 82.6% of the respondents from agreeing with the statement that sorcerers could make people ill or 65.1% from agreeing that ancestor spirits could make people ill. Substantially fewer, however, agreed that a sick person should consult a diviner before consult-

TABLE 1 *Responses to Items Relating to the Causation of Disease (Distribution 1 Percentage of Responses Excluding "Don't Know" Responses)*

em[a]	SA[b]	A[b]	U[b]	D[b]	SD[b]	D/K[c]
3. *Abatakati*[d] or *varoyi*[d] can make people sick	61.8	20.8	8.6	2.8	6.0	13
4. *Amadhlozi*[e] or *midzimu*[e] can make people sick	41.5	23.6	18.2	5.5	11.2	43
7. For certain kinds of sickness it is better to ask the help of the *nyanga*[f] rather than the medical doctor	38.2	24.2	11.0	10.0	16.6	20
4. If a man is sick he should go first to the *nyanga* to see what is wrong with him *before* he goes to a medical doctor	16.5	12.5	15.3	24.0	31.8	15
9. *Abatakati* or *amadhlozi* can make people cough blood	21.2	18.3	28.0	12.6	19.9	45
0. *Abatakati* or *amadhlozi* can make people have sores on their bodies that do not heal	21.3	23.0	27.5	13.2	15.0	61
1. *Abatakati* or *amadhlozi* can make people have difficulty in swallowing food	17.4	23.3	28.2	15.2	16.0	65
2. *Abatakati* or *amadhlozi* can make people have a lump that grows in the body	25.2	25.7	24.4	11.5	13.3	56
3. *Abatakati* or *amadhlozi* can make people pass blood in the water	11.5	11.5	29.1	22.1	25.7	55
4. *Abatakati* or *amadhlozi* can make people fall down in fits (*situtwani* or *zvipusha*)[g]	30.3	24.2	22.6	10.4	12.6	52

The item numbers shown are the actual item numbers in the questionnaire.

A = strongly agree, A = agree, U = uncertain (cannot decide), D = disagree, SD = strongly disagree.

/K = number of "don't know" responses.

hese are the actual words used in the items. The vernacular terms *abatakati* (Ndebele) and *varoyi* (Shona) for rcerers were used to make the meaning clear to the respondents, all of whom could understand these languages d many of them, both.

he vernacular terms *amadhlozi* (Ndebele) and *midzimu* (Shona) were used for ancestor spirits.

he vernacular word *nyanga* (Ndebele and Shona) was used for diviner.

he vernacular words *situtwani* (Ndebele) and *zvipusha* (Shona) were added to explicate the word "fits," which spondents may have had difficulty in understanding.

ing a medical practitioner or that sorcerers or ancestor spirits could cause specific symptoms of disease.[4] Irrespective of whether or not these responses reflect accurately what people really think about these conditions, the point of immediate interest is that there is a certain amount of variability in the responses. The problem may be rephrased in terms of the differences in response of subjects with varying social backgrounds and how far these differences were in accordance with what we might expect from our understanding of the positions these respondents occupy in the social system as a whole.

TRADITIONAL AND NONTRADITIONAL ORIENTATIONS TOWARD THE CAUSATION OF DISEASE

Regardless of the way in which respondents reacted independently to each of the ten items we have selected for analysis, it seems reasonable to argue that if a respondent consistently agreed, over all ten items, that diseases or specified symptoms of diseases (included in the survey) could be caused by ancestor spirits or sorcerers, then he was oriented, at least in the test situation, toward a traditional view of the etiology of disease. The extent to which respondents reacted to the items in a consistent way, of course, could be measured by product moment correlation coefficients.

Table 2 gives the correlations among these ten items. In order to compute the correlations, we assigned arbitrary values of 1 to 5 to the five categories of agreement/disagreement in accordance with the content of the item in such a way as to accord a "traditional" orientation toward the causation of disease a low score and a "nontraditional" orientation a high score. Where respondents had returned a "don't know" response, a value equal to the mean of the known responses to that item was inserted. It is immediately apparent that the correlations were all positive and that they ranged from 0.5770 to 0.0739.

It is possible mathematically to decompose each correlation in a set of correlations of this sort into a number of constituent parts, each of which is accounted for by a separate underlying general "factor." Furthermore, because of the mathematical procedures used to estimate these "factors," they are constrained to be independent numerically from one another; that is, the correlations among the "factors" themselves must all be zero. Applying an analysis of this sort to the correlations in Table 2 resulted in two "factors" of appreciable size.[5] The correlations of each of the separate items with the underlying factors, that is, the factor loadings, are given in Table 3.

From this table it is clear that all the items we have used in our analysis correlate positively with the first factor. Since these items refer to the belief that witches or spirits can cause symptoms of disease or to the role of the

Item	1	2	3	4	5	6	7	8	9	10
1. *Abatakati* or *varoyi* can make people sick	1.0000	0.4409	0.2205	0.2081	0.3117	0.3250	0.2870	0.3114	0.1718	0.3219
2. *Amadhlozi* or *midzimu* can make people sick	0.4409	1.0000	0.1945	0.2365	0.2984	0.2899	0.2797	0.2915	0.2006	0.2957
3. For certain kinds of sickness it is better to ask the help of the *nyanga* rather than the medical doctor	0.2205	0.1954	1.0000	0.3370	0.1439	0.1484	0.1198	0.1654	0.0739	0.1586
4. If a man is sick he should go first to the *nyanga* to see what is wrong with him *before* he goes to a medical doctor	0.2081	0.2365	0.3370	1.0000	0.2403	0.2039	0.2279	0.2118	0.1908	0.2192
5. *Abatakati* or *amadhlozi* can make people cough blood	0.3117	0.2984	0.1439	0.2403	1.0000	0.5011	0.5171	0.4519	0.4133	0.3738
6. *Abatakati* or *amadhlozi* can make people have sores on their bodies that do not heal	0.3250	0.2899	0.1484	0.2039	0.5011	1.0000	0.5770	0.5158	0.3547	0.4040
7. *Abatakati* or *amadhlozi* can make people have difficulty in swallowing food	0.2874	0.2747	0.1198	0.2279	0.5171	0.5770	1.0000	0.5490	0.4502	0.4306
8. *Abatakati* or *amadhlozi* can make people have a lump that grows in the body	0.3114	0.2915	0.1654	0.2118	0.4519	0.5158	0.5490	1.0000	0.3896	0.4778
9. *Abatakati* or *amadhlozi* can make people pass blood in the water	0.1718	0.2006	0.0788	0.1908	0.4133	0.3547	0.4502	0.3896	1.0000	0.4217
10. *Abatakati* or *amadhlozi* can make people fall down in fits (*situwani* or *zvipusha*)	0.3219	0.2957	0.1586	0.2192	0.3738	0.4040	0.4306	0.4778	0.4217	1.0000

Based on 2663 cases. "Don't know" or missing responses for items are replaced by mean values of known responses for those items.

TABLE 3 *Factor Loadings on Items Relating to the Causation of Disease*

Item	Factor 1	Factor 2
1. *Abatakati* or *varoyi* can make people sick	0.5026	0.3171
2. *Amadhlozi* or *midzimu* can make people sick	0.4855	0.3137
3. For certain kinds of sickness it is better to ask the help of the *nyanga* rather than the medical doctor	0.2791	0.3881
4. If a man is sick he should first go to the *nyanga* to see what is wrong with him *before* he goes to a medical doctor	0.3744	0.2966
5. *Abatakati* or *amadhlozi* can make people cough blood	0.6664	−0.0904
6. *Abatakati* or *amadhlozi* can make people have sores on their bodies that do not heal	0.6956	−0.1308
7. *Abatakati* or *amadhlozi* can make people have difficulty in swallowing food	0.7411	−0.2358
8. *Abatakati* or *amadhlozi* can make people have a lump that grows in the body	0.7002	−0.1186
9. *Abatakati* or *amadhlozi* can make people pass blood in the water	0.5514	−0.1928
10. *Abatakati* or *amadhlozi* can make people fall down in fits (*situtwani* or *zvipusha*)	0.6207	−0.0255
Percentage of variance explained	39.23	12.54

traditional healer (albeit to a lesser degree), we felt justified in treating this factor as one that would discriminate between those who thought of the causation of disease in traditional terms as opposed to those who saw it in nontraditional terms.[6]

The correlations of the items with the second factor were somewhat smaller than with the first. This factor separated the items relating to the symptoms of disease from more general considerations of causation, a fact which is interesting in itself but which we do not pursue here.

Having established the extent to which each item relates to a hypothe-sized underlying dimension concerning traditional or nontraditional notions about the causation of disease, we may now use the correlations of each item with this underlying dimension, together with the responses of each respondent on each of the ten items, to produce a score reflecting the extent to which the respondent fell toward the traditional or the nontraditional end of a continuum. The weights so derived, adjusted by the standard deviation

TABLE 4   *Weights Applied to Items to Determine Respondents'*
Positions along a Hypothetical Causation Orientation Continuum

Item	Weight
1. *Abatakati* or *varoyi* can make people sick	2.4512
2. *Amadhlozi* or *midzimu* can make people sick	1.9838
3. For certain kinds of sickness it is better to ask the help of the *nyanga* rather than the medical doctor	0.9907
4. If a man is sick he should go first to the *nyanga* to see what is wrong with him before he goes to a medical doctor	1.2308
5. *Abatakati* or *amadhlozi* can make people cough blood	2.8039
6. *Abatakati* or *amadhlozi* can make people have sores on their bodies that do not heal	3.1906
7. *Abatakati* or *amadhlozi* can make people have difficulty in swallowing food	4.4178
8. *Abatakati* or *amadhlozi* can make people have a lump that grows in the body	3.3572
9. *Abatakati* or *amadhlozi* can make people pass blood in the water	2.0369
10. *Abatakati* or *amadhlozi* can make people fall down in fits (*situtwani* or *zvipusha*)	2.5371

of each item, are presented in Table 4. These weights have been so adjusted that if a respondent were to disagree strongly with each item he would achieve a score of 100, whereas if he were to agree strongly with each item he would achieve a score of 0.[7] In other words, a score of 100 would represent the most extreme nontraditional position that a respondent could take, and a score of 0 would represent the most extreme traditional position. The actual scores of our respondents are shown in Table 5. These scores are, of course, entirely arbitrary: it would have been just as easy to arrange for the extremes to be reversed.

EFFECT OF BACKGROUND CHARACTERISTICS

Our immediate concern, however, was not with the interpretation of the scores per se but rather with the way in which the scores varied with combinations of different social backgrounds of the respondents. The material that can be collected on the social background of respondents in a test situation of this sort is, of course, limited to a number of fairly straightforward characteristics. Those that were included are listed in Table 6.

TABLE 5   *Distribution of Scores on Continuum for "Traditional"/ "Nontraditional" Orientation toward the Causation of Disease*

Orientation	Score	Number of Respondents
Extreme traditional	0–9	172
Traditional	10–19	224
	20–29	375
Mixed traditional and nontraditional	30–39	484
	40–49	482
	50–59	349
Nontraditional	60–69	203
	70–79	133
Extreme nontraditional	80–89	89
	90–100	72
		2583[a]

[a]The scores are for 2583 respondents because information on background characteristics was missing for 80 respondents and these have been excluded from the rest of the analysis.
    The distribution of scores is thus fairly even, with a mean of 42.15 and a standard deviation of 21.65. The majority of the respondents seem to occupy an intermediate position with respect to orientation toward the causation of disease, but nevertheless about one-tenth scored in the lowest range (say under 12) and one-tenth in the highest range (say over 75).

We are dealing here, as in all social analyses, with the operation of a large number of factors which we expect *ex hypothesi* to have some effect on the position of a respondent on the hypothetical attitudinal continuum relating to the causation of disease. All these variables operate simultaneously in the case of a single respondent. Analytically, however, we wish to separate the effects of one background factor from another so as to assess which of the factors is most likely to influence the position of the respondent along the continuum. There are several ways in which we could go about this, providing the approach handles the effect of all the measured factors simultaneously and not separately. We have elected to use regression analysis, mainly because the number of respondents is large enough to enable us to do so and because the techniques are well developed and reasonably robust. From a substantive point of view the procedure is constrained by the sort of variables we have been able to use in the analysis. Perhaps there were factors that would have had a much sharper effect on the respondent's orientation toward the causation of disease than those we have been able to include. This does not mean that they were not easily available to us, given the techniques of data collection we were using.

Considering that we are able to explore here only those variables included in our analysis, we are confronted with another difficulty. Normally regression analysis makes the assumption that the variables included in the analysis are continuous and measured on an interval scale. Quite clearly the material that we have to deal with cannot meet this assumption. Church affiliation, for example, or father's occupation could only be considered a nominal variable or at best an ordinal variable if, for instance, the religious groups or occupations could be arranged in some order in relation to the orientation toward the causation of disease. Recent developments in regression analysis in econometrics, however, have substantially overcome this difficulty even though they have not yet been used much in anthropological analyses. We refer here to what have come to be known as "dummy" variable procedures. In these procedures a variable that is not continuous and measured on an interval scale may be presented in a regression analysis as several distinct variables of a zero-one kind. If the respondent is a member of a particular Christian sect, for example, we could give him a score of unity on a dummy variable created to represent his religious affiliation. This implies that the respondent must of necessity be given a score of zero on other categories created to represent other religious affiliations, since we assume that the respondent can be a member of only one religious denomination. Using this procedure, we are able to represent variables of any complexity in a regression analysis. How we create the dummy variables, of course, will depend on what we are trying to achieve in the analysis. We would create the variables, for example, because we believe that a particular category is likely to be related to the dependent variable in a specific way.

In our analysis we did not use all the variables available to us partly because creating additional dummy variables would increase the number of variables we would have to handle and partly because we judged that they would not have any appreciable effect on the variable we wished to examine. The actual dummy variables we created and their effects on the score for orientation toward the causation of disease are given in Table 6.

Because of a technical problem concerned with solving for the effects of variables, one of the categories relating to each of the dummy variables must be excluded from the analysis.[8] We have marked with asterisks those which we have excluded. The choice of the category to exclude is purely arbitrary and makes no difference to the analysis except that if a category including only a very small number of cases is excluded, the determination of the effect of the remaining variables is likely to be unstable. The effect of the variables created as dummies is that the category excluded takes on a computed base value,[9] in this case a score of 45.49. The effects of the other categories in that variable (and in other variables as well) will be represented by departures from this value. For example, if we consider the variable relating to type of school, the excluded variable was large mission schools with teacher training facilities, which were attended by 62.3 percent of the respondents. Respondents at this type of educational establishment would have an expected score of 45.49. We see from Table 6, how-

TABLE 6 *Effects of Variables on "Traditional"/"Nontraditional" Orientation toward the Causation of Disease*

Variable	Proportion of Respondents in Category	Effect of Variable on Score
Type of school		
1. Urban secular schools	0.037	+ 9.41
*2. Large mission schools with teacher training facilities	0.623	45.49
3. Small mission schools without teacher training facilities	0.231	− 4.34
4. Rural secular boarding schools (technical and agricultural)	0.109	− 2.40
Respondent's educational level		
1. Nine or less years of schooling	0.377	− 1.24
*2. Ten to twelve years of schooling	0.552	45.49
3. Thirteen or more years of schooling	0.071	− 6.88
Type of course		
*1. Academic	0.424	45.49
2. Technical	0.537	− 2.66
3. Agricultural	0.039	− 1.22
Sex		
*1. Male	0.727	45.49
2. Female	0.273	+ 0.53
Age of respondent		
1. Sixteen years old and younger	0.502	+ 1.13
*2. Seventeen to twenty-one years old	0.348	45.49
3. Twenty-two years old and older	0.150	+ 1.20
Father's occupation		
*1. Rural agricultural (including subsistence)	0.438	45.49
2. Unskilled	0.041	− 2.02
3. Skilled	0.166	− 0.49
4. Supervisory	0.043	− 3.18
5. Business and trading	0.039	+ 1.33
6. White-collar and professional	0.189	+ 3.17
7. Not recorded	0.084	− 2.15

TABLE 6   (Continued)

Variable	Proportion of Respondents in Category	Effect of Variable on Score
Mother's occupation		
1. Rural agricultural (including subsistence)	0.061	+ 1.05
2. Unskilled (including housework)	0.775	45.49
3. Skilled	0.016	− 1.02
4. Supervisory	0.001	+13.86
5. Business and trading	0.002	+ 5.62
6. White collar and professional	0.120	+ 0.34
7. Unrecorded	0.025	+ 4.69
Ethnic group		
1. Ndebele	0.358	− 2.05
2. Shona and Kalanga	0.522	45.49
3. Zulu and Shangaan	0.019	− 0.03
4. Sotho and Tswana	0.041	− 1.72
5. Others	0.060	+ 1.05
Birthplace		
*1. Urban	0.186	45.49
2. Rural	0.814	− 0.78
Residence while attending school		
*1. At school	0.865	45.49
2. With own parents	0.097	− 2.10
3. With relatives and nonrelatives	0.038	− 1.20
Years attending particular school		
1. Less than one year	0.363	+ 2.61
*2. One to two years	0.505	45.49
3. Five years or more	0.132	+ 1.24
Residence during school holidays		
*1. With parents and relatives	0.925	45.49
2. With nonrelatives	0.007	+ 2.10
3. Elsewhere	0.068	+ 2.67
Father's educational level		
1. Nil	0.111	− 0.05
*2. Primary only	0.637	45.49
3. Secondary	0.189	− 1.54
4. Not known	0.063	− 0.76

(*Continued*)

TABLE 6 (Continued)

Variable	Proportion of Respondents in Category	Effect of Variable on Score
Mother's educational level		
1. Nil	0.142	+ 0.75
*2. Primary only	0.661	45.49
3. Secondary	0.101	− 2.92
4. Not known	0.096	− 2.49
Religious affiliation		
1. Roman Catholic	0.050	+ 1.17
2. Anglican	0.074	− 2.77
3. Dutch Reformed, Presbyterian, CCAP, Free Presbyterian Church of Scotland, Paris Evangelical, Lutheran	0.202	− 0.88
*4. Methodist, Congregationalist (LMS), Free Methodist, SAGM: Society of Friends, American Board Mission	0.295	45.49
5. Brethren in Christ, Salvation Army, Church of Christ, Baptist, Team, ELM	0.249	− 0.46
6. Seventh Day Adventist	0.090	+ 5.26
7. Jehovah's Witnesses and Full Gospel	0.003	0.00
8. Zionist, Zimbabwe, Apostolic Church, Mai Chaza, African Methodist Episcopal, Assembly of God	0.012	+ 1.71
9. Independent African Church, United African Faith Church, African Lutheran Church	0.002	− 3.01
10. No Christian affiliation	0.023	− 7.75

Asterisks indicate variables excluded from the analysis.

ever, that respondents at secular schools—the government schools in the town—would have an expected score some 9.41 points higher than this, that is, a score of 54.90, whereas respondents at small mission schools without teacher training classes would have an expected score 4.34 points less than 45.49, that is, a score of 41.15. Under the usual conventions of multiple regression, of course, it is assumed that the effects of all other variables included in the analysis have been allowed for in these scores. We may thus conclude that insofar as the attitude of respondents toward the causation of disease is concerned, the effect of different types of educational establishment may be interpreted as follows: Respondents at small mission schools without teacher training facilities have the most traditional orientation (score = 41.15); respondents at rural secular boarding schools have a slightly more nontraditional orientation (score = 43.09); students at large rural mission schools have a slightly more nontraditional orientation (45.49); but those at urban secular day-schools have the most nontraditional orientation of all. What in fact the use of dummy variables makes possible is an empirical determination of the effect of different categories of variables without assuming a direct linear relationship as do normal regression analyses using continuous variables. In particular, we are able to include, as a distinct category, respondents with "don't know" responses, which were appreciable in the items relating to mother's and father's occupations. This would have been impossible with normal regression procedures.

When the operation of all these variables is taken into account, only a small proportion of the variance in the scores relating to the orientation toward the causes of disease is accounted for.[10] The implication of this is that if there are major causal factors that influence the orientation toward the causation of disease, these factors have not been included in the variables we have been able to use. Even if the explanatory power of the variables used is low, however, we are nevertheless able to examine the *relative* effect of the variables we have used. To do this we need to examine the extent to which each of the variables succeeds in explaining the variance in the causation orientation score. We can do this most simply by computing the diminution in the proportion of variance explained when specified variables are excluded from the analysis. These effects are given in Table 7.

It is clear from this table that the type of educational institution (and to some extent therefore the type of course being followed) is associated most directly with changes in the score in the disease causation orientation score. Religious affiliation has the next most important effect and then father's occupation. At the other end of the scale we see that birthplace and sex have virtually no effect on the scores.

Since our set of respondents was not drawn from a universe in a way that would enable us to use sampling theory, we could not estimate the probability that the relationship between the dependent variable and the independent variables we found in our analysis was likely to exist in the general population. However, it is apparent from Table 7 that there is a sharp decrement in the proportion of variance explained when we exclude the first three variables, from "type of school" down to "father's occupation." It would seem reasonable therefore to confine our comments to the effects of these three variables.

The specific effects of the variables that are most closely associated with variations in the disease causation orientation score may be assessed by examination of the increment values in Table 6. But the effect of religious conviction on the scores was not so simple. From Table 6 we see that being a Seventh Day Adventist led to the most "nontraditional" expected score (50.75) of all the broad categories of religious persuasion. This group was followed by a category of fundamentalist sects with a score of 47.20, includ-

TABLE 7   *Percentage of Loss in Variance Explained When Specific Variables Are Excluded from the Analysis*

Variable Excluded	Percentage Loss
Type of school	0.880
Religious affiliation	0.864
Father's occupation	0.544
Respondent's educational level	0.251
Type of course	0.225
Mother's educational level	0.213
Years attending particular school	0.202
Ethnic group	0.195
Mother's occupation	0.175
Residence while attending school	0.098
Age of respondent	0.057
Father's educational level	0.052
Residence during school holidays	0.047
Birthplace	0.017
Sex	0.009

ing several, such as the Apostolic Faith Church, which believed in divine healing. At the other extreme of the range of scores were the adherents to a number of African Independent sects with a score of 42.48 and those who did not profess to be Christians with a score of 37.74. We had anticipated that membership in mission churches, that is, in overseas-based churches that maintained expatriate mission staffs in Rhodesia, would have the most "nontraditional" score, and we had expected that those who were members of local separatist sects and those who were not Christians would have scores indicating the most traditional orientation. While our expectations with respect to the non-Christians and to independent churches of what Sundkler (1948) would have classified as Ethiopian churches were borne out, our expectations with regard to the mission churches were not. On reflection, the nontraditional orientation of the Seventh Day Adventists seems reasonable since in general they are noted for their hard-headed, practical approach to Christianity, but we have no adequate explanation of why the members of the Anglican Church should have returned such a relatively high "traditional" expected score of 42.72, which is only slightly more "nontraditional" than the expected score of members of the Ethiopian-type Independent Churches.

Following the effect of school type and religious affiliation on the orientation toward disease causation score, the occupation of the respondent's father seems to have had most influence on the level of that score. In relation to respondents whose fathers were in rural agricultural occupations (including subsistence cultivation), those whose fathers were in white-collar or professional occupations tended to reflect a more nontraditional orientation toward the causation of disease (expected score of 48.67 versus 45.49), while those whose fathers were in supervisory occupations, with an expected score of 42.31, and those whose fathers were in unskilled occupations, with an expected score of 43.47, reflected a more traditional orientation toward the causation of disease. In general, the trend in the expected scores of respondents whose fathers were in different occupational categories followed the general level of education associated with those occupations in that there is a clear trend of increasing score, indicating a more nontraditional orientation, as one moves from the unskilled to white-collar and professional categories. The one exception to this is the supervisory category. The probable explanation for this is that because of their role in the government administrative system, the occupations of "headman" and "chief," both of which required no educational background and both of which were essentially related to rural contexts, were coded as "supervisory," a decision which in retrospect was unfortunate and could only be remedied by recoding the entire set of records.

CONCLUSIONS

In general, these findings are consistent with our expectations about the way in which people undergoing academic education and coming from homes in which parents are in white-collar or professional occupations would react to questions of this kind about the basic causes of disease. They are also consistent with our appreciation of how effective the teaching of fundamentalist sects can be in influencing the way in which their adherents react to questions of this type. The categories of respondents to which these expectations apply, however, are very different from one another. Although it is always easy to be wise after the event, we had not in fact anticipated the result we obtained from the Seventh Day Adventists.

But the exercise has been instructive in another way. We had included the original set of variables because we had anticipated on common-sense grounds that they would be related to the way in which young educated people appreciated medical services and to the factors underlying their beliefs about what made people ill. We had not anticipated that age or sex, for example, would make no difference at all to the way in which respondents reacted to the items. It is true that the age range of the respondents is small—the population was heavily selected from the younger ages of the population—but we had anticipated that respondents in the upper age range would have had more education and so would have reacted in a more nontraditional way than they did.

Our expectations with respect to respondents' living in boarding schools as opposed to home, their living in town as opposed to the country, the number of years of schooling they had had, and the level of education their parents had had were in general not confirmed.

We would not argue that the sort of analysis we have conducted here is a substitute for traditional anthropological fieldwork. Our view, rather, is that, providing appropriate analytic techniques are used,[11] surveys of this kind can be used to refine hypotheses and therefore to respecify questions that in the end may possibly only be answered using different methods of enquiry. There is clearly a dialectic between different methods of enquiry. Questions resolved by one method are likely to throw up questions of a different kind which can only be resolved by some other method.

NOTES

1. See, for example, Gelfand (1964: 134–143; 1973), in particular the histories he took of his own patients, the case history described by Mitchell (1964), the comments by H. F. Mitchell (1967), and the detailed analysis made by Chavunduka (1973).

2. The data were collected as part of the Geographic Pathology study of cancer in Rhodesia supported by the International Union Against Cancer and the British Empire Cancer Campaign. Preliminary results of the sociological findings of this study have been published in H. F. Mitchell (1967), which should be consulted for details concerning the original study.

3. We are grateful to the principals of the institutions concerned and to the students whose cooperation made the study possible.

4. It is interesting that a larger proportion agreed with the statement that sorcerers or ancestor spirits could cause "fits" or "lumps that grow in the body." This is almost certainly related to common beliefs about these conditions as against hematuria which, because of the widespread infestation of bilharzia, is quite common in Rhodesia.

5. "Appreciable size" here refers to factors with an eigenvalue of 1.0 or more. This is a standard commonly accepted for deciding whether it is worthwhile to take a factor into account or not.

6. These items were all worded deliberately to encourage respondents to react in terms of a traditional orientation toward the causation of disease. The object was to try to counterbalance the reluctance of relatively well-educated respondents to admit to beliefs in traditional causal mechanisms. It is possible that, had we included items phrased positively from the perspective of adherence to modern rather than traditional notions of causation, then separate factors relating to intensity or belief in traditional and nontraditional types of causation may have emerged. This possi-

bility is hinted at by the slightly lower loadings on factor 1 of the items that bear a reference to the "medical doctor." Our purpose, however, was not to examine the structure of beliefs per se but rather to try to point up factors that might influence the possible use of medical services. We felt justified in using the respondents' reactions to the totality of these items, suitably weighted as described in the text, to estimate the position of each respondent's orientation toward the causation of disease along a hypothesized "traditionalism" dimension. We have deliberately avoided referring to the "nontraditional" end of the dimension as "modern" precisely because we do not have the data to justify that usage.

7. The score for individual i was derived from

$$S_i = 100 \left(\frac{\sum\limits_{j=1}^{10} w_j (X_{ij} - X_{\min j})}{X_{\max j} - X_{\min j}} \right)$$

where $X_{\max j}$ is the maximum value item j could attain (i.e., 5), $X_{\min j}$ the minimum value item j could attain (i.e., 1), X_{ij} the score individual i had on item j, and w_j the weight, i.e., the factor coefficient derived from the first axis of a principal components analysis divided by the standard deviation for item j. If an individual returned a 5 response to all items his score would be 100, indicating a maximum orientation toward nontraditional views concerning the causation of disease. If he returned a 1 response to all items, his score would be 0, indicating a maximum orientation toward traditional views concerning the causation of disease.

8. This is based on the consideration that if all categories were included, then one of the categories, given the others, would be fully determined. In these circumstances there could be no unique solution of the regression equations.

9. In fact the intercept value.

10. The multiple correlation coefficient is 0.235, which implies that only 0.055 percent of the variance in the scores is explained by the variables that have been used in this study.

11. By "appropriate" we mean techniques that violate as little as possible the assumptions upon which the data were generated in the first instance. We look upon multiple regression using dummy variables as a technique of this sort, as is the related technique called multiple classification analysis. There has recently been a rapid extension of procedures for analyzing data which do not assume interval-type measures, and anthropologists do not seem to have availed themselves of the facilities that these techniques offer. One reason may be that a procedure like multiple regression using dummy variables rapidly expands the number of variables which must be used, and this can be a disadvantage if sample sizes tend to be small.

REFERENCES

Chavunduka, G. L. 1973. Paths to medical care in Highfields, Rhodesia. *The Society of Malawi Journal*, 26(2): 25–45.
Gelfand, M. 1964. *Witch Doctor*. London: Harvill Press.
———. 1973. The Shona Ng'anga as I know him. *The Society of Malawi Journal*, 26(2): 16–24.

Mitchell, Hilary Flegg. 1967. Sociological aspects of cancer rate surveys in Africa. *National Cancer Institute Monograph No. 25:* 151–170.
Mitchell, J. C. 1964. The meaning in misfortune for urban Africans. In G. Dieterlen and M. Fortes, eds., *African Systems of Thought,* pp. 192–203. London: Oxford University Press for International African Institute.
Sundkler, B. G. M. 1948. *Bantu Prophets in South Africa.* London: Butterworth.

Part Two

DATA REDUCTION

Multidimensional Scaling Applications in Anthropology

A. KIMBALL ROMNEY

The aim of this paper is to illustrate some uses of multidimensional scaling in anthropology. This will be done by presenting examples from recent investigations that differ widely among themselves and illustrate the flexibility and generality of the method.

Multidimensional scaling may be viewed as a tool that represents quantitative indices of similarity in terms of Euclidean distance. Such a representation frequently reveals structures of the data that might not otherwise be recognized. Any data that lend themselves to spatial representation may be considered candidates for multidimensional scaling.

Multidimensional scaling begins with a matrix of pairwise similarities among a set of objects of interest. These objects may be concepts, persons, traits, cultures, stimuli, groups, etc. In our first example they are intermarrying language groups. TORSCA (Young and Torgerson 1967), one of the more common programs, takes as input data the above-diagonal triangular half of an $n \times n$ distance matrix in which the n rows and n columns correspond to the same n objects. (Table 3, presented later, has intermarriage data in such a form.)

The analysis of data utilizing multidimensional scaling techniques provides the investigator with help in three related but distinct ways. First, the representation of the data in Euclidean space aids visual scanning and the discovery of previously unknown structures. Second, it provides an objective measure for comparing different studies or parts of the same study. Third, it provides a metric for testing empirical results against theoretical models. In the examples below we will attempt to explicate and illustrate each of the above uses of multidimensional scaling.

INTERMARRIAGE AMONG VAUPES LANGUAGE GROUPS

As part of a larger study, Professor Jean Jackson (1976) collected data on intermarriage among language groups in the Vaupés territory of southeastern Colombia. Table 1 presents the relevant raw data. The aim of multidimensional scaling analysis in this case was to analyze and gain insight into

71

TABLE 1   *Number of Marriages Between Selected Language Groups in the Vaupés (from Jackson 1976)*

Husband's Language Group	Wife's Language Group							
	Bará	Tuyuka	Tukano	Desana	Carapana	Tatuyo	Siriano	Yurutí
Bará (N = 77)	0	55	0	7	2	12	1	0
Tuyuka (N = 145)	58	0	71	3	0	6	7	0
Tukano (N = 127)	0	47	1	45	4	5	20	5
Desana (N = 55)	5	2	36	0	2	0	10	0
Carapana (N = 27)	3	0	6	4	0	10	2	2
Tatuyo (N = 20)	10	0	5	1	2	0	0	2
Siriano (N = 71)	2	8	27	14	5	1	0	14
Yurutí (N = 12)	2	0	2	0	1	1	6	0
Column N	80	112	148	74	16	35	46	23

the marriage preferences by representing them in Euclidean space. The aim was to represent groups with a high preference of intermarriage as being close to each other and groups with low or no intermarriage as being further apart. By constructing a picture that enables us to scan such data visually, we should be able to interpret the patterns of intermarriage more precisely and with greater ease than we can with the original data. Before presenting the analysis, let us give a little ethnographic background.[1]

The Bará are one of over twenty language-affiliated exogamous groups (henceforth referred to as "language groups") found in the Vaupés, Colombia. The Vaupés and adjacent Brazilian territory comprise the Central Northwest Amazon, a region characterized by linguistic exogamy. All semisedentary Vaupés Indians, including the Bará, are inhabitants of lowland tropical rainforests and live near streams or rivers. The men hunt, fish, and, using slash-and-burn techniques, clear fields in which the women grow bitter manioc and other crops. Multifamily longhouses are the traditional settlement type and are separated from each other by two to ten hours of canoe travel. Residence is patrilocal, and at present four to eight nuclear families inhabit a longhouse.

Vaupés social structure is segmentary and follows a rule of patrilineal descent. Its units, in ascending order, are the local descent group, the sib, the language group, and, although this is problematic, a possible phratric unit. The language group is a named patrilineal descent unit identified with a specific language. Membership is permanent and public; the one fact that will be known about an Indian before anything else will be his language group membership. If he marries a woman from far away, this is often the only information some of his relatives will have about her.

It should be stressed that Vaupés language groups do not occupy discrete territories. Nor are they corporate groups in any sense. The vast majority of interaction situations occur between Indians of more than one language group, mainly because of the effects of the exogamy rules. Furthermore, all Vaupés Indians, regardless of their language group membership, share a homogeneous culture. The few differences that coincide with language group boundaries besides the possession of a name and language are semimythical founding ancestors and rights to manufacture certain ceremonial objects and use certain chants. At present, the rule of language group exogamy and language affiliation are the most important characteristics of the language groups.

Our aim is to describe the patterns of intermarriage among the eight language groups represented in Table 1. We assume that the number of actual marriages among the various language groups is a function of two different variables. The first variable is the size of the groups involved. In general, the larger the group, the larger the number of marriages. The second variable involves some sort of preference. Our interest is to analyze these preference patterns as reflected in the actual marriages tabulated in Table 1.

In order to analyze the preference patterns, our first task is somehow to remove the effect of the first variable, namely the size of the group. In other words, we want to know the marriage preferences assuming that the groups are all the same size. A method for separating out the effects of size of groups from what we will call preference patterns is presented by Romney (Romney 1971: 191–213). Utilizing these techniques, we can look at the intermarriages among the eight language groups as they would appear if each group had exactly 100 females and 100 males. Table 2 presents the result of this operation. The data in this table reflect exactly the preferences inherent in Table 1 with the effects of differential size removed.

Our next step is to represent these preferences in a visual or spatial form. In order to do this we will assume that groups that intermarry frequently are "closer" to each other than groups that intermarry less frequently. This assumption depends in part on whether or not the data in Table 2 are symmetrical. In other words, the number of men and women exchanged between any two groups should be roughly equivalent in order for a spatial representation to make sense. If this symmetry did not hold, the distance between points would differ depending on direction, and therefore could not be represented in Euclidian space. An inspection reveals that the table is fairly symmetrical, and we assume no radical departures from symmetry.

Our input data derive from Table 2 and consist of the mean number of exchanges between each pair of language groups, regardless of sex. To convert these similarities to "distances," we subtract each cell value from 100. The results are presented in Table 3. Transformations of this sort are commonly used to obtain a distance matrix ready for analysis.

Figure 1 presents the three-dimensional spatial representation of the marriage preferences among the language groups derived from the values in Table 3. In this representation those groups that are close intermarry more frequently than those groups that are further apart. The probability of marriage among groups is a function of distance in the spatial representation.

The pattern that emerges from this representation is very obvious and clear-cut (and yet is not easily seen in the original data). The eight groups form four pairs, each of which has a high frequency of intermarriage. The next highest frequency of intermarriage occurs between groups that are adjacent in adjoining pairs.

With respect to the application of our findings to understanding Bará exogamy, we first note that the measure of symmetry, which shows that the number of men and women exchanged between any two groups is roughly equivalent, is in agreement with the statements of informants (and the expectations we would have on examining Bará kinship terminology) about bilateral cross-cousin marriage preferences and the preference for direct (sister) exchange in marriage.

The manner in which the marriage patterns among these groups relates to kinship and the wider social organization in the Vaupés is explored in

TABLE 2 *Normalized Data Showing Marriage Preferences among Eight Vaupés Groups Assuming Each Group Has Exactly 100 Males and 100 Females*

Husband's Language Group	Wife's Language Group							
	Bará	Tuyuka	Tukano	Desana	Carapana	Tatuyo	Siriano	Yurutí
Bará	0.00	59.22	0.00	11.35	6.81	21.63	1.05	0.00
Tuyuka	44.34	0.00	30.83	5.22	0.00	11.60	7.94	0.00
Tukano	0.00	27.33	0.21	39.42	7.36	4.86	11.42	9.42
Desana	9.45	5.71	38.65	0.00	18.08	0.00	28.04	0.00
Carapana	5.60	0.00	6.36	17.00	0.00	47.22	5.54	18.29
Tatuyo	28.99	0.00	8.23	6.60	27.73	0.00	0.00	28.40
Siriano	1.28	7.73	9.81	20.39	15.30	1.61	0.00	43.87
Yurutí	10.33	0.00	5.86	0.00	24.70	13.06	45.99	0.00

TABLE 3 *Marriage Preference Indices among Eight Vaupés Groups, Ready for Multidimensional Scaling*

Husband's Language Group	Wife's Language Group							
	Bará	Tuyuka	Tukano	Desana	Carapana	Tatuyo	Siriano	Yurutí
Bará	—	48.23	100.00	89.60	93.80	74.70	98.83	94.83
Tuyuka		—	70.91	94.54	100.00	94.20	92.16	100.00
Tukano			—	60.96	93.14	93.45	89.39	92.36
Desana				—	82.46	96.70	75.78	100.00
Carapana					—	62.53	89.58	78.50
Tatuyo						—	99.19	79.26
Siriano							—	55.06
Yurutí								—

FIGURE 1

Spatial Representation of Marriage Preferences among Eight Vaupés Language Groups

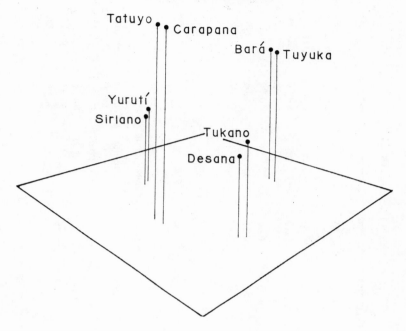

detail elsewhere (Jackson 1976). Here we wish only to point out that by using the methods outlined above we find we have a much clearer picture of what these patterns are with respect to the marriage preferences of eight language groups. We have found that such preferences can be demonstrated in actual marriage patterns, and we can with confidence broaden this to include all Vaupés language groups.

In this example the primary function of multidimensional scaling is to reveal patterns not previously discerned from the data in raw form. It can be seen that Figure 1 lends itself to a structural and functional interpretation to a much greater extent than the raw data as presented in Table 1. The exact nature of the intermarrying patterns can also be given definite quantification.

THE SEMANTIC STRUCTURE OF AMERICAN ENGLISH KINSHIP TERMS

The next example represents an application of the method to the semantic structure of American English kinship terms. Here distance represents similarity in terms of meaning. Those terms judged more similar in meaning are closer to each other than those terms judged less similar in meaning. In the example presented here, the method is used not only to compare one body of empirical data with another, but to make a comparison with a hypothetical model as well.

In a recent article entitled "Individual Variations in Cognitive Structures," Wexler and Romney (1972) presented some data on judged similarity among the eight male kin terms in English. Two sets of data were presented. The first consisted of responses from 116 high school students from Stanford, California, and the second from 155 undergraduates at the University of California, Irvine. In both cases the subjects "were given sheets of paper containing the 56 triads of the 8 male kin terms and told to pick the word in each triad which was the most different in meaning from the other two. The triads and words within triads were randomly ordered (but were the same for all subjects). The subjects were told to work quickly but to answer carefully. They were allowed as much time as they needed and none took longer than twenty minutes" (Wexler and Romney 1972: 77). The data were scored in terms of number of times each pair of kin terms was classed together over all triads.

In addition, Wexler and Romney derived predictions as to how the triad test would be answered on the assumption that a subject answered in terms of a specific process model. The model assumed was taken from Romney and D'Andrade (1964) and is presented in Figure 2. This model assumes that the terms are distinguished on the basis of three intersecting components or dimensions: direct versus collateral, ascending versus descending, and absolute generation. The details of this theoretical prediction may be found in Wexler and Romney (1972). The data for the two sets of subjects as well as the theoretically predicted results are presented in Table 4.

As indicated in the introduction to this paper, one of the major purposes

FIGURE 2

Theoretical Componential Model (from Romney and D'Andrade 1964)

	Direct		Collateral	
	− Reciprocal	+ Reciprocal	+ Reciprocal	− Reciprocal
G ± 2	Grandson	Grandfather		
G ± 1	Son	Father	Uncle	Nephew
	Brother		Cousin	

TABLE 4   *Values of* E(C) = *Mean Number of Times a Pair Is Classed Together (from Wexler and Romney 1972: 78)*[a]

| | Observed Data | | Theoretical Predictions from |
Kin Term Groups[b]	Stanford	Irvine	Romney–D'Andrade Model
Grso, Un	0.77	0.20	0
Grfa, Nep	0.81	0.31	0
Grso, Cos	1.10	0.81	0
Grfa, Cos	0.62	0.27	0
So, Un	0.63	0.32	0.33
Fa, Nep	0.61	0.26	0.33
So, Cos	1.43	0.75	0.50
Fa, Cos	0.55	0.25	0.50
Grso, Nep	1.68	1.38	0.67
Grfa, Un	1.56	0.92	0.67
Grso, Fa	1.62	1.88	0.83
Grfa, So	1.43	2.31	0.83
Grso, Br	1.55	1.36	0.83
Grfa, Br	1.00	1.01	0.83
Br, Nep	1.56	1.63	0.83
Br, Un	1.61	2.47	0.83
So, Fa	3.80	4.02	3.33
Fa, Un	1.95	2.13	3.50
So, Nep	1.23	1.02	3.50
So, Br	3.68	3.01	3.83
Fa, Br	2.32	2.31	3.83
Grso, So	3.17	4.04	4.00
Grfa, Fa	4.00	4.50	4.00
Br, Cos	1.75	1.75	4.00
Un, Nep	3.71	4.27	4.33
Un, Cos	3.48	3.86	4.33
Nep, Cos	4.24	4.71	4.33
Grso, Grfa	4.10	4.25	5.00

[a]The highest possible value is 6.00.

[b]Grso = grandson, Un = uncle, Grfa = grandfather, Cos = cousin, Fa = father, So = son, Nep = nephew, Br = brother.

of multidimensional scaling is to reduce complex data to a visual representation that aids and simplifies analysis. The data in Table 4 are very difficult to comprehend and visualize. For this paper we have run each of the three sets of numbers through a multidimensional scaling program (TORSCA) in order to illustrate how visual representation might aid in analysis. Figure 3 presents the results. Let us examine Figure 3 in some detail, with respect to both the degree of fit between the two sets of empirical data and the fit

FIGURE 3

Three-Dimensional Representation of Eight Kinship Terms Comparing
Theory to Stanford and Irvine Data

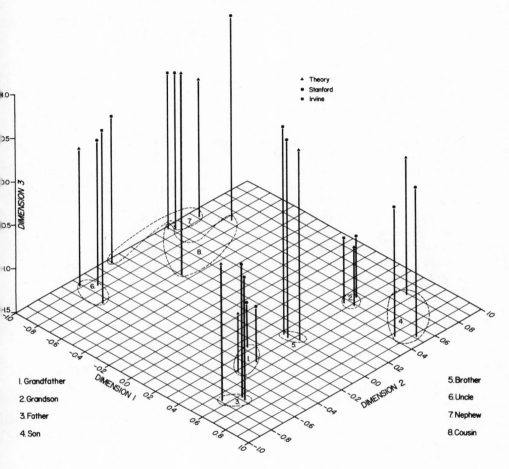

between the empirical data and the theoretically derived predictions.
Dashed lines enclose the points representing each individual kin term. For
example, the kin term "brother" is indicated by the number 5, and in the
figure the three points representing the concept "brother" are enclosed by
a dashed line.

Note that for the concept "brother" the data from Stanford and Irvine
are very close to each other relative to the total space. An examination of
each concept reveals that on a visual basis the data points are fairly close
to each other for all concepts except "nephew" and "cousin." Even these

two concepts differ primarily in dimension 2. We will comment on this discrepancy later. Our major overall visual impression is that the two sets of data correspond rather closely to each other, and therefore may be taken as fairly reliable indicators of some underlying stable structure.

A comparison of the theory with the data also reveals a fairly close fit. Let us now turn our attention to an interpretation of the overall structure and its relationship to the theoretical predictions. Dimension 1 seems to correspond very closely to the distinction between *direct* and *collateral* terms. All data and theory points with a positive value above 0.2 are *direct* terms, while all data and theory points with a value of less than −0.5 are *collateral* terms. We thus see that the distinction between direct and collateral terms in the theoretical model corresponds to a spatial distinction between these subsets in the picture presented by multidimensional scaling of judged similarity data. Dimension 2 corresponds to the ascending-descending or reciprocal dimension. In this case, neutral terms such as "brother" should have a value of zero, and reciprocals such as "father"-"son" should have similar values but opposite signs. Among *direct* terms this dimension is very clear-cut, while among the *collateral* terms there is some variability, as seen in the terms "nephew" and "cousin." Absolute generation is represented in dimension 3. Here those terms furthest removed from ego have negative values, those intermediately removed from ego have moderate values, and those terms in ego's generation have high positive values.

It is our feeling that Figure 3 represents the data of Table 4 in a very helpful and useful way. It makes immediately apparent areas in which the data are stable and correspond to the theory, and distinguishes such areas from the more unstable or unreliable areas. In this example the placement of the *direct* terms is more reliable and stable than that of the *collateral* terms. One might speculate that the closer and more important concepts are, in general, more stably cognitively placed than are terms that are more distant and less important. A similar methodology may be found in a paper by Nerlove and Burton (1972), entitled "A Further Examination of Cognitive Aspects of English Kin Terms."

THE SEMANTIC STRUCTURE OF ROLE TERMS

In the next example the semantic structure of roles is examined. Some years ago John Brim, a student at that time, became interested in judged similarity among English role terms. He selected 58 role terms from an original list of more than 1000. The role terms he selected for consideration are shown in Table 5. He printed each of these terms on small slips of paper and collected data from 108 high school subjects. Each of the subjects was given 58 slips of paper and asked to examine them for five minutes and then

TABLE 5 *List of Role Terms*

1. Artist	21. Fraternity brother	41. Musician
2. Aunt	22. Friend	42. Neighbor
3. Boss	23. Gambler	43. Newcomer
4. Brother	24. Gangster	44. Nurse
5. Carpenter	25. Gardener	45. Occupant
6. Cashier	26. Girl friend	46. Officer
7. Citizen	27. Grownup	47. Owner
8. Civilian	28. Gunman	48. Person
9. Classmate	29. Husband	49. Philosopher
10. Clerk	30. Intruder	50. Poet
11. Companion	31. Judge	51. Professor
12. Composer	32. Landlord	52. Secretary
13. Conspirator	33. Lawyer	53. Spectator
14. Cousin	34. Leader	54. Spy
15. Co-worker	35. Man	55. Stockbroker
16. Daughter	36. Manager	56. Stranger
17. Doctor	37. Mechanic	57. Woman
18. Executive	38. Member	58. Writer
19. Father	39. Mother	
20. Foreman	40. Murderer	

placed in the same pile while items less similar should be placed in different piles. The subjects were told that they might make as many or as few piles of words as they liked, and that they should feel free to change their minds about which terms belonged together. They were given forty minutes to work on this test. The results were coded, and a similarity score for each pair of words was derived. The methods are reported in an article entitled "Dissimilarity Measures for Unconstrained Sorting Data" (Burton 1975). This matrix of similarities was then analyzed through multidimensional scaling (TORSCA). The results are presented in Figure 4, which is simply a visual representation of the data analyzed. The interpretation of possible dimensions resulting from the analysis is in major part an intuitive proposition.

Let us examine Figure 4 in some detail. For dimension A we note first that very low values (around -1.0) tend to be "bad guys," such as "spy," "gambler," "conspirator," "gangster," "gunman," and "murderer." Those with very high values (say above 0.8) include such roles as "friend," "companion," and so forth. We could interpret dimension A as representing a "good"-"bad" dimension, with neutral values around zero being undefined.

Turning our attention to dimension B, we note that those clustered at the

FIGURE 4

Three-Dimensional Representation of Interpoint Distances among 58 Role Terms in American English

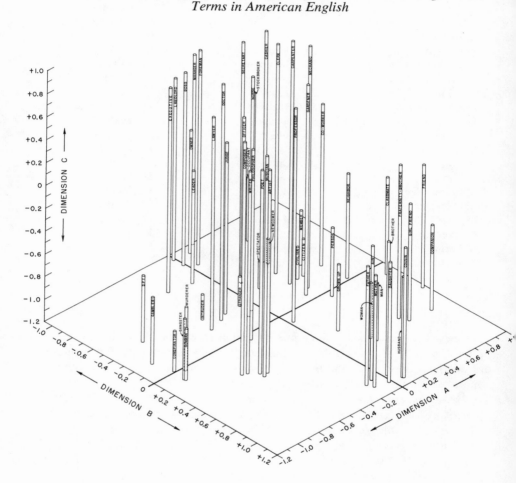

high positive end of the picture include kin terms and related roles such as "father," "aunt," "mother," "daughter," "cousin," and "husband." On dimension B roles with high negative values (around −1.0) include roles such as "executive," "landlord," "boss," "manager," "foreman," and so forth. We would tentatively interpret this dimension as going from roles involving familistic and particularistic relations to those that are universalistic and contractual. Neutral values around zero are again undefined.

Dimension C seems to represent occupations versus nonoccupations. Roles with high values in dimension C are occupations, while those with low values are nonlegitimate occupations. Again zero has an undefined value.

Note the cluster of five roles that occurs in the quadrant that is low on dimension A, medium-positive on dimension B, and high on dimension C, namely the cluster including "composer," "writer," "poet," "musician," and "artist." These are seen as legitimate occupations, since they are high on dimension C. However, they are not highly valued, since they tend to be toward the "bad" side on dimension A. Also they are more like families than like executives, since they are positive on dimension B.

This example demonstrates the usefulness of the method in representing a large number of data points in a way that can be immediately grasped visually. Figure 4 is derived from a matrix containing 653 entries. Further details may be found in Burton and Romney (1975).

The aim of this paper has been to illustrate some possible uses of multidimensional scaling in anthropology. In the first example the pattern of intermarriage among eight groups was revealed. In this case the primary use of the method was to reveal a previously unperceived pattern, and in this sense it contributed to the discovery process. In the second example, on kinship, the method provided a rather precise way of comparing empirical results with theoretical predictions. And finally, in a third example, it provided a convenient way of summarizing similarities among a large number of role terms. For those who are interested in the actual implementation of the method, Green and Carmone (1970) have perhaps the best single summary. A larger variety of examples and more advanced discussion of methods can be found in Shepard, Romney, and Nerlove (1972).

NOTE

1. The following data and discussion are from Jackson (1976). The multidimensional scaling analysis was a collaborative effort.

REFERENCES

Burton, M. L. 1975. Dissimilarity measures for unconstrained sorting data. *Multivariate Behavioral Research*, 10: 409–423.
Burton, M. L., and A. K. Romney. 1975. A multidimensional representation of role terms. *American Ethnologist*, 2: 397–407.
Green P. E., and F. J. Carmone. 1970. *Multidimensional Scaling and Related Marketing Analysis*. Boston: Allyn and Bacon.
Jackson, J. E. 1976. Vaupés marriage: a network system in the Northwest Amazon. In C. Smith, ed., *Regional Analysis*, Vol. 2, pp. 65–93. New York: Academic Press.
Nerlove, S. B., and M. L. Burton. 1972. A further examination of cognitive aspects of English kin terms. *American Anthropologist*, 74: 1249–1253.

Romney, A. K. 1971. Measuring endogamy. In P. Kay, ed., *Explorations in Mathematical Anthropology*, pp. 191–213. Cambridge, Mass.: MIT Press.

Romney, A. K., and R. G. D'Andrade, eds. 1964. Cognitive aspects of English kin terms. Transcultural studies in cognition. *American Anthropologist*, Special Issue, 66(3, Part 2): 146–170.

Shepard, R. N., A. K. Romney, and S. B. Nerlove, eds. 1972. *Multidimensional Scaling: Theory and Applications in the Behavioral Sciences*, Vols. 1 and 2. New York: Seminar Press.

Wexler, K. N., and A. K. Romney. 1972. Individual variations in cognitive structures. In R. N. Shepard, A. K. Romney, and S. B. Nerlove, eds., *Multidimensional Scaling: Theory and Applications in the Behavioral Sciences*, Vol. 2, pp. 73–92. New York: Seminar Press.

Young, F. W., and W. S. Torgerson. 1967. TORSCA, a FORTRAN IV program for Shepard-Kruskal multidimensional scaling analysis. *Behavioral Science*, 12: 498.

Part Three

PROBABILITY DISTRIBUTIONS

Statistical Husbandry: Chance, Probability, and Choice in a Reindeer Management Economy

T. INGOLD

According to a standard textbook on statistics, "the practical problem of the statistician is usually that of making a decision in the face of uncertainty" (Keeping 1962: 142). If that is so, we all share the statistician's problem for much of our decision-making lives. In the empirical context I wish to discuss it is the actors who are presented with problems of an inherently statistical nature. The task of the analyst, armed with a small kit of statistical equipment, is to define limits of knowledge, confidence, and rationality which it is impossible for the actor to exceed, though of course he may not reach them.

In our case the actors are reindeer owners: Skolt Lapps, representatives of a group of around 400 people now living in an area in the far northeast of Finland. The decisions are those of reindeer husbandry: the management by an individual owner of reindeer as a form of wealth and reproductive capital.[1] The parametric framework within which decisions are made is set by the results of herding campaigns, representing the collective effort of herders to bring animals under their owners' control, such that husbandry can take place at all. By introducing these parameters in his limit-setting functions, the analyst can simulate the effects of changes in the herding situation and predict possible consequences for the owners' husbandry decision-making.

I shall first outline the empirical situation and the nature of the decision-making problems with which a reindeer owner is faced. Then I shall translate these into formal terms which permit treatment by probability theory. The mathematics involved is no more complex than some simple properties of the binomial distribution.

THE EMPIRICAL PICTURE

Since 1960, there have been considerable changes in the form of reindeer management among the Skolts. Broadly speaking, these can be correlated with a change from intensive to extensive herding.[2] Under the intensive system deer, which were free to roam during the summer months, were gathered by herdsmen during autumn and winter. The collected herds were driven into roundup fences in which separation according to ownership took place. Only when the animals were delivered into his hands could the owner make husbandry decisions. The whole job required around four or five separations, each of which could last several weeks. At the end of each separation, an owner would lead his animals back to home-grazing pastures, where they were watched over intermittently for the rest of the winter. According to his requirements, the owner would select from his collected herd animals for slaughter, either for household meat supplies or to trade over the international border with Norway in exchange for other basic food supplies such as flour and butter. Come spring and calving time, pregnant female deer were tethered, and calving took place under close supervision. Within days of birth calves received earmarks specifying their owner. After calving, the herds were again free to roam in the forest.[3]

Under this intensive system, deer had a good deal of contact with their herders and were relatively well domiciled, recognizing established home areas to which they instinctively tended to return. However, in the early 1960s badly overgrazed pastures, together with a series of hard snowcrusts, forced herds to scatter in search of pasture, and this caused a gradual abandonment of the intensive system. Deer began to have less contact with men. Clashing economic interests of large and small owners, combined with the tendency of deer to follow along with the mobile, unsupervised herds, produced a snowball effect such that by around 1965 intensive herding had effectively broken down altogether. At the same time the snowmobile or motor-sledge was introduced into herding work in order to deal with the dispersal of the herds.[4] Without it the necessary area could not be covered; but the deer, now no longer drawn at a natural pace by following a "lead" animal but pursued from behind by mechanized force, began to develop their own tactics to avoid coming within reach of the herders. In this they have been rather successful. The relationship between man and deer has changed from a partially symbiotic to an entirely predatory form. The only remnants of herding are collective drives by force into fence-traps, while for their subsistence supplies men often go out in groups of two or three to hunt deer in the forest with firearms. The pastoralist value on deer as reproductive capital is thus combined with the techniques of hunting. I refer to this combination as *predatory pastoralism*.[5]

Since collected herds can no longer be controlled for any length of time, separations are nowadays small and frequent. Hundreds rather than thousands of deer are handled at a time. Separations can occur anywhere, in temporary fences, and at a moment's notice, lasting a day or less. In 1958–1959 there were five separations in the area; in 1971–1972 there were thirty, although fewer deer were handled overall. After separations the deer are immediately let loose again. Thus a man sees his animals only in the brief periods when they happen to turn up at separations, and all husbandry decisions concerning sale and slaughter must be made there and then. Outside the separations the herder has no control over his deer whatsoever. Even calving takes place in the wild, although in recent years summer separations have been held for the purpose of marking calves.

All reindeer management in Finland is organized on an associational basis. Each association of owners controls a defined pasture area on which the deer of its members are expected to graze. Matters of common interest, including the gathering of deer by herdsmen and their separation in the roundup fences, are organized by the association, which pays herders from subscriptions levied on members per head of deer owned. Deer should, in theory, keep within the territories of the associations to which their owners belong. In practice, however, there are always a number of "foreign" deer on every association's area. Territorial boundaries are sometimes of water, keeping deer apart in summer only; some are fenced, others open. The tendency for deer to follow customary routes prevents total dispersal of the herds, but these routes, though constrained by water boundaries and fences, are largely based on ecological zoning. Most of the Skolts' deer are found on the areas of three associations, A, B, and C (Figure 1). Association A has no Skolt members, whereas 88% of the members of association B are Skolts, and 43% of association C are Skolts. Since there is no fence between the territories of associations A and B on the overland boundary, and since deer tend to migrate from the high fell summer pastures in B to the low forest winter pastures in A, the deer of the two associations are thoroughly intermixed; whereas the deer of association C, whose territory includes both pasture zones, keep more effectively to their own area.

Figure 2 shows the total number of Skolt-owned deer found in separations from 1960 to 1972.[6] The yearly fluctuations far exceed the expected fluctuations from the balance of increase through calves and decrease through slaughter, while sharp drops cannot be accounted for by loss through natural death in hard winters when followed by rises of comparable magnitude. Evidently, a major component of this fluctuation is the yearly variation in the proportion of deer that are found and brought to the roundup fences during the winter. The figures, though by themselves inconclusive, support the contention that extensive, predatory herding has led to both a greater degree of fluctuation and a mean decrease in this proportion.

The production of calves is vital to the continuity of a herd. Calves follow their mothers from calving in May until around the following February. If the cow-calf pair is found during this period, the owner has the opportunity to mark his calf. Failing this, the grown calf may later be found in a separation as an independent unmarked animal (Finnish: *peura,* pl. *peurat*). Under intensive herding conditions, calf marking was fairly certain, taking place immediately after calving itself while the herds were still under super-

FIGURE 1

*Regional Sketch Map Showing Reindeer Association Boundaries and
Principal Ecological Zones*

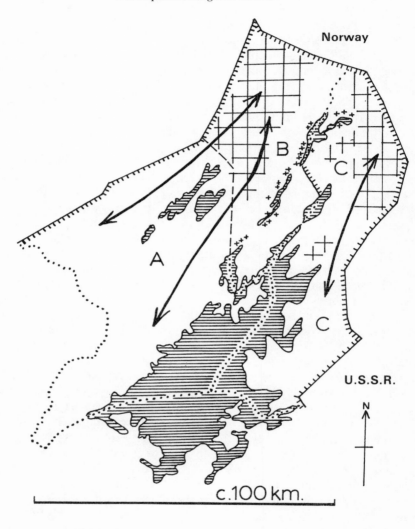

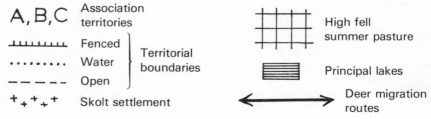

FIGURE 2

*Total Number of Skolt-Owned Deer Found and Recorded in Winter, 1959/
1960 to 1971/1972 (from Association Records)*

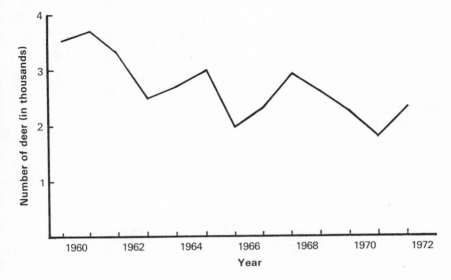

vision. Breakdown of intensive herding in the mid-1960s led to a considerable drop in the number of calves found and marked, and hence a high
supply of *peurat*. The summer separations, held at a time when herds tend
to be highly concentrated on open fell areas, provide an alternative setting
for calf marking. Although total finds in summer may be much higher than
in winter, summer herding is a chancy operation, and failure in some years
may cause temporary "bulges" in the *peura* supply.

The generation of *peurat* from calves is an irreversible process. A good
finding year following a bad one might return a man's adult, marked deer,
but the calves he lost will reappear as *peurat* over which he has no more
claim than anyone else. If the intake of calves is less than the number he
decides to slaughter, an absolute drop will be registered in his herd.

Peurat belong in the first place to the reindeer association on whose area
they are found. Reindeer men can then purchase these animals by auction
at the separations where they are found. *Peurat* thus form a medium of
investment whereby wealth is redistributed principally into the hands of a
few entrepreneurs prepared and able to take the risks of buying up deer in
large numbers. An example is the bachelor, owner B in Figure 3, who
wanted to build up his herd in the mid-1960s, just at the time when the
peura supply was at its peak. The growth rate of his herd is far greater than
that which could be achieved through reproductive increase. While he and

FIGURE 3

Yearly Recorded Holdings of an Unsuccessful Owner (A) Compared with Those of a Successful Owner (B), from 1959/1960 to 1971/1972

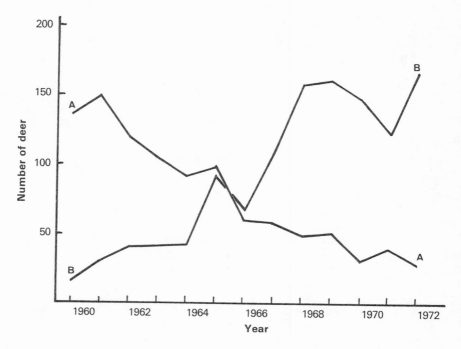

a few others gained deer through continual large-scale investment, older-generation men with already established herds, such as owner A in Figure 3, who had based their herd growth on reproductive increase, found themselves losing heavily. The result of this redistribution today is that while a few owners of large herds stand out prominently, the majority of Skolts own very few deer. The clear trend toward owning small herds is indicated in the histograms in Figure 4.

ESTIMATES AND DECISIONS

Given this background of the reindeer management situation, I shall now outline the husbandry problems confronting an owner and the contexts in which they emerge. These are summarized in Figure 5. An owner must decide whether or not, or to what extent, his reindeer economy must be supported by other food and money sources. For this he needs an estimate of the actual size of his herd, since he cannot know how many animals he

Number of Skolt Owners According to Number of Deer Owned (in Classes: 1–10, 11–20, 21–30, . . .), 1959/1960 and 1971/1972

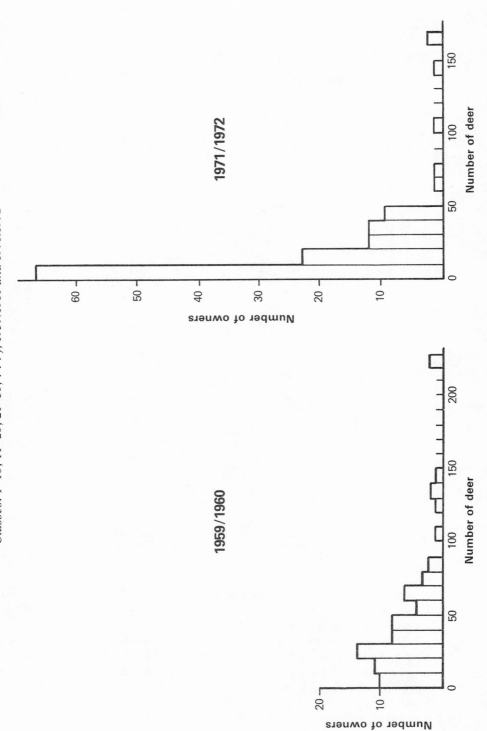

FIGURE 5

Decision Making, Estimation, and Information in Reindeer Husbandry

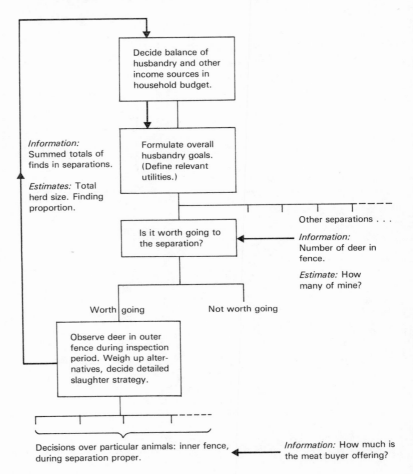

actually owns. The information on which he bases his estimate comes from finds of deer at previous separations; but since he cannot tell whether missing deer are merely lost or dead, estimates can be far off the mark.

Having determined the place of husbandry in his total household economy, the owner must define his overall husbandry goals, determining what factors he will consider when making husbandry decisions and the relative priority to be given to each; that is, he must make some kind of utility scale to apply as a general guide. Utilities will vary, for example, according to whether the owner is a young man most interested in building up his herd, an older small owner with a large family who needs to secure subsistence meat supplies, or an entrepreneurial large owner who wants to buy up *peurat* and to sell on the commercial market. Clearly, husbandry goals are largely set by the phase of development of the owner's household and the extent of his domestic obligations.

The next decision stage comes when the separation is announced. Nowadays getting to the separation may involve cost and inconvenience, and it is never certain that any of a particular owner's deer will show up in the fence. Given the news that so many hundred deer are in the fence, a man has to make an estimate of how many of his deer are likely to be there. If he decides to go, and arrives in good time, he will have the chance to pick out his animals while the herd is on display in the outer fence. Here he can make detailed decisions about what to do with his animals, though his plans are subject to last-minute provisos in view of buyers' prices. The final decision, made for each individual deer in turn, comes in the hectic period of the separation proper in the inner fence; the meat buyers are on the spot and something is known of prices.

The basic decision with which a man is faced in the separation is whether or not to slaughter. A decision to slaughter is an irreversible step often taken in the face of considerable uncertainty. This is especially so since the best time to slaughter, when prices are highest, is at the first separations of the season, when an owner has the least knowledge of his position concerning how many of his animals will be found in the future. Extensive, predatory herding has tended to cut back the options available to the small owner through the reduction of finds and the proliferation of separations; at the same time uncertain conditions encourage policies contrary to herd productivity and continuity.

The decline of reindeer management among the Skolts threatens the whole economic life of the community, and therefore presents a practical problem of some urgency. I suggest that the principal cause of this decline lies in the loss of control over herds, which has both changed the parameters of husbandry by replacing planned selection with random sampling and generated a situation of uncertainty in which, for the typical small owner, husbandry is a game that he is no longer prepared to play.

THE FINDING PERCENTAGE AND THE BINOMIAL DISTRIBUTION

An unknown but very great number of deer are at large in the forest. In practice, in the three associations we are concerned with, the number of deer is of the order of 15,000, of which around a quarter are Skolt-owned; the total number of owners is around 400, of whom one-third are Skolts. Since deer are not guided by earmarks in their own social grouping, and since, with the exception of a handful of old, tame deer, they are no longer domiciled on home pastures, we may imagine that the deer of different owners are effectively intermixed at random in the "forest," although the boundaries of the latter, viewed as the total area on which Skolt deer are found, remain somewhat indeterminate. Over each winter, herders attempt to round up deer into separation fences, and a record is kept of the numbers found in each fence, for every owner.

Deer may be listed only once in a season. On listing, a mark is cut in the hide so that previously counted deer may be recognized if they reappear in subsequent separations. At the end of the season, reindeer finds for every owner are totaled.

Every capture of a deer can be viewed in terms of probability as a success, every noncapture as a failure. The mean probability that a deer will be captured at least once during the season is equivalent to the proportion of the total herd that is found and listed. This we denote by the capture probability f or the finding percentage $F = 100f$. Since the total number of deer is very large, and since we assume the deer to be mixed at random, every trial—corresponding to every deer—may be taken to be independent.

The problem then resolves into a familiar one in probability theory. If the probability of success is f and the probability of failure is $1 - f$, what is the probability of achieving n successes in m trials? In other words, if a man owns m deer altogether, what is the probability that n deer will be found during the season? The man's deer thus form one sample from the total deer population.

This probability is given by the appropriate term of the binomial distribution:[7]

$$b(n) = \binom{m}{n} f^n (1 - f)^{m-n}$$

Figure 6A shows these probabilities for an owner of ten deer under two contrasting finding conditions: $F = 90\%$ (typical of traditional intensive herding) and $F = 60\%$ (typical of contemporary extensive herding).

Figure 6B shows the corresponding cumulative probabilities, that is, the probabilities of *at least* n successes in m trials:

$$B(n) = \sum_{u=n}^{u=m} b(u)$$

It can be seen that a smaller finding probability not only lowers the expected total find in proportion, but also reduces the degree of accuracy or confidence with which it is possible to predict the range of values that the actual find might take. A certain probability may be fixed as a confidence level defining minimum and maximum limits to the likely range of values such that the chances of the find falling below the minimum or above

FIGURE 6

(A) *The Probabilities* b(n) *and* (B) *the Cumulative Probabilities* B(n) *of a Find of n for an Owner of Ten Deer*

(A) The solid bars indicate probabilities when $F = 90\%$, the open bars when $F = 60\%$. (B) The scale on the right gives the probability $B(n)$ of a find of *at least* n, that on the left the probability of a find of *less than* n. The dashed lines at the top and bottom mark 2.5% confidence limits. The shaded bars indicate probabilities when $F = 90\%$, the open bars when $F = 60\%$.

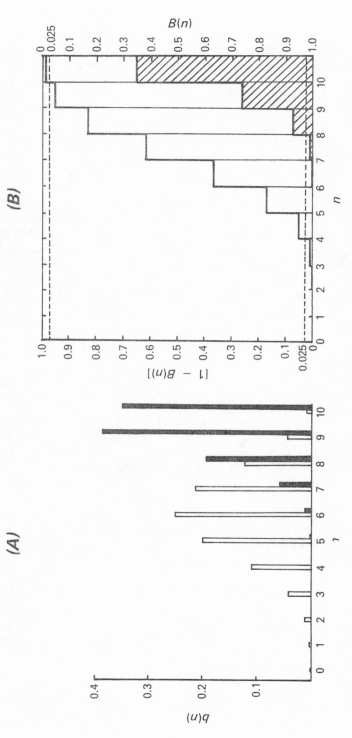

the maximum may be considered small enough to be insignificant. Thus, if in Figure 6 this confidence level were set at 95%, limits to the likely range of values would be set such that neither the probability of the find falling below the minimum nor that of its falling above the maximum would exceed 2.5%. The likely range of values would then be 7–10 inclusive when $F = 90\%$, and 3–9 inclusive when $F = 60\%$. In the former case the range includes only four numbers, in the latter it includes seven. As the finding percentage decreases, the same degree of accuracy may be maintained only at the expense of a drop in the level of confidence with which the range is delimited.

Calculation of binomial coefficients as m increases becomes laborious. However, it can be shown that the probability density curve generated by the binomial distribution approximates to the normal frequency curve as m increases. The approximation is least perfect when f is very close to zero or unity. By replacing the binomial distribution with the normal distribution of mean mf and variance $mf(1 - f)$, one can easily estimate limits to the range of find values according to a given confidence level for larger values of m, using ordinary statistical tables:

$$L_{max} \approx mf + z \sqrt{mf(1 - f)}$$
$$L_{min} \approx mf - z \sqrt{mf(1 - f)}$$
$$L_{max} - L_{min} \approx 2z \sqrt{mf(1 - f)}$$

where z is the value of the standard normal deviate corresponding to the ordinate $\Phi(z)$ of the cumulative normal distribution function, set by the chosen confidence level. The z value for a confidence level of 95%, with a Φ value set at 0.975, is 1.96. For example, when $m = 100$ and $f = (1 - f) = 0.5$, then $L_{max} = 60$ and $L_{min} = 40$, if we allow for the whole number correction. The range of likely finds thus includes 21 numbers.

Since the value of $\sqrt{f(1 - f)}$ reaches its maximum in the middle range when $f \approx (1 - f) \approx \frac{1}{2}$, it follows that for a given confidence level the range of likely find values increases as the finding percentage falls, so long as the latter does not fall far below 50%. If f is kept constant and we vary m, then it follows that

$$(L_{max} - L_{min}) \propto \sqrt{m}$$

We could further define the "relative range of find values" as

$$(L_{max} - L_{min})/m \propto m^{-1/2}$$

Thus, relative to the size of his total herd, the more animals a man owns, the more accurately he can delimit the range of possible numbers that may appear under given finding conditions.

In practice, it may be more important for a reindeer owner to know the probabilities of *at least* a certain number of deer being found. In the last resort a man needs a basic minimum number of found deer to satisfy domestic meat and money requirements, a minimum set not so much by the size of his herd as by the size of his family. For an ongoing husbandry strategy, enough animals must be found to allow the selection of suitable animals for slaughter, leaving others alive to secure the continuity of the herd. In the extreme case, it is the bachelor who has minimum requirements and hence the greatest freedom to develop his husbandry under fluctuating and uncertain herding conditions.

The probability of a find falling below a critical minimum for particular values of m and f can be calculated from the cumulative normal distribution function. For the sake of comparison, the graph in Figure 7 shows the probability of the find falling below a "basic minimum" of 15 deer under varying values of F for three owners: A with 100 deer, B with 50 deer, and C with 20 deer. From this graph we can read off how A, B, and C are affected as F decreases. Clearly, C is the first to feel the effect. When F is around 90%, owner C is still perfectly safe. When it drops to 80%, the risk (about 20%) is already considerable; at $F = 70\%$ it is severe (about 60%); and at $F = 60\%$, C will experience a crisis unless he has exceptional luck.

FIGURE 7

The Probability (p) of the Find Falling below a Basic Minimum of 15 under Variable Finding Conditions (F = 0–100) for Three Contrasting Owners: A with 100 Deer, B with 50 Deer, C with 20 Deer

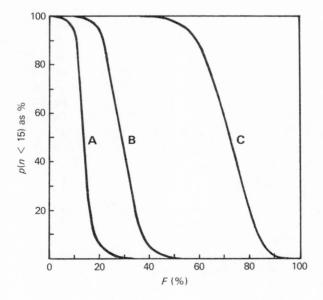

With F hovering around 70%, it is more or less a matter of chance how C manages. With repeated good luck he can continue, but a slight drop in the find can put the odds decisively against him. Owner B will not begin to be significantly affected until F has dropped to below 50%. Finds around 25–30% are critical. This is extremely low, and values of F on this level have probably never been reached. Thus Owner A is entirely safe under realistic conditions.

ESTIMATING THE FACTORS OF HUSBANDRY

A man can never know exactly how many deer he owns. Even if he keeps an exact record of the number he buys, sells, and slaughters, and the number of calves he has marked to his name, there is still a natural loss resulting from death from starvation, falling prey to predators, or simply wandering out of reach of the herders and eventually dying of old age. Yet a man must work with some estimate of total holdings as a basis for his general husbandry policy. In theory, it would be possible to make such an estimate only if records were kept of the finding history of each *individual* animal. Since in practice only the numbers and not the identities of found deer are listed, estimates of herd size cannot be made on the basis of finds alone. If I know the mean finding probability, I can make an interval estimate of my total herd size from the observed find. Alternatively, if I know the total number of my herd, I can make an interval estimate of the mean finding probability. Knowing neither totals nor probabilities, I can estimate nothing.

This inability to form estimates may account in part for the wide range of views held by the owners themselves, all of which can be made consistent with observation. On the one extreme, those who have experienced heavy irreversible losses, largely through the conversion of calves to *peurat,* maintain that the proportion of found deer has not dropped significantly from the high level assumed under former conditions, but that overgrazing, snowmobile herding, and sharp practices have led to massive losses through death by starvation and fatigue, or robbery. On the other extreme are those who are well aware of the place of *peurat* in the total picture, often quoting the huge herds handled in a successful summer separation as evidence that the winter find may be anywhere between 30% and 60% of the total herd.

Both theories contain a measure of truth; but the sharp upward as well as downward trends in the graph of total Skolt holdings, as well as the rapid rise of the present large owners, can be accounted for only in terms of the second "reversible" theory. The observed size of collected herds in summer lends additional weight to this argument; besides, it is evident that deer, which are highly mobile animals, will tend to wander abroad in search of pasture rather than stay at home and starve, and will attempt to escape the net of the herder rather than allow themselves to be driven to exhaustion by the snowmobile.

A running estimate of the number of animals owned could be constructed by adding the number of calves and subtracting the number slaughtered from the previous year's figure. However, not only does an estimate of this kind require an unknown "starting figure," but it ignores a number of unknown quantities which, although tending to balance each other out, could be significant. Ignoring the loss through natural death[8] tends to make the estimate too large, while ignoring the flow of *peurat* into private ownership and the increase through calves marked in summer but not recorded in winter tends to make it too small. One way of judging the reasonableness of estimates made in this way would be to test the hypothesis that the sample m_A of successes and failures that gives one owner A an estimated finding proportion of f_A and the sample m_B giving another owner B an estimated finding proportion of f_B in the same year were both drawn from the same population. If the hypothesis is true, the confidence limits for the value of $(f_A - f_B)$, found from the normal distribution with mean $(f_A - f_B)$ and variance $[f_A(1 - f_A)/m_A + f_B(1 - f_B)/m_B]$, include zero. If the estimates are reliable, this hypothesis should hold good for every possible comparison.

Let us imagine that an owner A wishes to construct an interval estimate for the actual finding probability, based on his own find (n) and his own estimate (m) of his total number of deer. Using the normal curve as an approximation to the binomial distribution we have

$$(n - \tfrac{1}{2}) - mf_{\min} \approx z[mf_{\min}(1 - f_{\min})]^{1/2} \tag{1}$$

$$mf_{\max} - (n + \tfrac{1}{2}) \approx z[mf_{\max}(1 - f_{\max})]^{1/2} \tag{2}$$

Equations 1 and 2 can be solved as quadratics for $f_{\min}$ and $f_{\max}$ respectively. For large values of m, reasonable approximations are given by

$$mf_{\min} \approx n - zn^{1/2}(1 - n/m)^{1/2}$$

$$mf_{\max} \approx n + zn^{1/2}(1 - n/m)^{1/2}$$

Alternatively, owner A may make a guess at f and may wish to make an estimate of m. This may be similarly calculated from the normal distribution at a given level of confidence by holding f constant and inserting $m_{\min}$ and $m_{\max}$ in equations 1 and 2, respectively:

$$z = (m_{\max}f - n)/(m_{\max}f[1 - f])^{1/2} = (n - m_{\min}f)/(m_{\min}f[1 - f])^{1/2}$$

If n is large, it can be shown that

$$m_{\max} - m_{\min} \approx 2z[n(1 - f)]^{1/2}/f$$

When f is held constant, $(m_{max} - m_{min})$ is approximately proportional to the square root of the find—a result similar to that concerning the range of likely values, which is, in a sense, the same problem in reverse: given the total, what will be the find?

It is obviously ridiculous to suggest that the reindeer owner should perform such elaborate calculations as we have here. Nor are these techniques of much use to the analyst, since one key parameter has to be given an assumed prior value, be it the finding probability or the total number of deer, if any calculations are to be performed at all. On the other hand, they do tell something about the maximum precision with which herd parameters can be estimated. They tell us the minimum amount that an owner *cannot* know about his herd, with or without the introduction of purely subjectively based parameters. They also show how these minima respond to real or imagined variations in the total size of the herd and the finding probability, such that we can construct a model that predicts the effects of, for example, a reduced find on an owner's predictive confidence.

The distinction between real and imaginary is important. We have three major parameters: f, m, and n, of which only n is fully known. If an owner reasons in terms of an imaginary m value that is very different from the unknowable, real m value, the results may be surprising, but can be easily accommodated by altering f to fit. In a sense, the owner is free to choose the parameters of his own game, to play according to them, and to interpret the results accordingly. But play the game he must, unless he decides to opt for an all-slaughter policy. As with all of us, the basic parameters of decision making for the husbandman, the things he believes or insists he knows, are just those things that are, in principle, unknowable. The things he does not insist he knows about in advance are those he observes to be variable.

GOING TO THE SEPARATION?

One final problem of estimation remains to be considered. An owner hears news—by telephone or gossip—that a certain number of deer have been gathered in a fence. The separation is due to start the next day. If the fence is near at hand, the owner will reason that there is nothing to lose by going. Frequently, however, getting to the separation may involve a long trip by snowmobile, bus, or taxi, and the cost may be considerable. In addition, for a man involved in wage work, going to the separation may mean loss of a day's wages. Usually the association sends its own representatives to distant separations, and these men are responsible for handling members' deer. Nevertheless, an owner would generally prefer to make his own decisions concerning his animals. In order to decide whether or not to go to the separation, the owner must estimate the number of his deer, if any, that might be in the fence, on the basis of the information he receives. This information is normally limited to an observer's rough estimate of the total herd gathered in the fence, usually to the nearest 100, or 50 for small separations.

The ratio of the total number of a particular owner's deer (m) to the total number of deer in the forest (M) may be assumed to be very small (of the order 10^{-2} to 10^{-3}). If, say, X deer are collected for separation, we can imagine that each deer in the fence represents one independent trial to capture one of the owner's deer, when the mean probability of success (m/M) is very small. For example, if there are 300 deer in the fence, of which two are mine, then two successes will have been registered out of 300 trials. The 300 deer caught in the fence represent a random sample from the total deer population.

The normal distribution cannot be used as an approximation for the binomial when the parametric probability is close to zero or unity. However, it can be shown that when the number of trials (X) is large and the probability of success very small, the binomial probabilities approximate to the Poisson distribution:

$$p(x) = e^{-\mu}\mu^x/x$$

where μ is the mean number of successes and $p(x)$ is the probability of x successes. An important property of this distribution is that it depends only on μ ($=Xm/M$), but not on X and m/M independently.

The numbers of the owner's deer that turn up at each separation provide successive estimates of μ. If every separation handled exactly the same number of deer, we would expect the frequencies of finds of so many deer for a particular owner to follow a Poisson distribution. This picture is complicated by two factors: first, different separations handle different quantities of deer; second, the probability of capture of a Skolt owner's deer does fall off toward the indeterminate limits of "the forest." Thus, in theory, every separation site would have a different μ value.

Let us assume, for simplicity, that we can apply a definite value for the mean number of successes, reckoned per 100 deer. In an empirical example, for a typical Skolt owner, this value came to 0.28. A separation is announced with 800 deer. How many of his deer will the owner expect to find? The value of μ for 800 trials will be $0.28 \times 8 = 2.24$, and the probability of finding x deer is

$$p(x) = e^{-2.24} (2.24)^x/x! = 0.1065 \times (2.24)^x/x!$$

The results are shown in Figure 8A. The risk that no deer will be found, which works out at about 11%, is considerable; but there is a 98% chance that the number found will lie between 0 and 5 inclusive.

This example is typical of contemporary conditions. In the days of intensive herding, there were fewer, larger separations. Warning was given well

FIGURE 8

The Probability of a Find of x *Deer in a Separation According to the
Poisson Distribution for an Owner with a Mean Find of 0.28 per 100 Deer*

(A) For a separation of 800 deer (μ = 2.24); (B) for a separation of
3000 deer (μ = 8.4).

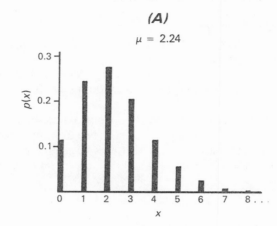

(A)

μ = 2.24

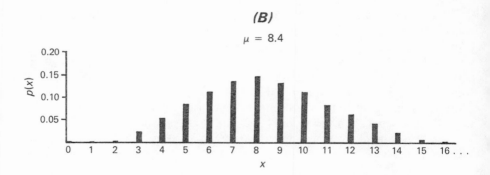

(B)

μ = 8.4

in advance, and the cost of transport to the fence by reindeer sledge was
small. Thus, the problem of deciding whether or not to go to the separation
hardly arose. Figure 8*B* shows the probabilities for an owner of the same
number of deer, who would expect a mean of 8.4 deer in a separation of
3000 animals. In this case, the risk of less than three deer appearing in the
fence is negligible, so that a journey made to the separation would almost
certainly prove worthwhile.

The problem may be stated in a more formal way in terms of utility values. If an owner attaches a utility value V_x to the opportunity to make his own decisions with respect to x deer appearing in a separation, and if the utility cost of making the journey to the fence is C, then the expected net utility of going to the separation will be positive if

$$\sum_{x=0}^{x=m} p(x)V_x > C$$

If V_x is made some function of x, it is possible to express the sum on the left-hand side of the inequality as a function of μ by substituting the Poisson distribution for $p(x)$ and summing the resulting expression for all values of x from zero to infinity.

THE RANDOMIZATION OF HUSBANDRY

Every single deer found in a separation presents its owner with a binary choice: to slaughter it for sale or home consumption, or to keep it alive. According to a variety of criteria, such as age, meatiness, tameness, fertility, and breeding quality, the owner will assign to the deer a value of, say, 0 (leave alive) or 1 (slaughter). From all the possible sequences of 0's and 1's, he will choose that giving the highest utility according to his evaluation criteria.

Under ideal intensive herding conditions, every one of a man's deer would be found in autumn, and over winter he would have his herd together on home pastures, where he would be able to judge every animal according to its merits before arriving at a final slaughter strategy. Such ideal conditions have never existed in practice. Even prior to the breakdown of intensive herding, a few animals would always remain unfound, and a few might die natural deaths. In such cases, planned husbandry decisions are replaced by the chance outcomes of herding and the action of natural forces. A reduction in the find correspondingly reduces the number of deer subject to the owner's decision making. If, say, out of a herd of ten deer, one dies a natural death while three survive but are not found in a particular season; this is equivalent to picking out one deer at random from ten and assigning it the value 1, then picking out a further six deer at random from the nine remaining and automatically assigning the value 0 to the three that are still left. For the six that are picked out, the owner may make his own decisions without resorting to random selection procedures.

The total number of possible selection strategies available to an owner with respect to those of his deer that are found, that is, the number of possible sequences of n 0's and 1's when n deer are found, is 2^n. In the example above, this number is $2^6 = 64$. Limitations on the range of possible selection strategies, however, may be imposed by the owner's minimum slaughter requirements. Thus, if he reasons that he must slaughter *at least*

t deer for domestic meat and cash needs, then the number of admissible sequences can be defined as the number of ways of drawing at least t individuals from a population of size n. The number of ways of drawing x from n is given by the binomial coefficient

$$\binom{n}{x} = \frac{n!}{x!(n-x)!}$$

The number of ways of drawing at least t from n is therefore given by the sum of coefficients for values of x from t to n inclusive:

$$S(n, t) = \binom{n}{n} + \binom{n}{n-1} + \binom{n}{n-2} + \cdots + \binom{n}{t+1} + \binom{n}{t}$$

These coefficients can be found from Pascal's triangle:

```
                    1       1
                1       2       1
            1       3       3       1
        1       4       6       4       1
    1       5      10      10       5       1
1       6      15      20      15       6       1
    •       •       •       •       •       •       •
•       •       •       •       •       •       •       •
```

$$S(6, 2) = 15 + 20 + 15 + 6 + 1 = 57$$

If, in our example, the owner, six of whose deer are found, *must* slaughter at least two, then the total number of admissible sequences is reduced by 7 from 64 to 57. The relative impact of fixed minimal requirements clearly increases as the number of found deer decreases. Thus, had all ten of the owner's deer been found, only 11 out of 1024 possible sequences would have been excluded. A poor find, by placing a greater number of deer outside the scope of planned decision making, also tightens the constraints limiting choice of selection strategy with respect to those deer that do appear.

The range of options of the small owner, whose minimal requirements make up a significant proportion of the total herd size, is most sensitive to reduced finds. The proliferation of small ownership during recent years (cf. Figure 4) has further inhibited the exercise of husbandry choice. A number of independent decision makers, each aiming to select a certain minimum number for slaughter from their own found deer, are more restricted in their range of options than would be the case were finds and requirements pooled under a single decision maker. This may be expressed formally by the inequality

$$S(N, T) > S(n_1, t_1) \cdot S(n_2, t_2) \cdot \ \cdots \ \cdot S(n_j, t_j)$$

where

$$N = \sum_1^j n_x \quad \text{and} \quad T = \sum_1^j t_x$$

Besides reducing finds, the breakdown of intensive herding has led to a fragmentation of decision making. Since the herd can no longer be maintained on home pastures, all slaughter decisions have to be made at the separation site itself. As separations become smaller and more frequent, the number of separate decision events increases, and the number of deer involved each time decreases. Single on-the-spot decisions cannot be extended to cover deer found in previous separations that have already been handled, nor to cover deer that might be found in future separations, about which the owner has no prior knowledge. The effect of this fragmentation is to transform a situation of straightforward utility maximization into one of risk or uncertainty, in which the number of unknowns, greatest at the start of the season, gradually falls off toward the end. In the early separations, the owner has to consider whether to slaughter for his basic requirements immediately or risk waiting in the hope that possibly more suitable deer might appear in the future. If he takes the risk and no better deer are found later, he will be forced to slaughter unsuitable animals or, in the worst case, he may be unable to satisfy basic requirements. The safer solution, though possibly less profitable, is to concentrate essential slaughtering in the earlier separations. This is also a time when domestic needs tend to be greatest and when the deer are in the best condition for slaughter, therefore fetching the highest prices. In contrast, toward the end of the season, the condition of the deer is often so poor that their meat is no longer considered edible, and meat buyers cease to attend separations.

The imposition of a requirement that a certain minimum number of deer be slaughtered from the first separations implies the elimination of certain selection sequences that would be admissible were the whole herd simultaneously available for inspection. Thus, the results of husbandry come to depend not only on *whether* particular deer turn up during the season, but on *when* they appear in the fence, if at all, and on the number and kind of deer that happen to appear along with them in the same separation.

Consider again, for example, the owner with a herd of ten deer. Each successive separation in which his deer appear represents a random sample of a certain number from all of his animals that have not previously been eliminated through slaughter or natural death. Those that fail to be selected

on any of these occasions are automatically left alive (value 0) unless they
die natural deaths (value 1). For simplicity, we may disregard the possible
reappearance in subsequent separations of deer left alive in previous separations, which in practice may allow an owner to reassess earlier decisions.

Let us say that out of ten deer, seven are listed over the season, and that
these seven appear for the first time in five different separations: one in the
first separation, two in the second, two in the third, one in the fourth, and
one in the fifth. The owner's minimum requirement is to slaughter three
deer. If all his found deer were simultaneously available for consideration,
he would be able to select from $S(7, 3) = 99$ possible sequences. However,
when decisions are spread over a number of different separations, he may
introduce the additional order requirement that he must slaughter at least
one deer from each successive separation until at least three deer have been
slaughtered altogether. We can list all the possible combinations of numbers of deer slaughtered in each separation that would satisfy these requirements. The number of admissible sequences according to each combination
may be found by multiplying the appropriate binomial coefficients. Thus,
for the combination which states that 1, 1, 1, 0, 1 deer should be slaughtered
from separations in which 1, 2, 2, 1, 1 deer appear respectively, the number
of admissible sequences is

$$\binom{1}{1} \cdot \binom{2}{1} \cdot \binom{2}{1} \cdot \binom{1}{0} \cdot \binom{1}{1} = 1 \cdot 2 \cdot 2 \cdot 1 \cdot 1 = 4$$

The total number of admissible sequences can be found by summing for
every possible combination. In this example, possible combinations are

$$
\left.
\begin{array}{ccc}
1 & 1 & 1 \\
1 & 1 & 2 \\
1 & 2 & 0 \\
1 & 2 & 1 \\
1 & 2 & 2
\end{array}
\right\}
\left\{
\begin{array}{cc}
0 & 0 \\
0 & 1 \\
1 & 0 \\
1 & 1
\end{array}
\right.
$$

The sum of admissible sequences for every combination comes to 40. In
summary, while the effect of a minimal slaughter requirement is to reduce
the number of sequences from 2^7 (= 128) to $S(7, 3)$ (= 99), the effect of
breaking down the find into separate samples and the introduction of an
order requirement specifying the timing of slaughter further reduces this
number to a value of 40.

One further chance factor is introduced under contemporary conditions.
Deer are widely scattered, and separations may be held anywhere rather
than at a few central points. Deer appearing in distant fences are usually
slaughtered, especially if the owner has not considered it worth his while

to attend the separation himself or has no means to return his deer to his own association's territory. Another possibility may be that deer cannot be slaughtered for sale because of the failure of a meat buyer to reach the site. In either case, the fate of a deer comes to depend to an increasing extent not only on *whether* and *when,* but also *where* it turns up.

The husbandry situation has been presented here in a rather idealized form, with small numbers being used for simplicity. However, these examples suffice to show how, under contemporary conditions, slaughter decisions are based increasingly on the application of rules derived from the constraints of domestic requirements and physical distance to a series of samples drawn at random from the herd, while those deer remaining unfound are placed outside the scope of planned husbandry altogether. Whereas under intensive conditions decisions could be based almost entirely on the application of absolute standards, defined according to husbandry goals and to the quality of each animal, today the results largely depend on whether, when, and where each animal turns up, and leave far less scope for the exercise of "pure" husbandry choice based on the quality of the deer alone. If a man is lucky, the outcome may not differ markedly from that which he might have chosen under ideal conditions; but it is equally probable that random selection procedures specify policies both unproductive and detrimental to the continuity of the herd. The numerical computation of admissible sequences, although hardly undertaken in practice, gives quantitative expression to the randomization of husbandry.

RISK AND UNCERTAINTY

The changes that have occurred in reindeer management in recent years can be viewed in terms of two alternative paradigms. According to the first, these changes represent qualitative breakdown. A herding situation which for all intents and purposes could be treated as one of *certainty* has transformed into one of total *uncertainty,* in which the factors of husbandry are impossible to predict. The opposition of certainty and uncertainty is absolute: this paradigm does not include concepts of degree. According to the second view, the contemporary situation is more *risky* than before. The concept of risk admits degrees of variation from "high" to "low." This paradigm is based on the quantitative notion of probability. The way in which a reindeer owner arrives at his slaughter decisions will depend on which of these alternative paradigms he holds.

In principle, the reindeer owner can be likened to a gambler playing a "one-armed bandit." He knows how many coins he has in his hand. Does he withdraw from the game with the certainty of having at least so much, or does he feed his coins back into the machine, risking loss but hoping for further gains? Let us imagine that the owner has to make a decision on a reindeer-cow, which is expected to calve the following season. If he leaves it alive, and the cow-calf pair is found in the following season, he will realize a good profit. If the pair is not found, he will not get the calf, but the cow may turn up in subsequent seasons. On the other hand, there is always the possibility of natural death.

We can assign utilities in this situation as below:

Value of cow = V
Value of calf = u
Value of realizability of utility (i.e., of having the animal available such that its value may be realized) = e

There are three possible outcomes:

X: Cow and calf found next season
Y: Cow not found, but still alive
Z: Cow dies natural death

The two alternative strategies are:

0: Leave alive
1: Slaughter

Utilities according to the different strategies and outcomes are tabulated below. Obviously the value for strategy 1 is fixed: if the deer is slaughtered, what happens next season is irrelevant. This strategy represents withdrawal of one deer from the game.

		Outcome	
	X	Y	Z
Strategy 0	$V + u + e$	V	0
1	$V + e$	$V + e$	$V + e$

If we view this problem as a situation of risk, our approach would be to make a reasonable guess at the next season's finding probability (f) and at the probability of natural death (q), and estimate the expected utilities of alternative strategies according to Bayes' method. Since the probability of outcome X is estimated as f, that of outcome Z as q, and that of Y therefore as $(1 - f - q)$, the expected utility of strategy 0 will be

$$f(V + u + e) + (1 - f - q)V + q(0)$$

If this exceeds the utility for strategy 1 $(V + e)$, then the owner can argue that the gamble (strategy 0) will pay off in the long run. The condition for choosing 0, then, is that

$$f(V + u + e) + (1 - f - q)V > V + e$$

that is,

$$f > (e + qV)/(u + e)$$

Thus, while lower estimates of f, higher estimates of q, and greater immediate needs (higher values of e) will tend to favor strategy 1, higher values placed on the continuity of the herd (u) will tend to favor strategy 0.

If, on the other hand, the owner reasons in terms of the paradigm of certainty and uncertainty, the most rational solution would be to adopt the minimax principle of the theory of games. The game can be imagined as a three-cornered match between men, reindeer, and the set of unpredictable forces that can be called Nature. This view involves the assumption that all three parties are plotting against each other. The reindeer wishes to avoid capture and slaughter, and Nature is envisaged as a predator hoping to catch the reindeer for herself. Outcome X is a gain for the owner and a loss to both the reindeer and Nature. Outcome Y is a gain for the reindeer and a loss to the owner and to Nature. Outcome Z is a gain for Nature but a loss to the owner and to the reindeer. Utility tables similar to that above could be constructed to show utilities for Nature and for the reindeer. If the minimax principle is to be applied, a zero-sum game must be assumed.

Under all possible circumstances, the minimax solution is clearly strategy 1, which ensures a utility gain of $(V + e)$ regardless of what happens in following seasons. Clearly, this "slaughter every time" solution, stemming from an inability to predict the unknown factors of husbandry in the framework of the paradigm of uncertainty, is a formula for the abandonment of husbandry, and marks the reversal from a herding to a hunting economy. It is a formula that an increasing number of older-generation Skolts seem to apply. The validity of the game theoretic assumptions may, however, be questioned. The assumption that the reindeer is acting strategically to avoid the herder, inapplicable under former conditions, is increasingly justified in view of the transformation from symbiotic to predatory pastoralism. This assumption implies that deer that are found must necessarily have been outwitted in herding campaigns. The assumption of a malevolent Nature is not so easily justified. Nature, after all, provides the food for the deer to eat. However, surveying the overgrazed pastures, an owner might even doubt that: lichen always grows whiter on the other side. The game theoretic assumptions do, indeed, negate the very foundations of any pastoral economy.

MEN AND MATHEMATICIANS

It often happens that when mathematics is introduced into sociological or anthropological analysis, any remaining hints of realism tend to be sacrificed in favor of the elegance of mathematical logic which requires no data to support it. The men disappear behind the mathematics. In our presentation, it seems that we have made the men into mathematicians. It can well be argued that this is equally unrealistic. One can hardly believe that our image of the statistically minded husbander, conversant with the properties of the binomial distribution, has any real counterpart.

Nevertheless, a formal mathematical treatment enables us to specify the limits of knowledge, confidence, and rationality within which the husbander of necessity operates. These limits define the problem of husbandry, and are set by the results of herding operations. We have shown how a change from intensive symbiotic pastoralism to extensive predatory pastoralism alters these limits such as to generate a form of husbandry that may be perceived as either qualitatively uncertain or quantitatively risky according to the paradigmatic framework in which it is handled.

Reindeer lend themselves to quantitative treatment. There are a lot of them, and they can be counted. On the other hand, reindeer are only amenable to counting under specific conditions. If total counts of deer could be made "in the forest," the whole structure of the situation would be altered, and the degrees of freedom would be reduced from 2 to 1. In general, reindeer can only be counted when they are in fences. Not all these counts are accessible to the anthropologist, but as an observer he has a broader perspective, based on an overall survey of the records, whereas the interpretations of the individual reindeer owner are heavily colored by his own personal fortunes and recollections. Thus, neither actor nor anthropologist has the power to reduce the degrees of freedom, but each makes inferences from a different range of data and views these data from a different angle. In one respect, the actor's judgment far outweighs that of the anthropologist, for his experience enables him to perceive the qualitative uniqueness of every animal.

If we wished to have a complete analysis of the situation of a man playing a "one-armed bandit," we would need, on the one hand, to find out as much as we could about what goes on in the mind of the player; on the other hand, we would want an accurate specification of the machine itself: its mechanism, structure, and dimensions. Similarly, we have attempted to give the specifications of husbandry. We have seen that the husbander is, up to a point, free to define his own parameters and thus adapt the game to his own requirements. To complete the analysis, we need to know much more about the players—the reindeer owners themselves. This complementary aspect of the problem has not been covered in this paper, and the approach we have adopted here would not be appropriate to deal with it.

The systematic investigation of "ethnomathematics" as applied by the reindeer owners in the context of husbandry unfortunately lay outside the scope of my original field work. I can therefore only put forward an impressionistic picture, based on various informants' presentations of the husbandry problem. The older-generation Skolt, brought up in a tradition of highly intensive small-scale herding, is accustomed to certainty. His values stress cool, reserved judgment and experience and skill in handling animals. In his personal relations he tends to be quiet and somewhat withdrawn. Recent years, however, have seen the emergence of a quite different kind of character: an extrovert and reckless gambler, noisy and sociable, a man who is prepared to throw all his fortunes and personal energies into a risky enterprise. A classic example of the "big man," he is the very antithesis of the older-generation owner, whose experience and judgment are rendered largely obsolete under contemporary conditions. Owners A and B in Figure 3 are examples of these two types.[9]

The traditional mathematics of certainty, lacking concepts of risk, probability, and proportionality, sees general losses in irreversible and absolute terms rather than relative to herd size, and cannot handle the fluctuations of contemporary conditions. The foundations of husbandry appear to have disintegrated; and the search for certainty in uncertainty leads to the logic of game theory, which in turn instructs the husbander to withdraw, leaving the field clear for the operations of the "big man." The latter, whose career would not be possible under conditions of certainty, thrives on risk. Although in terms of traditional logic the enterprise of the "big man" appears to be an entirely irrational gamble, in terms of his own paradigm, based on probability and expected utility rather than minimax, his strategy appears perfectly rational. We can suggest, then, that developments in reindeer management in the recent past favor the emergence of the hot-headed risk-taker, while the careful man, whose mathematics of certainty is inadequate to handle the situation, withdraws.

In this paper, I have explored the logical consequences of a number of variations on a single basic idea: that the capturing of reindeer, on which husbandry depends, represents a process of random probability sampling. I hope that these ideas will be further developed in two directions. On the one hand, empirical comparison would be interesting. Perhaps the chaotic state of Skolt reindeer management is somewhat exceptional, but I feel sure that many of the diverse forms of economic life we describe, not only among pastoralists, can be reduced to formal problems of the same kind which would bear comparison. On the other hand, there is room for theoretical development with regard to the general study of decision-making processes beyond the level attempted here.

ACKNOWLEDGMENTS

Field work was carried out among the Skolts between May 1971 and September 1972, and was supported by studentships from the Social Science Research Council (U.K.) and Churchill College, Cambridge, and a grant from the Emslie Horniman Anthropological Scholarship Fund.

I am grateful to Dr. R. C. Campbell and Professor J. A. Barnes for suggestions and criticisms on the original draft of this paper. Responsibility for the present version rests entirely with its author.

NOTES

1. I am here following the distinction made by Paine (1970) between *husbandry* as "the growth of herd capital and the formation of profit" and *herding* as "the control and nurture of animals in the terrain."

2. The distinction between *intensive* and *extensive* herding is also taken from Paine (1972).

3. A description of intensive herding as it was among the Skolts in the late 1950s is given by Pelto (1962).

4. The pros and cons of the snowmobile are discussed by Pelto, Linkola, and Sammallahti (1969).

5. Cf. Ingold (1974). A more comprehensive account of the contemporary transformation of Skolt reindeer economy is contained in Ingold (1976: Part 1).

6. These figures are taken from association records kept by the central organization for Finnish reindeer management, showing the number of listed deer for each owner. The accuracy of the figures for the first few years is questionable, as there is clear evidence of "fixing" of the figures for certain owners.

7. The term $\binom{m}{n}$ is the standard form of the binomial coefficient:

$$\frac{m!}{n!(m-n)!}$$

where $n!$ is shorthand for the multiplication $1 \cdot 2 \cdot 3 \cdot 4 \cdot \cdots \cdot (n-2) \cdot (n-1) \cdot n$.

8. Under certain circumstances, attempts may be made to search the whole territory for dead animals in order to establish claims for compensation payments. However, it is never possible to establish with certainty the total extent of natural death.

9. This contrast is explored further in Ingold (1976: 64–73).

REFERENCES

Ingold, T. 1974. On reindeer and men. *Man*, n.s., 9: 523–538.
———. 1976. *The Skolt Lapps Today*. Cambridge: Cambridge University Press.
Keeping, E. S. 1962. *Introduction to Statistical Inference*. New York: D. Van Nostrand.
Paine, R. 1970. Lappish decisions, partnerships, information management, and sanctions: a nomadic pastoral adaptation. *Ethnology*, 9(1): 52–67.
———. 1972. The herd management of Lapp reindeer pastoralists. *Journal of Asian and African Studies*, 7: 76–87.
Pelto, P. J. 1962. *Individualism in Skolt Lapp Society*. Kansatieteellinen Arkisto 16. Helsinki: Suomen Muinaismuistoyhdistys.
Pelto, P. J., M. Linkola, and P. Sammallahti. 1969. The snowmobile revolution in Lapland. *Journal de la Société Finno-Ougrienne*, 69: 1–42.

Polygyny as a Measure of Social Differentiation in Africa

PAUL SPENCER

What is popularly known as Pareto's law refers to the unequal distribution of wealth within many societies whereby a minority of the population control the major part of the resources. In this chapter I wish to explore an inequality of this kind, using numerical data from 50 African societies, in order to consider the problems of sociological inference and interpretation.

This unequal distribution may be envisaged in graphic form as a humped curve with a relatively low maximum value (the less affluent bulk of the population) and a long upper tail (the privileged rich and excessively rich). Where the distribution of wives or clients or dependents is considered as an index of wealth, however, a stepped profile would be more appropriate than a curve because the data are discontinuous. Thus area is a continuous variable, and a landowner may have 2½ hectares of land; but he cannot have 2½ wives. For heuristic purposes, the distinction may be of little importance: a continuous distribution may be presented in the form of a stepped histogram, while a discontinuous distribution (or *series*) may be thought of as approximating to a particular curvilinear form. However, mathematically they are quite distinct, and this distinction is basic to the present exercise. Two hypothetical distributions of probability are especially relevant here: the continuous *gamma curve* and the discontinuous *negative binomial series*. Each has the characteristic low maximum and long upper tail, and they are illustrated in Figure 3. The negative binomial series is relatively unknown among social scientists, yet it seems to have an especially wide range of application to social phenomena. This is therefore an opportunity to consider its relevance.

I have chosen the specific topic of polygyny because its incidence in various societies is well recorded and has been related by many writers to sociological factors; and Africa is an especially suitable area in which to explore the theme because of the wide prevalence of polygyny.[1]

THE DISTRIBUTION OF POLYGYNY IN 50 AFRICAN SAMPLES

A representative view of the high regard for polygyny in Africa has been expressed by Phillips in his *Survey of African Marriage and Family Life*

117

(1953): "Where the traditional outlook still prevails, the possession of a number of wives is normally a mark of importance and success in life and— for this among other reasons—is something which the average African man would gladly achieve if he could: in other words, monogamy is for the majority who are in fact monogamous, a matter of necessity rather than choice" (p. xiv). In her contribution to that survey, Mair echoes the theme, but with a deliberate shift in emphasis, noting the extent to which polygyny remains an ideal in those areas where it is still an economic asset rather than a liability, but has dwindled in those areas where the education of children and other modern expenses have altered the economic advantages and have encouraged alternative modes of converting wealth to prestige. The point is well taken. Here I am concerned with samples from 50 of the more traditional African societies (rural and urban), selected because their rates of polygyny have been recorded and are relatively high. However, this is not to deny that in other areas a comparable distribution of prestige may exist, manifesting itself in other ways. Relevant data from the samples are summarized in Appendix I, and their distribution in Africa is shown by Map 1.

As an initial step toward analysis, we may consider two parameters. The first is the average rate of polygyny. For the 50 samples this *mean* varies from 1.12 wives per married man among the Hima to 2.36 wives among the Mende.

This immediately raises the problem of the availability of surplus women associated with the higher levels of polygyny. A number of writers[2] have pointed out that the most significant feature that accounts for this surplus is not any intrinsic unbalance in numbers between the sexes, but a delay in the age of first marriage of men. In other words, while there are generally about equal numbers of each sex, the glut of married women in a highly polygynous society is associated demographically with a queue of unmarried men who must wait as bachelors for a period, an underprivileged sector biding their time. Here I shall refer to the married men as *elders*. Thus the average polygyny rate of a society is often an indirect measure of the delay in the age of marriage of young men, a measure of the extent to which the elders can maintain a monopoly over marriage and over the privileges associated with this.

In this sense, the mean rate of polygyny, m, may be generally regarded as a measure of the distribution of power and prestige between old and young. For our present purposes, this measure will be referred to as *gerontocracy*. This is not to suggest that this mean is the only measure of gerontocracy or even the best one. Among the Hima, for instance, gerontocracy manifests itself not in high polygyny rates, but in older men actually denying themselves further wives in order to tie their own sons down with early marriage and family responsibilities.[3] Conversely, there are societies in which a high rate of polygyny is associated not with gerontocracy, but

MAP 1

Distribution of Sample Areas in Africa

rather with the virility and economic drive of younger men; the Gonja and Yakö are in this category but appear to be atypical (E. Goody 1973: 82–83; Forde 1941: 77–80). "Gerontocracy," then, is a useful though occasionally misleading label for this variable. The development of this model, however, hinges primarily on the second parameter, to which I now turn.

The second parameter is the measure of the spread of polygyny among elders, that is, the extent to which the available surplus of women is monopolized by a few men or is widely shared. The interpretation of this spread has been well expressed by Nadel (1942) in relation to different communities among the Nupe.

In Nupe as in most polygamous societies in which marriage is by bride-price (and high bride-price at that) the number of wives a man possesses becomes an infallible index of wealth and status. In the peasant districts, where we find comparatively little inequality of wealth, the range of polygamy also varies within narrow limits.

But in Bida, the royal capital,

the great inequality of wealth and status is reflected in the widely varying range of polygamy. In the houses of the *talakaži,* the "poor ones," monogamy is the rule; in the "middle class" the conditions are much the same as in the peasant districts, but as regards the men of substance and rank, though it would be correct to say that they have rarely less than four wives, the upper limits of their polygamy are very fluid, and cannot even be ascertained with any accuracy. Popular notions attribute to certain royal princes and, above all, to the kings of Nupe, numbers of wives varying between 100 and 200 [p. 151].

One may note the contrast between remote areas where a mild degree of polygyny is the privilege of many and the royal capital where monogamy is the lot of many and excessive polygyny the prerogative of a few.

For present purposes, it is convenient to define the spread of the incidence of polygyny as the ratio of variance to mean (s^2/m), and this is referred to here as *variability, d.* Consistent with the interpretation of the mean polygyny rate as a measure of social differentiation between elders and younger unmarried men, one may interpret variability in the distribution of wives as another measure of inequality, but this time among the elders themselves; here this variability is given the label *social differentiation among elders.* Those who possess several wives are assumed also to have associated privileges at the expense of others who are less fortunate. Once again, it has to be emphasized that while this interpretation is consistent with many studies of African societies, it is only an initial approximation and exceptions can be cited. A modified interpretation is suggested later in this paper.

At this point, one has a clear choice in measuring the level of polygyny. It can be expressed either as the number of wives of each elder, or as the number of further wives after his first marriage. The former is the more usual measure; the Nupe village of Mokwa, for instance, had an average of 1.55 wives per elder. In terms of further wives, on the other hand, this would be expressed as an average of 0.55 further wives per elder. For reasons that should become clearer in a subsequent section, the second measure is adopted here. One may note a certain logical consistency in this. On this scale, a completely monogamous society would show an average of no further wives ($m = 0$), implying no delay in the age of marriage of young men and no gerontocratic restrictions on first marriage; in this sense a nil rating is logical. So far as variability is concerned, the measure focuses on the distribution of surplus women, and so again in a sense it is the number of further wives that is more directly relevant for analysis. To express it in a slightly different way, we are considering societies in which in general every adult man has a certain right to a wife, and a mature bachelor is regarded as somewhat anomalous. Monogamy is a man's inherent right, whereas polygyny is a measure of his ability to achieve an ideal. For the development of a man's independence from his senior kin and the founding of a family, his first marriage is of course extremely significant. However, in the tacit competition for prestige and the building up of a polygynous family, the first marriage may be regarded as a man's entry into a new game.

In Figure 1, the 50 societies are plotted according to the values estimated for their parameters m and d. If one accepts the above interpretations of these parameters, this raises certain questions of comparison between neighboring societies. For example: (1) The Maasai, whose independent egalitarianism is legend, appear to be rather more socially differentiated than most other groups, such as, for instance, their distant kinsmen the Samburu. (2) Gulliver's (1955) comparison of the Turkana and Jie suggests a more gerontocratic control among the Jie, but this appears to be contradicted by the higher polygyny rate among the Turkana. (3) In comparing LoDagaba and LoWiili domestic groups, Jack Goody (1958) focuses his attention on the units of production rather than of reproduction and partly justifies this choice on the grounds that there is little difference between the two societies in the distribution of wives among adult men: "There seemed to be no differences of any significance between the figures for the LoDagaba, the LoWiili and the Tallensi" (p. 57, in reference to the figures on p. 89). But it is apparent in Figure 1 that there is a substantial difference in variability of polygyny between the LoDagaba and the LoWiili, and in the average polygyny rate when compared with the Tallensi. (4) In his notional continuum between town and country among the Nupe, Nadel would have placed the royal capital to the extreme right of Figure 1, and the remoter villages such as Mokwa, where the "chief's rank is merely the highest in the order of village ranks," toward the left. Somewhere in the middle would be the less remote villages of Doko and Kutigi, where commoners are a class apart from the ruling dynasty and there is a degree of social differentiation. This is reflected, he suggests, in the polygyny rates (Table 1), which show a wider range in Doko and Kutigi than in Mokwa (Nadel 1942: 50–51, 54, 55, 63, 151).[4] However, as in the example cited by Goody, the figures are deceptive, and Figure 1 shows Doko and Kutigi actually to have *less* variability than Mokwa. Whether such differences are significant or not is considered further in the next section.

Finally, the distribution of points in Figure 1 may be considered in relation to a generalization made about traditional African societies. Jack Goody has suggested that there is a certain association between high poly-

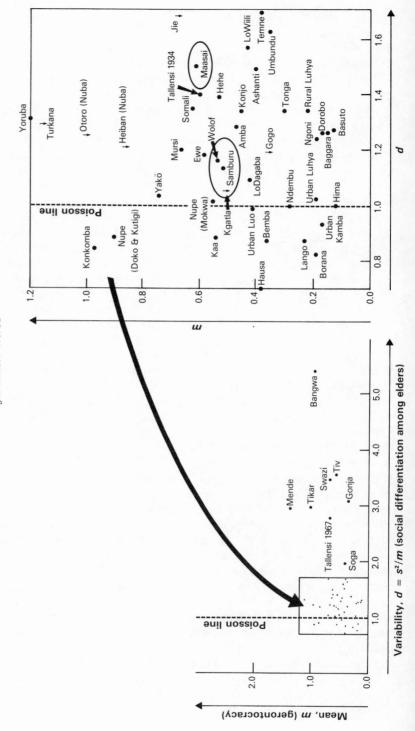

FIGURE 1

Social Differentiation in 50 African Samples Indicated by the Distribution of Further Wives

TABLE 1   *Polygyny Rates among the Nupe*

| Village | Number of Further Wives | | | | | | Total | Parameters | |
	0	1	2	3	4	5+		*m*	*d*
Mokwa	44	28	3	3			78	0.55	1.55
Doko and Kutigi	68	96	20	11	1	1	197	0.90	0.87

gyny rates and lack of social differentiation, since in highly polygynous societies wealthy men disperse their wealth by paying for more wives and having more children to inherit from them (1973: 10–11, 13, 17–18).[5] While this argument is well sustained by reference to particular African societies, if it is generally true and one accepts the interpretation put forward here for the parameters in Figure 1, then it should be reflected by a certain clustering of points along a diagonal from the upper left to the lower right.

By way of contrast, one may consider an alternative hypothesis. If "gerontocracy" is a theme that is pervasive in some societies and generally absent in others, then one could expect to find a high rate of polygyny (emphasizing the differentiation between elders and bachelors) associated with a high "social differentiation" between the older elders who have been stockpiling wives for many years and younger elders who find considerable difficulty in acquiring a second wife; even as elders they still face gerontocratic restrictions. This would tend to produce a clustering along the other diagonal, from upper right to lower left.

Visually, neither pattern of clustering appears to predominate in Figure 1. A correlation test, however, reveals that a distinct positive correlation does in fact exist, lending support to the second (pervasive gerontocracy) hypothesis.[6] The fact that the points are nevertheless widely scattered leaves open the possibility of other less dominant patterns. It is quite feasible that the first (dispersal of wealth) hypothesis holds good, but that the present manner of presenting the data masks the underlying pattern. Were polygyny data available for a single age group in all these societies, then it is conceivable that there would be a negative correlation, lending support to Goody's hypothesis.

CONSISTENCY AND THE LIMITS OF CONFIDENCE

Figure 1 invites comparative analysis on a wide number of possible issues. It is necessary therefore to query the accuracy of the estimates for each parameter as a next step toward pursuing any questions that are raised. One has to rely on the data available and the form in which they are presented, extrapolating if necessary when, for instance, there is a grouping of "more than five wives" (as in Table 1) that obscures the profile of the upper tail. One also has to rely on the context in which each sample was collected and accept the possibility that, because of shortcomings in the techniques of collection, this is not representative of the wider society. Thus the larger samples may be statistically preferable, but they may also have been collected with less concern for accuracy.[7] Terminal polygyny rates derived from genealogies of ancestors would be higher than polygyny rates derived from an existing community, where many men will still take on further wives.[8] In societies where polygamous families are dispersed, polygynists are more likely to be included in a local survey than monogamists.[9] Again it is not always clear whether concubines or inherited widows or separated wives have been counted as wives for the purpose of sampling.[10]

Without a doubt, a major weakness of the current exercise rests with these reservations. Apart from those samples that clearly fall short of the ideal, most of the remainder are suspect in that there is no clear statement of sampling procedure or apparent awareness of the pitfalls. To develop the model beyond the limited aims of this exercise would require a more careful selection of samples.

If some convention had to be proposed for collecting data relevant to this study, I would suggest that a sample should cover the current wives of each elder in a defined area and those concubines and inherited widows who de facto (if not de jure) are comparable to full wives. It should exclude wives that are separated or living elsewhere, unless it is quite clear that the elder in question maintains control over separate households. In such a case (following Barnes 1949) the elder's presence would be notionally divided between his various wives for purposes of the survey, and the fraction of the elder associated with those wives who live outside the survey area should be excluded.

Above and beyond these doubts concerning the mode of collecting data on polygyny, there is also the question of the statistical confidence that can be placed in the results as they stand. The points in Figure 1 are only best estimates for the parameters of the parent population, often limited by the smallness of the samples. The true values for each parameter might be anywhere in the vicinity of these points. The ovals around the points for the Maasai and Samburu on the diagram represent the estimated limits of a 68% probability that the "true" parameters in question lie somewhere inside these areas.[11] As a probability estimate for the true values of each parameter, this is not particularly impressive. However, of the remaining 32% (outside the oval) for the Maasai, the "true" parameters are just as likely to be further away from the Samburu oval (16%) as they are to be closer (16%). Similarly, the "true" Samburu parameters are as likely to be further away from the Maasai oval (16%) as they are to be closer (16%). Thus the chances that the "true" Maasai and Samburu parameters broadly correspond—that the "true" Maasai point lies beyond its oval toward the

Samburu *and* that the "true" Samburu point lies beyond its oval toward the Maasai—is about 2.5% (=16% × 16%), and this is strong evidence that the Maasai are indeed the less egalitarian society. *If two ovals do not overlap, there is at least a 97.5% probability that the societies are dissimilar.*

Additional ovals representing the same limits of confidence are shown in Figure 2, although to avoid congestion and confusion I show only a selection of societies.

With regard to the comments on individual societies in the preceding section, it is evident that the Turkana appear to be significantly more gerontocratic than the Jie. The LoDagaba appear to be significantly more egalitarian than the LoWiili, and both appear to be significantly less gerontocratic than the Tallensi. Among the Nupe, on the other hand, Mokwa village does not appear to be significantly more differentiated than Doko and Kutigi despite Nadel's conclusion drawn from his table. Clearly, if one accepts the present interpretation of the parameters, these examples pose further questions regarding the data and the societies in which they were collected that were not considered by the authors. At a 97.5% level of probability, these conclusions cannot be dismissed on the grounds of chance and the smallness of the sample sizes.

CHARACTERISTICS OF THE NEGATIVE BINOMIAL SERIES

So far in this exercise the techniques adopted for analysis have essentially been borrowed from those most appropriate for the analysis of the normal curve, a continuous and symmetrical distribution. However, polygyny frequencies are discontinuous and asymmetrical. The shape or *profile* of each sample may vary, providing, in effect, a third dimension for analysis and further insights.

Among the various discontinuous distributions are a class that can collectively be referred to as binomial series. These can be defined in terms of the parameters m and d, which together determine the precise profile. Thus, corresponding to each point on Figure 1, there is a binomial profile that matches the recorded polygyny data in terms of mean and variability, and can be compared with these data to see how closely it matches also in terms of shape. This section is primarily concerned with the implications of such a match where it occurs.

For the "true" binomial profile, the value of d is invariably less than 1.0; and in the context of sampling theory, it is common statistical practice to regard the Poisson profile as a limiting instance, at which point the variability attains the value of 1.0. Here, in a different context, I prefer to regard the Poisson profile as the midpoint in a spectrum that stretches beyond to a less well-known series in which d is greater than 1.0. The series at this end of the spectrum are known as *negative binomial series*. Mathemati-

FIGURE 2

Social Differentiation in 50 African Samples Indicating the 68% Limits of Confidence in Parameter Values for Selected Societies

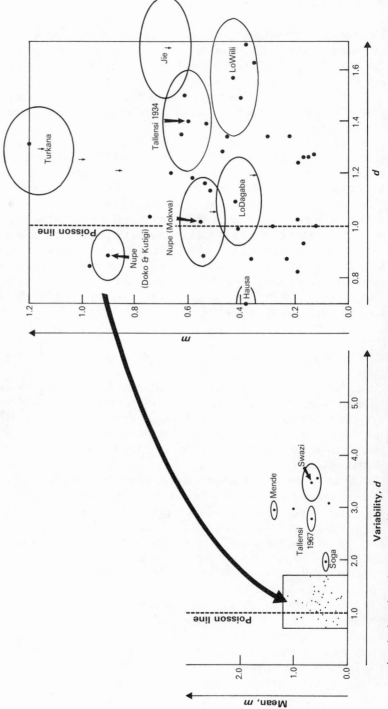

Assuming that each sample represents a wider society, there is a 68% probability that the parameters *m* and *d* for that society lie within the area of the ellipse. Where two ellipses do not overlap, there is a 97.5% probability that

cally, the true binomial, the Poisson, and the negative binomial series are logically linked in a continuum, and in Figures 1 and 2, a vertical line with a value of $d = 1.0$ is labeled "Poisson line." To the left of this line is the area associated with the true binomial series; to the right is the area associated with the negative binomial series. In Appendix II a graphic model is used to summarize some of the properties of this continuum.

The historical development of the negative binomial series from the Poisson series has considerable relevance for the argument pursued here. The Poisson series concerns the recurrence of chance events when the probability of each recurrence remains constant. Thus, given the average daily rate of accidents within a population (accidents per day), one can predict with considerable accuracy the number of days in the year on which there will be 0, 1, 2, 3, . . . accidents. Poisson distributions of this kind have been widely observed in natural phenomena.

However, early attempts to apply this series to insurance-company data, in order to predict the profile of accident rates for individuals within a population (accidents per person), indicated a different pattern with a greater variability; d was altogether greater than 1.0. This suggested that the probability of having an accident was not uniform throughout the population, and that a minority was altogether more prone to accidents than the remainder. It was therefore necessary to infer the distribution of proneness so as to develop a new series that had the observed parameters m and d. The assumption that this skewed continuous distribution of proneness followed a *gamma curve* stemmed primarily from the convenient and flexible properties of this curve. The gamma curve was then used to generate a new hypothetical distribution of accident rates, which was found to correspond well with the observed profile when the recorded parameters m and d were used for the curve (see Appendix II). Because this new series could be shown mathematically to have an inverted relationship with the already established binomial series, it was dubbed the "negative binomial" (Greenwood and Yule 1920).

Figures 3a–3c show typical negative binomial profiles and the corresponding gamma curves portraying the hypothetical distribution of, for instance, proneness that would give rise to this series. For each profile, the horizontal axis refers to the frequency of events, such as accidents during a fixed period of time ($r = 0, 1, 2, 3$, etc.), and the vertical axis to the population associated with these frequencies. The value for m remains constant in these diagrams while the value for d is reduced, thereby increasing the compactness of both the negative binomial and especially the gamma curve. If d were reduced further to 1.0, then the profile would become a Poisson distribution and the gamma curve would reduce to a single vertical line at a value of m, indicating no variation in proneness.

Thus the statisticians inferred an underlying property of proneness distributed among the population to account for the observed profile of acci-

FIGURE 3

Negative Binomial Profiles and Gamma Curves

Negative binomial profiles

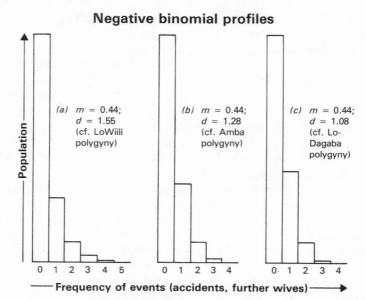

(a) $m = 0.44$;
$d = 1.55$
(cf. LoWiili
polygyny)

(b) $m = 0.44$;
$d = 1.28$
(cf. Amba
polygyny)

(c) $m = 0.44$;
$d = 1.08$
(cf. Lo-
Dagaba
polygyny)

Population

0 1 2 3 4 5   0 1 2 3 4   0. 1 2 3 4

Frequency of events (accidents, further wives)

Associated gamma curves

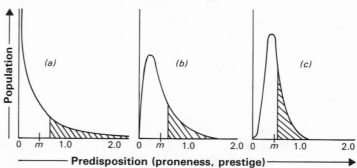

Population

(a)   (b)   (c)

0 *m* 1.0 2.0   0 *m* 1.0 2.0   0 *m* 1.0 2.0

Predisposition (proneness, prestige)

Other distributions

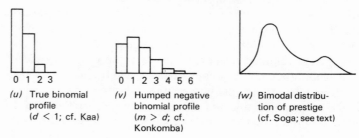

0 1 2 3   0 1 2 3 4 5 6

(u) True binomial
profile
($d < 1$; cf. Kaa)

(v) Humped negative
binomial profile
($m > d$; cf.
Konkomba)

(w) Bimodal distribu-
tion of prestige
(cf. Soga; see text)

dent rates. Clearly, however, similar reasoning could apply to a wide range of social phenomena: visiting rates to a doctor could indicate an underlying proneness to become ill (or anxious); moves to new houses or jobs could indicate a basic mobility; consultations with colleagues could indicate a basic sociability. Research into each of these has, in fact, demonstrated a negative binomial profile, lending credibility to the assumption of an underlying range of proneness, mobility, and sociability.[12]

With regard to the analysis of polygyny rates, this has an immediate relevance since it has already been assumed that the distribution of further wives reflects an underlying distribution of prestige. The data considered so far have concerned the frequencies of further wives, whereas the inferred distribution of prestige would normally be continuous, and an underlying gamma curve could be very appropriate (and certainly convenient) to describe this. The three profiles shown in Figures 3a–3c are, in fact, closely similar to those recorded for polygyny among the LoWiili, Amba, and LoDagaba, and the associated gamma curves would be the inferred distributions of prestige.

A possible objection to this argument is that wives are not only the culmination of prestige as accidents are of proneness; they can also be a source of prestige and ultimately perhaps of further wives. A partial answer to this is that the available data refer to polygyny rates at a point in time, a snapshot view, whereas the objection extends beyond this to a more dynamic view for which data are generally not available. An attempt is made later in this chapter, however, to consider the time dimension.

A second objection is that the hypothesis would apply only to those samples whose variability d is greater than 1.0. It could not account for a possible Poisson or a true binomial profile among the remainder. While this problem concerns only a minority of the samples, it will be shown to provide a vital clue in the development of the hypothesis.

Inquiry into the sociological relevance of the gamma curve and the negative binomial distribution echoes the insights of Durkheim and Pareto. Durkheim (1952) recognized the chance events that precipitate individual suicides but sought the underlying social causes that could be inferred from comparing suicide rates. His "predispositions" that run through any society may be equated with a collectively induced distribution of proneness. It would not be wholly inappropriate to discuss prestige and polygyny in terms of a collectively induced predisposition to have wives. It is the predisposition rather than the wives that one wishes to measure.[13]

One may cite again Pareto's law, noted at the beginning of this chapter: the popular notion that 20% of a population (or thereabouts) control 80% of the resources. In relation to the possession of wives as resources, it is possible to be more precise than this. In the three examples of Figure 3, the most polygynous 20% of the elders have 78%, 72%, and 67% of the further wives, respectively. If, however, one wishes to infer the hypothetical distributions of prestige that underlie the possession of wives, then it is to the corresponding gamma curves that one must turn, and this suggests a greater contrast between the three examples: the most prestigious 20% of the elders are inferred to possess 52%, 43%, and 33% of the available prestige, respectively; this 20% is shown as the shaded areas in Figure 3. Clearly, the gamma distribution provides a more sensitive and in some ways more meaningful indication of social differentiation. However, it can only be inferred as an assumed social characteristic underlying the observed data.

Thus the gamma curve and the negative binomial series are not especially new to our ways of thinking, but rather may be used to give mathematical expression to familiar concepts.

THE NEGATIVE BINOMIAL PROFILE AND THE 50 SAMPLES OF POLYGYNY

Having established the general characteristics of the negative binomial series in relation to the gamma curve, I now propose to examine further the profiles of the 50 polygyny samples in order to assess how closely they approximate to this series, and to explore to a greater extent the underlying patterns.

As a first step, one may note that the earlier decision to consider only the distribution of further wives simplifies the problem. The negative binomial series invariably requires some estimate of the population whose frequency is nil, for example, no wives or no accidents ($r = 0$). If one is considering only the distribution of further wives among married men, then clearly the population with no further wives is the monogamists. If, on the other hand, one is considering the distribution of *all* wives among *all* men, then the task becomes more complex, since it is not at once apparent whether the class of bachelors ($r = 0$) should include only eligible men, or all males, or some intermediate sector. Moreover, various authors have adopted different conventions as to which bachelors, if any, should be included in their samples. Apart from the logical consistency of excluding bachelors, it is also a matter of expediency in order to consider the negative binomial profile.

The parameters calculated for each sample (as plotted in Figure 1) were used as a basis for generating a negative binomial (or, where appropriate, a true binomial) series for comparison with the observed profiles of polygyny. The method adopted is described in Appendix II, and a selection of the results is shown in Table 2, in which the observed profiles are compared with the calculated series and the degrees of divergence are noted.

For the 50 profiles, the task of fitting a true or negative binomial series was trivial in seven instances: the polygyny rates were low and uniform,

TABLE 2 *Profiles of 15 Polygyny Samples and the Negative Binomal Series*
O: Observed Polygyny Profiles (Yielding Parameters m *and* d*);*
E: Negative Binomial Series (with Parameters m *and* d*)]*

Sample[a]		Number of Further Wives (%)						Original Sample Size	Significance of Chi-Square Divergence
		0	1	2	3	4	5+		
Nupe (Doko and Kutigi)[b]	O:	34.6	48.8	10.2	5.6	0.5	0.5	197	0.5%
	E:	38.2	39.4	17.6	4.4	0.6	0.1		
Kaa[b]	O:	56.5	33.8	9.0	0.7			278	Not at 50%
	E:	56.3	34.7	8.3	0.9	0.1			
Nupe (Mokwa)[c]	O:	56.5	35.9	3.9	3.9			78	30%
	E:	56.6	31.3	8.7	1.6	0.2			
LoDagaba	O:	67.4	25.4	6.0	1.5			67	Not at 50%
	E:	66.9	26.0	6.0	1.1	0.2			
Samburu	O:	62.4	26.9	9.3	1.1	0.6		186.5	Not at 50%
	E:	61.8	28.1	8.1	1.8	0.4	0.1		
Somali	O:	56.8	29.2	9.5	4.7			127	Not at 50%
	E:	56.5	30.8	10.3	2.8	0.6			
Basuto	O:	89.0	9.8	1.2	0.3	0.1		64,324	0.1%
	E:	89.3	9.3	1.4	0.3				
Amba	O:	68.0	20.3	9.1	2.8			143	50%
	E:	66.5	25.8	7.8	1.9	0.5	0.1		
Hehe[d]	O:	62.3	27.7	7.0	2.0	0.8	0.4	3,028	0.5%
	E:	63.9	25.3	8.1	2.4	0.7	0.3		
Tallensi 1934	O:	60.4	27.0	5.4	6.3	0.9		111	30%
	E:	60.0	26.2	9.3	3.1	1.0	0.4		
Ashanti	O:	70.6	22.5	5.7	1.0	0.2	0.2	473[e]	10%
	E:	72.6	19.2	5.8	1.8	0.6	0.3		
Maasai	O:	59.4	27.5	8.3	3.6	0.7	0.7	558	Not at 50%
	E:	60.6	25.0	9.4	3.4	1.2	0.6		
LoWiili	O:	71.5	19.6	6.9	0.0	2.3		87	50%
	E:	71.4	19.6	6.2	2.0	0.7	0.3		
Soga	O:	74.1	18.1	6.4	0.4	0.4	0.9	455	5%
	E:	76.2	15.2	5.3	2.1	0.9	0.7		
Swazi	O:	68.8	17.0	9.7	1.6	0.0	3.2	124	30%
	E:	72.1	13.7	6.1	3.2	1.9	3.2		

[a]The profiles are listed in order of increasing variability.

[b]True binomial series.

[c]Almost a Poisson series.

[d]To achieve a closer approximation, a second negative binomial series was generated with the variability *d* reduced by 0.06.

[e]Estimated.

and an almost perfect fit could be obtained without in any way testing the present hypothesis. Of the remaining 43 profiles, three diverged from the hypothetical series with a significance of well below 1%, and seven others with a significance of 10%. Had I used a computer to search for parameters giving a closer fit, the amount of divergence would have been reduced, but only up to a point. At the other extreme, 22 of the 43 profiles did not diverge even with a significance of 50%; and by definition if the parent populations are in fact distributed in (negative) binomial form, one could expect this figure to be about 21 or 22.

The initial hypothesis that there is an underlying gamma distribution of prestige reflected in a negative binomial distribution of further wives, then, appears to have some substance for most of the 50 societies.

A number of questions remain to be considered.

1. What is the interpretation of those polygyny profiles that approximate to a Poisson series?
2. What is the interpretation of those polygyny profiles that approximate to a true binomial series (where no underlying distribution of prestige can be inferred)?
3. Can one discern any pattern of divergence among those polygyny profiles that do not approximate to a negative or true binomial series?

In the course of answering these, a further question can be considered.

4. Can one relate these profiles diachronically to the accruing of prestige and wives with age?

THE INTERPRETATION OF PROFILES THAT APPROXIMATE TO A POISSON SERIES

A Poisson profile would imply a uniform distribution of prestige throughout the entire population of married men. Nine of the 50 samples conformed quite closely with such a profile (urban Luhya, Kamba, and Luo; Hima, Ndembu, Nupe (Mokwa), Kgatla, Yakö, and LoDagaba). This would imply at first sight that the laws of chance play a stronger role in the acquisition of further wives than any other law. Certainly, there are early reports of West African peoples who gambled for wealth and ultimately wives, and their fortunes, determined by chance, might logically generate a Poisson distribution of wives (Siegel 1940: 16–20; Chapple and Coon 1947: 624–625). Nevertheless, for the more fully and recently described societies, however fluid some of them may be, this is an odd notion, to say the least. Some skill, some quality, or some other attribute that is not uniformly distributed could be expected to be relevant to the acquisition of further wives.

One should note, however, that there are undoubtedly random factors affecting polygyny in all these societies: barrenness in one wife will induce the husband to take on another; mortality strikes at random; some elders have difficulty in obtaining further wives; some, idiosyncratically perhaps, do not want them; other relatively inconspicuous elders may accrue several wives, possibly as a result of inheritance windfalls, or of having a number of marriageable sisters for direct or indirect exchange. And, of course, there are always the idiosyncratic choices of the ethnographer in devising his scheme for data collection, and of his informants for providing information, all of which will introduce additional random factors in the data available for analysis.

Moreover, a Poisson series is not inconsistent with a complex system in which the interplay of different forces obscures any obvious pattern and gives the appearance of random behavior. Thus polygyny profiles that approximate to a Poisson distribution do not deny the possibility of differences in prestige within the society. However, they do imply that there is little evidence in the samples as they stand of social differentiation between elders, and one must analyze the data further or consider other explanations. For the Yakö, at least, this is consistent with the remark that "there is little emphasis on the number of wives as a direct impression of a man's importance and prestige" (Forde 1941: 77). The extent to which the Yakö diverge from the other societies in this survey has already been noted.

THE INTERPRETATION OF PROFILES THAT APPROXIMATE TO A TRUE BINOMIAL SERIES

In seven samples, the variability d was well below 1.0; and because of the lack of variety, the exercise of fitting a true binomial series to the profile tended to be trivial: other mathematical series might almost as easily have been made to fit. The exercises for the Bemba, Borana, Hausa, and Lango were trivial in this sense; for the Kaa and Konkomba there was no significant divergence from a true binomial profile, but the exercise was more demanding; for the Nupe (Doko and Kutigi) there was a significant divergence. But trivial or otherwise, this profile cannot be derived logically from some underlying gamma distribution of prestige or predisposition, and some alternative interpretation is necessary. Two explanations are considered.

The first is to note that random error in any of the samples could conceivably have distorted what might otherwise be a negative binomial profile. However, this is exceptionally unlikely in the instance of Hausa (see Figure 2), and to argue that the other six samples are *all* distorted in the same manner is to stretch a weak point further. One may argue with equal logic that the nine samples that approximate to a Poisson distribution are in fact distorted true binomials. The argument can work both ways.

In order to seek an alternative explanation, it is necessary to revise the basic model and to reinterpret the horizontal dimension of variability in a quite different way. Given some tendency for societies to diversify, the interpretation of the spread of 34 points in Figure 1 to the right of the Poisson line in terms of a negative binomial seemed feasible. The approximation of nine points to a Poisson distribution could be grasped with some difficulty and even incredulity. Beyond that we are confronted with seven other points that appear to reflect an underlying "negative proneness," and at first sight such a concept is elusive or even meaningless. It is as if, despite the laws of chance, which would tend to distribute further wives somewhat unevenly, and the existence of inequality, which would make the distribution still more uneven, there are certain forces acting in the opposite direction that ensure a more even distribution. The Islamic restriction on four concurrent wives could produce this effect among the Hausa, for instance, but in the present sample no man has so many wives, and it is as if there is some prescribed limit below this number.

The apparent switch in emphasis is away from a measure of social differentiation implying a tacit competition for prestige and toward a certain conformity with a norm. Thus, instead of portraying this dimension simply in terms of "social differentiation among elders," one is now tempted to substitute a scale representing some balance between *competition* (to the right) and *conformity* (to the left). Questions that were previously couched in terms of the evidence for greater social differentiation among the Lowiili and Maasai than among their neighbors may alternatively be couched in terms of greater opportunity for successful competition and lower pressures toward conformity.

Seen from this point of view, the Poisson line becomes the point along the scale of variability where the contrary pressures toward competition on the one hand and conformity on the other exactly balance. Neither predominates, and the observed profile has the appearance of an underlying random process.

This revised model, however, raises new problems regarding societies in which a high degree of differentiation is ascribed and not the product of unbridled competition; this is discussed more fully in a later section. Here the point to emphasize is that in an unbridled free-for-all, success will breed more success, and there will be a wide difference in achievement between the successful and the unsuccessful (d is high); whereas in the opposite situation, differences will be inhibited and the successful individual will be under greater constraint to conform (d is low).

Logically, although the gamma curve has no positive meaning when d is less than 1.0, one could expect some other mathematical curve to be related to a true binomial profile in a way that parallels the relationship between the gamma curve and the negative binomial profile. Intuitively, the whole argument has to be inverted, and the inverse of a distribution of prestige that encourages diversity—if it has any meaning at all—would seem to imply a distribution of pressures that penalize those who deviate from a norm. In terms of polygyny, this would restrict the distribution of further wives, and the restrictiveness would increase as the value of d decreased. Precisely what the inverted mathematical argument might be I cannot say.

Thus this exercise initially developed a model based on the notion of proneness in relation to the negative binomial distribution. But the total array of available polygyny data has forced us to extend the explanation from the negative binomial sector of the spectrum, through the Poisson series, to the true binomial sector. An underlying gamma distribution of prestige is still tenable, but now it is seen as more applicable to situations in which there is an element of competition: prestige has to be achieved at the expense of other players. At the true binomial end, any association between prestige and plural marriage achieved in a free-market situation is inhibited: the emphasis is on constraint. At points along this spectrum, there is a changing balance between these two countervailing forces.

This twist in the argument is fundamental, and at the risk of belaboring the point, it may be reiterated in a different context. Suppose one were examining the distribution of wild beehives found in the African bush by members of a society. As an initial hypothesis, one might assume that this is a matter of luck determined solely by chance. If so, then the distribution of finds over a period of time among the population would be a Poisson series. Indeed, knowing the average number of finds for the whole population, one could predict the number of people expected to have found 0, 1, 2, 3, . . . beehives. However, skill may also be relevant, and as an alternative hypothesis, one might predict that this skill is distributed in some gamma curve, in which case the distribution of finds would conform to some negative binomial distribution; and by searching for the best negative binomial fit, one would be in a position to infer the underlying gamma distribution of skill in the human population. The more closely the profile of finds approximates to a Poisson series, the less important the element of skill and the greater the element of chance.

Among the Bemba, however, we are told that there is a certain resentment toward undue success: for a man to be much better off than his fellows is dangerous, and he may be considered to have achieved his good fortune by some form of sorcery. In Bemba terms, to find one beehive in the bush is luck, to find two is very good luck, and to find three is witchcraft (Richards 1939: 188, 215, 232; cited by Gluckman 1965: 59). In such circumstances one would not expect a man to push his luck (or skill) too far: he would feel under a wider constraint. This would inhibit the degree of variation between the most and the least successful collectors of honey, and one could hypothesize a true binomial distribution of finds, indicating the strength of the social pressures toward conformity. Switching from beehives to marriage, one may note that for the Bemba, at least, the distribution of wives among commoners is indeed a true binomial.

At this point we are in a position to examine changes in the balance of pressures toward conformity and competition in relation to the life cycle of the individual.

THE GROWTH OF PRESTIGE AND THE FAMILY DEVELOPMENTAL CYCLE

The usual model of African society—with the Yakö and Gonja as obvious exceptions—is of polygyny increasing with age associated with family development and the prestige of the family head. The advantages of older men in the market for further wives may be regarded in terms of both social differentiation among elders and gerontocracy; the two dimensions of Figure 1 are not wholly independent. Younger men cross their first hurdle on their initial marriage, only to find themselves still in a relatively junior position among elders (see page 123 above).

If, therefore, any of the larger samples could be divided into two or more age groups, then a graph could be drawn illustrating this developmental process with age. Altogether 18 of the 50 samples (excluding the Yakö) may be considered from this point of view. In order to simplify analysis, the samples have been divided into three types in Figure 4 according to the slopes of the graphs, since they imply different patterns of development. Inevitably, this refinement entails small subsamples for each age group and lower limits of confidence. To emphasize this point, 12 of the graphs are shown as continuous; in these cases at a 2.5% level of confidence (i.e., 97.5% level of probability) one can assume that the graphs slope in the direction shown—that is, they probably belong rightly to the figure (4a, 4b, or 4c) in which they appear and the implications for development remain valid. For the remaining six graphs, however, there can be no such confidence; since they could conceivably belong to one of the other figures, they are shown as dashed.

The clear impression one has from the graphs of Figure 4a is of a pressure toward conformity on younger men which relaxes with age as they become increasingly self-reliant elders and able to assert themselves. One may regard the Poisson line as a stage which each age group transcends at some point as the pressures toward conformity are outmatched by tendencies toward individualism and assertiveness in the pursuit of wives and prestige. The Tallensi would exemplify such a pattern well: they have a moral concept of *Yin* or personal destiny which is weak among younger men, but grows more powerful as they grow older and wish to assert some independence from their fathers (Fortes 1949: 227). The process is more dramatically illustrated by Hart's 1967 sample (personal communication) than by Fortes' 1934 sample in the same community, and suggests that the older men are increasingly free of constraint.[14] Similarly, Dorobo men were

FIGURE 4

Patterns of Development of Polygyny with Age

(a) Societies in which variability increases with age, compared with logarithmic growth (dotted lines). (b) Societies in which variability decreases with age, implying increasing constraint. (c) Societies that show no consistent trend with age. (Samburu: i, all elders; ii, three age groups; iii, less worthy clans; iv, more worthy clans.)

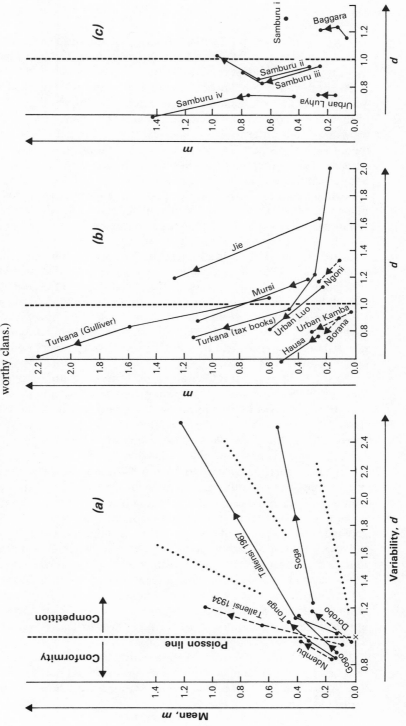

seen by their Samburu neighbors to reach an early independence, breaking free of family constraint and exhibiting a greater degree of competitiveness; this earned them a local reputation for sorcery (Spencer 1965: 285, 286).

The dotted lines that appear to radiate from the point marked × in Figure 4a require some explanation. Logarithmic or compound growth has been observed in economic and natural phenomena where the absolute rate of growth of an enterprise or species in an unrestraining environment increases with its size. It seems logical, therefore, to enquire whether this pattern of growth applies also in relation to prestige, linked as it is to economic acquisition. It can be shown (in Appendix II) that if there is an underlying gamma distribution of prestige that tends to increase logarithmically for each elder, then the parameter points for each successive age group will lie along a line that appears to radiate from the point at which $m = 0$ and $d = 1$ (marked × on Figure 4a).

In relation to these dotted lines, the Tallensi graphs are again the most striking. Hart's 1967 figures suggest a process not unlike the development of a game of Monopoly, where all the players start off on equal terms, but cumulative variations in success occur between the "haves" and the "have-nots." (R. K. Merton has dubbed this the Matthew Principle: to him that hath. . . .) The slow starters are left behind, their *Yin* perhaps predestining them for a mediocre future, while the front runners bound from success to inevitable success.

Figure 4b appears to reflect an opposite trend, with competition among younger men giving way to increasing constraint as they grow older. It is as if they were competing in an obstacle race in which the obstacles get harder the further they go, thereby inhibiting the front runners. A recurrent theme among the Turkana is of secession by younger men asserting their independence from their older kinsmen (Gulliver 1955: 5, 136–137).[15] Among the Mursi, according to Turton,[16] there is no restriction on the age of first marriage of young men; it depends entirely on their wealth or the wealth of their families. In the subsequent constraints, one would expect economic factors to play an important role. Certainly among other pastoral societies where the degree of polygyny is linked to the size of the herd, polygyny beyond a certain point necessitates dispersal into smaller viable units. As a measure of a man's worth, polygyny has certain attractions, but it increases his problems of management, and elders may be inhibited from taking on further wives beyond a certain point. There may be parallel constraints in urban situations to account for other graphs in this figure. Again at this stage I would prefer to use such patterns to ask questions rather than to propose any hasty answers.

Figure 4c shows some intermediate graphs in which there is no consistent change in the balance between conformity and competition with age. The significance of presenting several graphs for the Samburu in this figure is discussed in the next section.

The broad impression from these various studies is that the analysis of polygyny data can provide alternative models of growth in relation to the family developmental cycle and the changing balance of pressures between conformity and competition with age. As a tool for comparative analysis, this would seem to offer considerable opportunities. It bears out a point raised by Fortes when stressing that

> numerical data are essential for the analysis of the developmental cycle of the domestic group. Each phase of the cycle can be thought of as the outcome of a set of "pushes" and "pulls", antecedent and contemporaneous. They come in part from within the domestic domain and in part from the external structure of society. Numerical data provide a means of assessing the relative strength of these forces and of describing their configuration at a given phase [in J. Goody 1958: 13].

THE CONTEXT OF CONFORMITY AND COMPETITION

A notional scale ranging from conformity to competition is hardly new. Mead proposed a typology of societies along these lines in 1937, and the notion has been toyed with by a number of writers. One point that Mead emphasizes is that "no society is exclusively competitive or exclusively cooperative." The very existence of highly competitive groups implies cooperation within the groups, and again there may be a lively rivalry within a cooperative activity (Mead 1937: 460; Gluckman 1965: 77). It should be stressed therefore that any interpretation of conformity or competition among the various societies considered here refers only to the context of acquiring further wives; it does *not* assume that these societies are inherently conformist or competitive in every respect. To emphasize the relevance of this point, I consider three instances in which it can be raised: the Samburu graphs in Figure 4c, the urban samples in Figure 1, and recent discussions on bridewealth.

In Figure 4c, Samburu polygyny rates are shown in several forms. First there is a single point (Samburu i) representing all elders and corresponding to the point plotted in Figure 1. In part the variability of this point reflects differences in polygyny rates between younger and older elders, and when the data are presented for separate age groups (as in the graph marked Samburu ii), there is a shift toward uniformity (*d* low): there is less variety within each age group. Finally, there is a graph of two less worthy clans (Samburu iii) which contrasts with the graph for two very worthy clans (Samburu iv). The very worthy clans have a higher polygyny rate for each age group (*m* high), which is a clear indication of the extent to which they are preferred as husbands when several men contend for the same woman (a usual occurrence): their reputation for worthiness as eligible suitors is measured in their polygynous success. Worthiness is upheld by concerted effort, supporting the suits of weaker members, restraining the more ambitious and irascible members, and proclaiming the highest ideals of Samburu society. Within such a clan elders are under constraint, conformity is an ideal, and this appears to be reflected in the lack of variety in the polygyny rates of these worthier clans (d low). Less worthy clans adopt a similar stance, but their claims have less credibility, their marriage suits are less welcome, and their polygynous achievement is lower. The extent to which they do not succeed in supporting their less desirable members' marriage suits or in restraining their more ambitious members appears to be reflected in the higher degree of variability for each age group (m low, d high). [In Samburu terms, the Dorobo (Figure 4a) are seen to represent a further shift in the same direction (m lower and d higher).] Thus conformity is present up to a point *within* all Samburu clans, and there is competition *between* them; but within the less worthy clans (and especially among the Dorobo), there is an element of competition that tempers their reputation and success.[17]

One may also consider Parkin's three Nairobi samples in Figure 1 (Luo, Kamba, and urban Luhya). These are close to the Poisson line, and are clearly less competitive than the majority of rural samples, including those collected in an earlier era for the Luhya. The striking feature is not just the consistency between these three urban samples on the horizontal scale, but also the apparent contradiction with the general notion that life in urban areas tends to be more achievement oriented and less constrictive than life in many rural societies. Banton notes that "in the city an individual has to compete for place and promotion. . . . In the new social order of the city, roles and status are more and more being assigned in accordance with individual achievements and this trend will doubtless continue" (1957: 80). One might therefore expect the urban samples to lie toward the competitive end of the scale, assuming that urban competitiveness is reflected in marriage patterns. Parkin, however, emphasizes the extent to which the main focus of competition in Nairobi—especially for jobs and housing—is between the major ethnic groups, and this entails a very strict control over marriage and strong rural links. Far from there being a free market for wives in a detribalized urban competition, there were virtually no interethnic marriages in Parkin's samples, and among the Luo and Luhya the freedom of women was firmly held in check by their close kin (Parkin 1974: 126, 129, 132).

Each of these examples, the Samburu and the urban samples, illustrates Mead's point that competition at one level may entail a degree of cooperation (and hence constraint) at a lower level, and the importance of considering the context of plural marriage to which the sample relates. The Samburu competed against other clans, but had to conform to clan ideals to achieve this; the urban ethnic groups studied by Parkin competed against one another, but had to maintain an internal discipline. The focus of competition varies from society to society, and it is only meaningful in the present exercise when we know the precise context of its relation to polygyny.

The context of conformity and competition appears also to be relevant when one tries to bring together various views on the topic of marriage payment. On the one hand, bridewealth may be seen primarily in terms of a competitive free market, implying a formalist approach; thus "the types and quantities of property available, and the proportions of the sexes and their relative marriage-ages, may by the laws of supply and demand affect the marriage payment and the divorce rate" (Gluckman 1950: 192); or again, "there is an interesting link between economic calculation and the prevalence of plural marriage. . . . Bridewealth and polygyny play into each other's hands," and "standard payments seem to fluctuate in relation to the cattle population, so that an increase in the herds does not lead to cheap marriages" (J. Goody 1973: 10–12). On the other hand, a more substantivist approach may envisage bridewealth in the hands of the privileged as coupons whose acquisition and restricted use controls the rationing of wives (Douglas 1967: 127–129); and in certain instances "bridewealth acts in favour of the equal distribution of women; it is a substitute for sister exchange, a form of sexual rationing" (J. Goody 1973: 18). The notion of rationing neatly conveys constraint in the distribution of wives rather than free competition. Each approach accepts that women are in short supply, but focuses on diverging ways in which they may be distributed, and each approach may be substantiated with reference to selected societies. It is tempting again to see the differences in terms of the poles of the scale of variability, and to explore the extent to which bridewealth is comparable with coupons in societies at the lower conformist end of the scale and with a less restricted currency at the upper competitive end. Whether or not this is so, and whether one might resurrect the term *brideprice* for the more competitive situations, are not strictly relevant to the present exercise. What is relevant is the importance of defining the contexts in which bridewealth and women are exchanged in any attempt at arriving at generalizations.

SAMPLES THAT DIVERGED SIGNIFICANTLY FROM A (NEGATIVE) BINOMIAL PROFILE

Ten samples diverged from a (negative) binomial profile with a significance of less than 10%. They are Ashanti and Mende (10%); Gonja, Soga, and Tallensi 1967 (5%); Nupe (Doko and Kutigi) and Plateau Tonga (2.5%); Bangwa (1%); Hehe (0.5%); and Basuto (0.1%).

There was a broad correlation between the size of the samples and the extent to which they diverged from a (negative) binomial profile. The Basuto sample was more than ten times larger and diverged more strikingly than any other sample. Of the other 13 samples of more than 300 elders, five diverged significantly; of the 36 smaller samples, only four diverged significantly.

One reason for this is that the statistical tests for significance are more precise for the larger samples and reveal more clearly any departure from a (negative) binomial profile. As this calls into question the validity of this exercise, I prefer to discount the probability that the actual data in the larger samples, often derived from tax books and official censuses, reflect less concern for accuracy than most of the smaller samples, and also Mitchell's editorial words of comfort that for larger samples, this test of fit is perhaps too exacting (p. 15 above). Rather than dismiss the larger samples as possibly misleading, the aim here is to discern some regularity in the patterns of divergence. One point should be stressed at the outset: the fact that a number of larger samples diverge significantly from a negative binomial profile does not imply that such a profile is a bad first approximation, but rather emphasizes that it is only a first approximation. Table 2 should be viewed with this point in mind.

Two themes recur in the analysis of these divergences. The first is that there are more elders with a large number of wives than any feasible (negative) binomial distribution would lead one to expect: for the observed values of the mean and variability, the upper tail is unduly pronounced. In the samples in which this may be especially noted, one also has good evidence that the populations from which the samples were drawn were not homogeneous, but entailed in each instance a discontinuity between a privileged elite with a high polygyny rate and the remainder of the population. Where one has in effect two contrasting populations within one sample, one would not expect a regular gamma distribution of prestige, but rather a bimodal distribution with a second smaller hump at the high prestige end of the scale, as indicated in Figure 3w. In other words, the conditions of homogeneity underlying the negative binomial hypothesis do not exist.

Such a bimodal distribution is explicitly indicated or broadly implied for the Soga (Fallers 1956: 163), Nupe (Doko and Kutigi) (Nadel 1942: 51, 63), Ashanti (Fortes 1954: 292), Basuto (Ashton 1952: 80), Gonja (E. Goody 1973: 82–83), and Bangwa (Brain 1972: 146). In these instances, the evidence does not simply point to a wide range in the distribution of wealth between rich and poor, which is allowed for in the model of homogeneity, but also indicates a cleavage, a separate set of rules that applies to the elite and not to the remainder of the population.

The second theme is that there are more polygynists with one further wife and fewer polygynists with two further wives than expected. This is especially marked among the profiles for the Nupe (Doko and Kutigi), Hehe, Tallensi 1967, and Tonga, and to a lesser extent among the Ashanti and Soga. It is as if in these societies there is a tacit barrier through which an elder must pass before he can obtain his second further wife.

Seen from a purely male point of view—and these are male-oriented societies—this theme could reflect the problems of polygyny in relation to the management of resentful co-wives. This problem was expressed vividly by the highly polygynous Bangwa: " 'A compound of wives is like a handful of poisonous snakes. The tighter you hold them the more they squirm; the more they escape; the more they bite. I say two wives are one too many. But we go on marrying them just the same' " (Brain 1972: 148). It could be argued that three wives are very much worse than two. In sociometric terms, two wives have only one communication link through which to quarrel or form an alliance against the elder, whereas three wives have three such links. The prospect of a threefold increase in their problems of domestic management could deter a number of bigamists from further marriage regardless of prestige. Thereafter, with successive wives, the problem may not increase so steeply: four wives (with six links) entail only a twofold increase, and five (with ten links) an increase by 67%. As he accumulates more wives, the deterrent for the elder who can cope, thrive, and even triumph would diminish. With his tenth wife, his problems increase only by 25%, and this is reduced to 10% by his 22nd wife, and to 1% by his 202nd wife. Long before this point is reached, however, some internal organization of his harem will be necessary, and it will be possible to separate wives who are jealous of each other or who collude against him, and to delegate responsibilities for internal management to certain senior co-wives as an enticement for their collaboration. Indeed, when he has passed the critical point of three wives, a division into two independent pairs, each internally ranked, becomes possible, and the problems of a shrewd elder are simplified. In other words, it is suggested that in societies such as these a man can expect to cope with two wives on an ad hoc basis. More than this, however, demands a certain flair for management, and a pause for second thoughts.

It is possible to measure the recurrence of the two themes throughout the exercise. Each component value (or partition) of each chi-square test represents an instance in which the (negative) binomial series provided an overestimate or an underestimate of the observed figure. This is most clearly shown for the Basuto in the bottom rows of Table 3, whose combined total horizontally gives the chi-square estimate of 113.7. The remainder of the table has been formed by repeating this exercise for each of the other samples, compiling a list, and then in effect adding the totals vertically rather than horizontally for divergent and nondivergent samples separately. The values in bold type are those that consistently reflect the two themes at each level of divergence.[18]

This is not to conclude that the (negative) binomial series provides a bad approximation to the observed data, but rather to suggest that in any refinement of this exercise, one would look for a similar distribution that could give more emphasis to these characteristic themes and thereby provide a

TABLE 3   *Reaggregated Partition Values* $[(O - E)^2/E]$ *for Underestimates* (E < O) *and Overestimates* (E > O)

Significance of Chi-Square Divergence	Number of Further Wives					
	0	1	2	3	4	5+
Not at 10% (32 samples)						
Underestimates	0.7	12.7	7.0	17.3	10.2	11.6
Overestimates	1.7	3.5	19.1	10.5	14.4	4.4
0.5–10% (9 samples)						
Underestimates	0.1	50.1	2.2	0.7	0.6	19.2
Overestimates	6.5	0.0	20.7	10.5	8.4	1.8
0.1% (Basuto)						
Underestimates	0.0	20.0	0.0	5.2	15.7	41.5
Overestimates	1.1	0.0	30.2	0.0	0.0	0.0

Note: The first theme is reflected in the column for 5+ further wives, the second theme in the columns for 1 and 2 further wives.

closer fit. It could well be that the basic shortcoming of this exercise is not the assumption that there is a gamma distribution of prestige within any homogeneous population, but rather the assumption that each sample represents a homogeneous population in the first place.

CONCLUSION

There is an extensive literature on the statistical nuances of the negative binomial distribution: Johnson and Kotz (1969) list 65 references. This appears to be matched by a wide range of social phenomena that approximate to a negative binomial profile. Here, as a nonstatistician, I have considered some of the problems of sociological inference with specific reference to polygyny in Africa, for which extensive data are available.

In attempting to fit a mathematical curve or series to observed data, one is exploring the inner logic of the system under scrutiny. Ideally, one would posit a wide range of hypotheses regarding the nature of the underlying social forces and chance factors, and translate each hypothesis into a theoretical distribution of probability that could then be compared with the observed data. The best fit should then indicate the most plausible hypothesis.

In practice, however, this approach assumes that data have been collected with full regard for statistical cautions and accuracy, which is rare, and that polygyny patterns can be reduced to a single, well-defined hypothesis, which is unlikely. This leads one to suggest that in the final resort it is the most flexible theoretical distribution that can be readily moulded like a piece of putty into a required shape that has the best chance of fitting the observed data. The hypothesis then shifts from a concern for the nature of the observed system to the nature of the problem of fitting a theoretical distribution. The negative binomial series (like the gamma curve from which it derives) has precisely this property of flexibility, whence perhaps its wide range of relevance.

Having made this reservation, one is then forced to admit that the observed distribution of polygyny in any one society cannot be reduced entirely to matters of chance: luck, careless recording, and a multiplicity of independent forces. If this were so, then the distribution would reveal itself as a Poisson series. (Even taking account of the fact that older men have had more time to accumulate wives would not affect this pattern: older men might show a different Poisson series from younger men, but the aggregate would still be a Poisson series.) Therefore one is forced to search for some underlying explanation other than age differences to account for the fact that the majority of samples clearly approximate to a wide range of negative binomial series and not of Poisson series.

The initial temptation was to follow the lead of others who have considered the social relevance of this distribution and to posit some form of "proneness"—in this case an underlying distribution of propensity within each population to take on further wives. While this seemed plausible, it did not explain those few samples that appeared to approximate to a Poisson distribution and even less those that approximated to a true binomial distribution, for which there was no ready hypothesis. The problem was comparable to that of a child learning to subtract: at first he finds it easy to take 3 away from 5 but difficult to take 5 away from 3 because he has not grasped the concept of negative numbers. At this stage in his reasoning, zero is seen as the limiting case in a range of positive numbers rather than as a transitional point that leads on to a new and inverted range of numbers that at first can only be intuitively grasped. Similarly, taking the proneness hypothesis, one has a wide range of possible distributions, with the Poisson series as the (highly unlikely) limiting case. However, according to the data, the Poisson series appears to be a transitional point in a continuum, and one therefore requires a further hypothesis that inverts the argument and yet still makes sense in order to account for the samples that approximated to a true binomial series. Intuitively and without mathematical support, it was suggested that this reflects a scale between the extremes of competition and conformity in the acquisition of further wives, with the Poisson series representing a midway point where the two forces exactly balance. As one moves from this neutral midpoint toward the competitive extreme, one increasingly encounters a situation in which success breeds further success and failure breeds further failure. As one moves toward the conformist extreme, success brings a handicap and failure brings encouragement, each reflected in the distribution of wives. The notion of proneness at one end of the scale has to be complemented by the notion of immunization at the other. Where one has a poor (negative) binomial fit, this often appears to reveal a discontinuity in the population from which the sample was drawn, namely, a successful elite with a large number of wives and an underprivileged majority. Here stratification dominates any underlying pattern of open competition or conformity within any of the strata, and one has a more complex situation, obscured by the way in which the sample was drawn.

The development of the argument follows quite closely the successive stages in my own understanding of the problem. As the number of societies considered was increased, the distributions of recorded polygyny rates invited comparisons, tested the generalizations and comments of various authors, and led eventually to a transformation of the initial model.

In the societies we study, we are surrounded with distributions of various kinds. Occasionally, we even record them. But the attempt to probe their inner significances as a means of testing our hunches has hardly begun.

APPENDIX I: DETAILS OF THE 50 AFRICAN SAMPLES

A full key for these otherwise abbreviated notes is given for the Amba only.

AMBA (or Bwamba). *Location:* Uganda. *Period when the polygyny data were collected:* 1950–1952. *Source:* Winter 1956: 37. *Sample size, t* = 143. *Parameters with 68% confidence limits: mean, m* = 0.47 ± 0.06; *variability (with Bessel's correction), d* = 1.28 ± 0.15. *Degree of correspondence between the observed polygyny rates and the theoretical negative binomial series:* no significant divergence; chi-square = 3.70; with 4 degrees of freedom (df = 4).

ASHANTI. Agogo town, Ghana, 1945. Fortes 1954: 286. t = 473 (estimated); m = 0.40 ± 0.04; d = 1.49 ± 0.10. Significant divergence from a negative binomial series at 10%; chi-square = 13.78; df = 7. The author's fertility survey was of all adult women present in the village, who were each asked how many wives their husbands had. The collation of replies, therefore, indicates the distribution of answers to the question and only indirectly the rate of polygyny. Following Barnes (1949: 42–43), the actual polygyny rate has been calculated by weighting the different replies. Thus 81 women replied that their husbands had three wives, which is taken to be equivalent to a sample of 27 polygynists with three wives. Again, "The 10 women married to men with seven or more wives are all wives of the chief" indicates *one* man with 10 wives. In the calculations it has been assumed that this is the correct estimate for the chief and not the lower figure of eight wives which is implied on p. 291 or of seven wives implied in Table 39.

BAGGARA. Sudan, 1961–1962. Henin 1969: 259. t = 779; m = 0.15 ± 0.02; d = 1.26 + 0.07 or − 0.06. No significant divergence from a negative binomial distribution; chi-square = 2.80; df = 4.

BANGWA. Bella chiefdom, Western Cameroons, 1965. Brain 1972: 147. t = 42; m = 0.93 ± 0.34; d = 5.40 + 1.24 or − 1.11. Significant divergence from a negative binomial at 1.0%; chi-square = 16.56; df = 5. The larger sample of homesteads close to Fortem palace was disregarded because it specifically excluded a considerable number of related monogamists who had moved further afield.

BASUTO. Lesotho, 1936. Basutoland 1937. t = 64,314; m = 0.13 ± 0.00; d = 1.27 ± 0.01. Significant divergence from a negative binomial series at <<0.1%; chi-square = 113.72; df = 5. The extent of this divergence is due to the sample size, which makes the test altogether more demanding. As a first approximation, the negative binomial provides a useful fit; see Table 2.

BEMBA. Zambia, 1939. Richards 1940: 119. t = 209; m = 0.36 ± 0.04; d = 0.87 + 0.09 or − 0.08. While there is no significant divergence from a true binomial series, the exercise of fitting such a series was trivial because of the relatively low variability.

BORANA. Ethiopia, 1962–1963. Legesse 1973: 297–315. t = 119; m = 0.19 ± 0.04; d = 0.82 + 0.11 or − 0.10. While there is no significant divergence from a true binomial series, the exercise of fitting such a series was trivial because of the low variability of a low polygyny rate. In collating data from Legesse's survey print-out, I found no obvious correlation between polygyny rates and *gada* (age-set) status. In other words, any prestige that might be gained through polygyny appears to be quite independent of the political system in which *gada* status is all important.

DOROBO (Suiei). Kenya, 1959. Spencer, unpublished. t = 139; m = 0.17 ± 0.04; d = 1.26 ± 0.15. No significant divergence from a negative binomial series; chi-square = 0.54; df = 3. These data were collected from tax books. For further information regarding the Suiei Dorobo, their pattern of marriage, and the tax book census, see Spencer 1965: 283–285, 319; and 1973: 206–208.

EWE (Anlo). Ghana, 1962–1963. Nukunya 1969: 158. t = 222; m = 0.59 ± 0.06; d = 1.18 ± 0.11. No significant divergence from a negative binomial; chi-square = 3.23; df = 5.

GOGO. Tanzania, 1961–1963. Rigby 1969: 181. t = 195; m = 0.35 ± 0.05; d = 1.19 ± 0.12. No significant divergence from a negative binomial series; chi-square = 3.50; df = 4. Polygyny rates for dependent elders in Cilungulu are omitted, and m is therefore inflated. In Figure 4a the two points determining the graph are homestead heads and dependent elders, respectively.

GONJA. Ghana, 1956–1957. E. Goody 1973: 82. t = 172; m = 0.33 ± 0.08; d = 3.09 + 0.34 or − 0.32. Significant divergence from a negative binomial series at 5%; chi-square = 11.43; df = 5.

HAUSA. Northern Nigeria, 1949–1950. Smith 1955: 23. $t = 198$; $m = 0.38 \pm 0.04$; $d = 0.70 \pm 0.07$. While there is no significant divergence from a true binomial series, the exercise of fitting such a series was trivial because of the low variability of the polygyny rate. These figures refer to a traditional craft and market center on an old trade route (Census G). Data are also provided for a more prosperous and self-contained settlement of ex-slaves and their owners' families (Sample A); the greater diversity and polygyny rate in this second sample presumably stem from the less open character of this community ($t = 81$; $m = 0.48 \pm 0.07$; $d = 0.94 + 0.15$ or $- 0.14$).

HEHE. Tanzania, 1933. Brown and Hutt 1935: 107. $t = 3028$; $m = 0.53 \pm 0.02$; $d = 1.39 \pm 0.04$. Statistically there is a significant divergence from a negative binomial series; chi-square $= 21.32$; df $= 7$; significant at 0.5%. The extent of this divergence is due to the sample size, which makes the test altogether more demanding. As a first approximation, the negative binomial provides a useful fit; see Table 2.

HEIBAN (Nuba). Sudan, 1938–1940. Nadel 1947: 116–117. $t = 103$; $m = 0.87 \pm 0.10$; $d = 1.21 + 0.17$ or $- 0.16$. No significant divergence from a negative binomial series; chi-square $= 2.93$; df $= 5$. A minor discrepancy in the author's total has been ignored. Data were obtained from genealogies, and m is therefore inflated.

HIMA. Uganda, 1965–1967. Elam 1973: 24. $t = 154$; $m = 0.12 \pm 0.03$; $d = 1.00 + 0.12$ or $- 0.11$. While there is no significant divergence from a Poisson series, the exercise of fitting such a series was trivial because of the low variability of the polygyny rate.

JIE. Uganda, 1950–1951. Gulliver 1955: 242. $t = 144$; $m = 0.68 \pm 0.09$; $d = 1.68 + 0.20$ or $- 0.19$. No significant divergence from a negative binomial series; chi-square $= 3.72$; df $= 6$. Polygyny figures include dead wives, and m is therefore inflated.

KAA. Botswana, 1850. Livingstone, cited by Schapera 1940: 99. $t = 278$; $m = 0.54 \pm 0.04$; $d = 0.88 + 0.08$ or $- 0.07$. No significant divergence from a true binomial series; chi-square $= 0.49$; df $= 4$.

KAMBA (urban sample). Nairobi, Kenya, 1968. Parkin, personal communication. (Polygyny rates for 0, 1, or 2 further wives, respectively: men over 40 years of age—37, 15, 1; younger men—66, 4, 0.) $t = 123$; $m = 0.17 \pm 0.04$; $d = 0.93 + 0.12$ or $- 0.11$. While there is no significant divergence from a true binomial series, the exercise of fitting such a series was trivial because of the low variability of a low polygyny rate. The sample is of household heads, and excludes married lodgers whose wives would normally live in the rural areas. See also Parkin 1974, Tables 2 and 3.

KGATLA. Botswana, 1929–1934. Schapera 1940: 99. $t = 74$; $m = 0.50 \pm 0.08$; $d = 1.05 + 0.18$ or $- 0.16$. No significant divergence from a negative binomial series; chi-square $= 0.64$; df $= 4$. Data were obtained from genealogies, and m is therefore inflated.

Konjo. Uganda, 1952. Taylor 1969: 91. $t = 1677$; $m = 0.48 \pm 0.02$; $d = 1.34 \pm 0.05$. No significant divergence from a negative binomial series; chi-square $= 3.59$; df $= 3$. It was, however, necessary to interpolate for polygyny rates above three further wives and hence the chi-square test could not be rigorously applied.

Konkomba. Ghana, c. 1951. Tait 1961: 166. $t = 96$; $m = 0.97 \pm 0.09$; $d = 0.84 \pm 0.12$. No significant divergence from a true binomial series; chi-square $= 2.52$; df $= 4$. At first sight this sample would appear to be of a Muslim area, with a sharp cutoff at four wives producing a low variability. However Tait (p. 11) notes that he knew of no Muslims in the area.

Lango. Uganda, 1966. Curley 1973: 29. $t = 96$; $m = 0.23 \pm 0.05$; $d = 0.87 + 0.13$ or $- 0.12$. While there is no significant divergence from a true binomial series, the exercise of fitting such a series was trivial because of the low variability of a low polygyny rate.

LoDagaba. Ghana, 1950–1952. J. Goody 1958: 89. $t = 67$; $m = 0.42 \pm 0.08$; $d = 1.09 + 0.18$ or $- 0.17$. No significant divergence from a negative binomial series; chi-square $= 0.04$; df $= 3$.

LoWiili. Ghana, 1950–1952. J. Goody 1958: 66, 89. $t = 87$; $m = 0.43 \pm 0.09$; $d = 1.57 + 0.25$ or $- 0.23$. No significant divergence from a negative binomial series; chi-square $= 3.20$; df $= 4$.

Luhya (urban sample). Nairobi, Kenya, 1968. Parkin, personal communication. (Polygyny rates for 0, 1, 2, or 3 further wives, respectively: men over 40 years of age—64, 22, 0, 0; younger men—110, 12, 1, 1.) $t = 210$: $m = 0.19 \pm 0.03$; $d = 1.02 \pm 0.10$. No significant divergence from a negative binomial series; chi-square $= 4.85$; df $= 3$. The sample is of household heads, and excludes married lodgers whose wives would normally live in the rural areas. See also Parkin 1974, Tables 2 and 3.

Luhya (rural sample). Vugusu, Kenya, 1934–1938. Wagner 1949: 50. $t = 5339$; $m = 0.22 \pm 0.01$; $d = 1.34 \pm 0.03$. No significant divergence from a negative binomial series; chi-square $= 9.89$; df $= 7$. The author's figures for the south Maragoli have been excluded from the exercise because of the marked degree of monogamy in an area of intensive mission activity ($m = 0.066$).

Luo (urban sample). Nairobi, Kenya, 1968. Parkin, personal communication. (Polygyny rates for 0, 1, 2, or 3 further wives, respectively: men over 40 years of age—72, 54, 15, 1; younger men—134, 28, 4, 1.) $t = 309$; $m = 0.41 \pm 0.04$; $d = 0.99 \pm 0.08$. No significant divergence from a true binomial series; chi-square $= 0.52$; df $= 4$. The sample is of household heads, and excludes married lodgers whose wives would normally live in the rural areas. See also Parkin 1974, Tables 2 and 3.

Maasai. Tanzania, 1939. Fosbrooke 1948: 44. $t = 558$; $m = 0.62 \pm 0.04$; $d = 1.50 \pm 0.09$. No significant divergence from a negative binomial series; chi-square $= 3.31$; df $= 5$.

MENDE. Sierra Leone, c. 1934. Crosby 1937: 259. $t = 842$; $m = 1.36 \pm 0.03$; $d = 2.94 \pm 0.14$. Significant divergence from a negative binomial series at 10%; chi-square $= 7.63$; df $= 3$. It was necessary to extrapolate polygyny rates above two further wives, and hence the chi-square test could not be rigorously applied.

MURSI. Ethiopia, 1970. Turton 1973: 146. $t = 389$; $m = 0.66 \pm 0.05$; $d = 1.20 + 0.09$ or $- 0.08$. No significant divergence from a negative binomial series; chi-square $= 2.56$; df $= 6$. The mean figure may have been slightly inflated by the inclusion of wives living outside the census area and also of (rarely) divorced wives (Turton, personal communication).

NDEMBU. Zambia, c. 1953. Turner 1957: 282. $t = 158$; $m = 0.28 \pm 0.04$; $d = 1.00 + 0.12$ or $- 0.11$. No significant divergence from a Poisson series; chi-square $= 1.54$; df $= 3$.

NGONI. Zambia and Malawi, 1948–1949. Barnes 1951: 24. $t = 98$; $m = 0.19 \pm 0.05$; $d = 1.24 + 0.18$ or $- 0.17$. No significant divergence from a negative binomial series; chi-square $= 2.29$; df $= 4$.

NUPE. Doko and Kutigi villages, Nigeria, 1934–1936. Nadel 1942: 151. $t = 197$; $m = 0.90 \pm 0.06$; $d = 0.88 \pm 0.09$. Significant divergence from a true binomial series at 0.5%; chi-square $= 18.45$; df $= 5$.

NUPE. Mokwa village, Nigeria, 1934–1936. Nadel 1942: 151. $t = 78$; $m = 0.55 \pm 0.08$; $d = 1.01 + 0.17$ or $- 0.15$. No significant divergence from a negative binomial series; chi-square $= 4.34$; df $= 3$.

OTORO (Nuba). Sudan, 1938–1940. Nadel 1947: 116–117. $t = 92$; $m = 1.01 \pm 0.12$; $d = 1.25 + 0.19$ or $- 0.18$. No significant divergence from a negative binomial series; chi-square $= 8.45$; df $= 5$. Data were obtained from genealogies, and m is therefore inflated.

SAMBURU. Kenya, 1958. Spencer 1965: 319–320. $t = 186.5$; $m = 0.51 \pm 0.06$; $d = 1.13 + 0.12$ or $- 0.11$. No significant divergence from a negative binomial series; chi-square $= 1.13$; df $= 4$. For Figures 1 and 2, the more accurate settlement census was used. For Figure 4, where a larger population was necessary, the tax book census was used.

SOGA (Basoga). Uganda, 1950–1952. Fallers 1956: 75. $t = 455$; $m = 0.40 \pm 0.04$; $d = 1.99 \pm 0.13$. Significant divergence from a negative binomial series at 0.5%; chi-square $= 14.24$; df $= 7$.

SOMALI. Somalia, 1955–1957. Lewis 1961: 142. $t = 127$; $m = 0.62 \pm 0.08$; $d = 1.35 + 0.17$ or $- 0.16$. The Islamic restriction on polygyny may have slightly stunted the observed distribution of frequencies beyond four wives, but with the relatively small sample this has not led to a significant divergence from a negative binomial series;

chi-square = 2.98; df = 4. Only the author's frequencies for concurrent unions are relevant to the present exercise; cumulative marital experience of successive unions (p. 143) has been ignored here.

SWAZI. Swaziland, 1934–1937. Kuper 1947: 37. $t = 124$; $m = 0.65 \pm 0.13$; $d = 3.46 + 0.45$ or $- 0.42$. No significant divergence from a negative binomial distribution; chi-square = 12.23; df = 9.

TALLENSI 1934 (Tongo). Ghana, 1934. Fortes 1949: 65. $t = 111$; $m = 0.60 \pm 0.09$; $d = 1.40 + 0.19$ or $- 0.18$. No significant divergence from a negative binomial series; chi-square = 6.13; df = 5.

TALLENSI 1967 (Tongo). Ghana, 1967. Hart, personal communication. (Polygyny rates for 0, 1, 2, 3, . . . , 11 further wives, respectively: men over 45 years of age— 51, 33, 13, 4, 0, 1, 1, 1, 0, 1, 0, 1; men between 31 and 45 years of age—53, 17, 6, 1; younger men—36, 2.) $t = 221$; $m = 0.65 \pm 0.09$; $d = 2.76 + 0.27$ or $- 0.26$. The divergence from a negative binomial series is significant at 5%; chi-square = 15.68; df = 8. This sample refers only to nonmigrants. Hart has provided separate data for migrants, but these have not been incorporated here because they demonstrate a different polygyny profile, indicating different constraints on marriage. A more elaborate model than that discussed in the present paper would have been necessary to combine the two populations. (For the migrant sample, $t = 143$; $m = 0.24 \pm 0.08$; $d = 3.49 + 0.42$ or $- 0.40$.)

TEMNE. Sierra Leone, 1954. Littlejohn, cited in Banton 1957: 198. $t = 61$; $m = 0.38 \pm 0.10$; $d = 1.69 + 0.32$ or $- 0.29$. No significant divergence from a negative binomial; chi-square = 2.15; df = 4.

TIKAR. Central Cameroons, c. 1938(?). Schmidt, cited in McCulloch, Littlewood, and Dugast 1954: 46. $t = 473$; $m = 1.00 \pm 0.08$; $d = 2.96 + 0.20$ or $- 0.19$. No significant divergence from a negative binomial series; chi-square = 4.91; df = 4.

TIV. Nigeria, c. 1950. Bohannan 1954: 64–66 (abstracted). $t = 48.8$; $m = 0.56 \pm 0.20$; $d = 3.56 + 0.74$ or $- 0.67$. No significant divergence from a negative binomial series; chi-square = 1.98; df = 4.

TONGA (Plateau Tonga). Zambia, 1946–1950. Colson 1958: 96. $t = 309$; $m = 0.30 \pm 0.04$; $d = 1.34 \pm 0.11$. Significant divergence from a negative binomial series at 2.5%; chi-square = 9.40; df = 3. It has been necessary to interpolate polygyny rates above three further wives, and hence the chi-square test could not be rigorously applied.

TURKANA. Kenya, 1948–1950. Gulliver 1955: 243. $t = 92$; $m = 1.16 \pm 0.13$; $d = 1.29 + 0.19$ or $- 0.18$. No significant divergence from a negative binomial; chi-square = 2.61; df = 6. Polygyny figures include dead wives, and m is therefore inflated.

UMBUNDU. Angola, c. 1933(?). Childs 1949: 30–31. $t = 37$; $m = 0.35 \pm 0.12$; $d = 1.62 + 0.39$ or $- 0.35$. No significant divergence from a negative binomial series; chi-square $= 5.43$; df $= 4$.

WOLOF. Senegambia, c. 1954(?). Massé, cited in Gamble 1957: 53. $t = 299.6$ (estimated); $m = 0.54 \pm 0.05$; $d = 1.16 + 0.10$ or $- 0.09$. No significant divergence from a negative binomial series; chi-square $= 0.86$; df $= 5$.

YAKÖ. Nigeria, 1939. Forde 1941: 78. $t = 121$; $m = 0.74 \pm 0.08$; $d = 1.03 + 0.14$ or $- 0.13$. No significant divergence from a negative binomial series; chi-square $= 2.21$; df $= 4$. The Yakö contrast in a number of respects with other societies considered here. They did not delay the marriage of younger men; polygyny was not the prerogative of older men; and it was not directly associated with prestige. On the other hand, it is also clear that it was associated to some extent with wealth and that a larger number of children could bring a man prestige within his patrilineage (Forde 1941: 77–81).

YORUBA. Nigeria, 1951–1953. Galletti, Baldwin, and Dina 1956: 70–74. $t = 757$; $m = 1.20 \pm 0.05$; $d = 1.32 \pm 0.07$ (estimated). No significant divergence from a negative binomial; chi-square $= 0.68$; df $= 3$.

APPENDIX II: A GRAPHIC MODEL FOR GENERATING NEGATIVE BINOMIAL AND OTHER SERIES

In referring to the negative binomial series, one usually uses another parameter, k, rather than d, and this is defined as $k = m/(d - 1)$. It is harder to interpret a precise meaning for k, but it is very closely linked to the shape of the gamma curve from which a negative binomial can be derived. In Figure 3, gamma curve a is representative of instances in which k is less than 1.0, curve b of instances in which k lies between 1.0 and 2.0, and curve c of instances in which k is greater than 2.0.

Each term of a negative binomial series may be calculated from the previous term. If the population with a frequency of r is defined as $P(r)$, then

$$P(r) = \frac{m}{m + k}\left(1 + \frac{k - 1}{r}\right) P(r - 1) \tag{1}$$

Figure 5 is a graphic model derived from this formula in which the ratio $P(r):P(r - 1)$ is portrayed on a vertical scale and r is shown on an inverse horizontal scale ranging from 1 to ∞. It follows from Equation 1 that the successive points of a negative binomial series plotted on this scale would lie in a straight line intersecting lines AB and CD, respectively, at values $mk/(m + k)$ and $m/(m + k)$. These correspond to m/d and $(d - 1)/d$ with the earlier parameters. The lines a, b, and c correspond to the lie of the points for the three profiles a, b, and c of Figure 3.

Thus the point at which such a line cuts CD corresponds to a specific value of d independently of m; the lower the intersection, the more restricted the variability. It also follows from Equation 1 that the lie of points will intersect diagonal AC at a notional value of $r = m + 1$. This again is independent of the other parameters.

FIGURE 5

Graphic Model for Generating Series

r = frequency of events $(0, 1, 2, 3, \ldots)$; $P(r)$ = population associated with frequency r. The lines a, b, c, u, and v correspond to the lie of the points for the profiles of Figure 3. The lines e, f, g, and h represent the following special series: (e) Poisson $(d = 1.0, k = \infty)$; (f) symmetrical binomial $(d = 0.5)$; (g) geometric (cf. Jie, $k = 1.0$); (h) triangular numbers $(1, 3, 6, 10, \ldots)$.

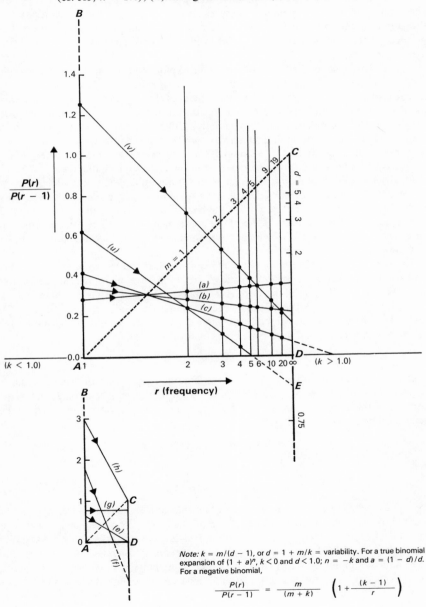

Note: $k = m/(d - 1)$, or $d = 1 + m/k$ = variability. For a true binomial expansion of $(1 + a)^n$, $k < 0$ and $d < 1.0$; $n = -k$ and $a = (1 - d)/d$. For a negative binomial,

$$\frac{P(r)}{P(r-1)} = \frac{m}{(m+k)}\left(1 + \frac{(k-1)}{r}\right)$$

Examples *a, b,* and *c* were chosen with the same value of *m,* hence their common intersection on the diagonal. Intersection at a point closer to *C* along this diagonal would imply a higher value of *m.* Finally, it follows from Equation 1 that if the lie of the points is extended to line *AD* (also extended), it will intersect *AD* at a distance $k/(k - 1)$ from point *A,* independently of the other parameters. Hence, if in the modification of a negative binomial series, one of the parameters is kept constant, then the lie of the points will appear to hinge on the corresponding point on the graph unique to this value of the parameter in question. Comparing alternative graphic models, we note that each point in Figure 1 corresponds to a line in Figure 5 and vice versa.

Figure 5 was developed in relation to an exploration of the negative binomial series, and has been used for this exercise as a simple device for generating each negative binomial series from the initial estimate of the parameters provided by each marriage sample. The method was sufficiently accurate for our present purposes, and it reduced the calculations to a minimum. Other series noted in this exercise can, however, also be related to the figure, which supports the notion that the negative binomial, Poisson, and true binomial series form a continuum. If one envisages a negative binomial profile whose mean *m* remains constant while its variability is gradually reduced, it will appear to hinge on a point on diagonal *AC* while its point of intersection with line *CD* will fall toward point *D.* At point *D* the value for variability *d* will be 1.0 and the profile will become a Poisson profile. If the variability *d* is lowered further, then the lie of the points will be cut off at some point along base *AD,* as shown by line *u,* which corresponds to the true binomial profile shown in Figure 3*u,* and *k* becomes negative.

The dimensions of Figure 5 have a different significance in sampling theory. For a true binomial series representing the distribution of chance in a succession of samples, the cutoff point along base *AD* would be at some point *r,* where $(r - 1)$ represents the sample size *n.* If the lie of the points is extended to intersect line *CD* (extended downward) at point *E,* then the distance *DE* would be *u,* where the binomial series is derived from the expansion of the equation

$$(1 + u)^n \qquad (2)$$

It can be shown that in the context of the binomial expansion of this equation, a negative binomial series entails negative values of *n* and *u* in Equation 2; and in the context of the profiles examined in this exercise, a true binomial series would be generated by Equation 1 where

$$k = -n \text{ (and is always negative)}$$

and

$$m/(m + k) = -u = (1 - d)/d$$

A series whose points lie in a straight line that intersects line *CD* at *C* or some point above *C* would not constitute a finite profile. As an infinite series, however, it can still have some meaning. One such series, formed by the so-called triangular numbers $(1, 3, 6, 10, 15, \ldots, \Sigma n, \ldots)$, was relevant in considering the increase in communication links between wives with increasing polygyny. Plotted in the figure, these points lie in a line extending from a value of 3.0 on line *AB* to point *C.* The decrease in height corresponds to the de-escalating problems of a compulsive polygynist.

In relation to the enhancement of an elder's prestige, the possibility of some form of logarithmic growth has been considered. This assumes that there is a gamma distribution of prestige that underlies the negative binomial distribution of further wives. The gamma curve corresponding to a negative binomial with parameters m and k is

$$y = Cx^{k-1}e^{-kx/m} \tag{3}$$

where C is a constant and y is the population with prestige x.

If there is logarithmic growth, then any small increase in prestige at each level is in proportion to the value of this level: $\delta x/x = \text{constant} = a$. If $z = x(1 + a)$, then the distribution of prestige becomes

$$\overline{y} = Cx(1 + a)^{k-1}e^{-k(1+a)x/m} = Cz^{k-1}e^{-kz/m}$$

which is clearly still a gamma distribution.

Expressed in terms of x, we let the parameters of this new distribution be $\overline{m}$ and $\overline{k}$, with a standard deviation $\overline{s}$:

$$\overline{m} = \frac{\int_0^\infty zy\,dz}{\int_0^\infty y\,dz} = \frac{(1+a)^2 \int_0^\infty xy\,dx}{(1+a)\int_0^\infty y\,dz} = (1+a)m$$

and

$$\overline{s^2} = \frac{\int_0^\infty y(z-\overline{m})^2\,dz}{\int_0^\infty y\,dz} = \frac{(1+a)^3 \int_0^\infty y(x-m)^2\,dz}{(1+a)\int_0^\infty y\,dx} = (1+a)^2s^2 = \text{variance}$$

But the variance of a gamma curve is m^2/k; hence

$$\overline{s^2} = \frac{\overline{m}^2}{\overline{k}} = \frac{(1+a)^2m^2}{\overline{k}} \tag{4}$$

But

$$\overline{s^2} = (1+a)^2s^2 = (1+a)^2\frac{m^2}{k} \tag{5}$$

From Equations 4 and 5 it follows that

$$\overline{k} = k$$

The modified gamma distribution would therefore become

$$y_1 = Cx^{k-1}e^{[-k/m(1+a)]x}$$

Thus with logarithmic expansion, k would remain constant while m increased. Expressed in terms of the parameters of Figure 4a,

$$k = \text{constant} = m/(d-1) \qquad \text{(by definition of } k\text{)}$$

In other words, $(d - 1)$ increases in proportion to m, and in Figure 4a this would appear to trace out a line radiating from the point ×, where $m = 0$ and $d = 1.0$. In Figure 5, on the other hand, this logarithmic increase would be seen as a lie of points that appears to hinge about a point on the extended base AD corresponding to the value of k. This hinging line would approach point C as the parameters m and d increased.

ACKNOWLEDGMENTS

I would like to express my thanks to colleagues at Oxford, Manchester, and the School of Oriental and African Studies, London, with whom I have discussed this paper, and especially to Drs. Keith Hart, David Parkin, and David Turton, who in addition have provided unpublished data. Finally, my greatest debt is to Mr. John Wright, who in an earlier joint exercise stimulated my initial interest and lay understanding of the negative binomial series. In preparing the present paper, I have sought further advice from Mr. Wright. Any statistical misinterpretations are, however, my own. For further analysis of the negative binomial series, see Spencer and Wright (1971) and Mr. Wright's appendix to that work.

NOTES

1. Clignet (1970: 17) notes that the Human Relations Area Files indicate a lower percentage of monogamous cultures in Africa than elsewhere, with three-fourths of the recorded societies characterized by a general polygyny.

2. Wilson (1950: 112); Mair (1953: 56); Dorjahn (1959: 109); Spencer (1965: 96); Bohannan (1966: 158); Clignet (1970: 27–28); Brain (1972: 143).

3. If one regards resident daughters-in-law as further wives attached to the households of the older Hima men, then the effective polygyny rate would increase from 1.12 to 1.50 wives per elder. (Abstracted from Elam 1973: 24, 37, 187–188. Cf. also Spencer 1965: 15.)

4. In Table 1 I have assumed that the numerical errors are in Nadel's totals and not in his recorded frequencies for polygyny.

5. There are, as Goody notes, exceptions in which high polygyny rates are associated with low bridewealth payments (e.g., the Samburu), and one might add that there are others in which the emphasis on primogeniture inhibited the dispersal of the family estate (e.g., the Luhya; see Wagner 1940: 231).

6. Six samples in Figure 1 for which the value of m was overestimated were omitted from the exercise (see note 8 below). For the remaining 44 samples, the correlation coefficient $r = 0.42$ was obtained, and this was significant at 0.5% (student's $t = 3.04$ with 42 degrees of freedom).

7. Where the census is thought to be related to tax liability, there would be a tendency to understate the number of wives (Wagner 1949: 50; Mair 1953: 25; Dorjahn 1959: 90); conversely, if it is thought to be related to prestige, then the tendency could be to exaggerate.

8. Rates recorded for the Jie, Kgatla, Otoro, Heiban, Gogo, and Turkana are inflated for this reason. The bias is indicated in Figure 1 by recording the mean polygyny rate as a downward arrow; the true figure would be below this point.

9. Barnes (1949: 42–43) discussed this point and suggested that polygynists should be notionally divided between their homesteads so that, for instance, a man with two dispersed wives only counts as one-half of an elder in each homestead. [See also Spencer (1965: 318) and Appendix I for the adjustment to the available Ashanti data.]

10. Among the Nupe, for instance, because of Islamic limitations on polygyny, concubines appear to be wives in all but name (Nadel 1942: 151–152). Among the Jie, Gulliver was uncertain how far he was successful in omitting inherited widows from his data. However, one may plausibly argue that widows who were so absorbed into other men's households as to be perceived as wives could also be regarded as wives for present purposes (Gulliver 1955: 114, 243). The simple expedient of ignoring separated wives in surveys of this kind may also be the most appropriate; one would be less concerned with problems of precise marital status, and one could seriously question whether a man's inability to retain his wife would reflect a higher prestige. In line with this, surveys that relate to cumulative marital experience (serial polygyny) have not been included in the present exercise.

11. Since all the polygyny samples include more than 30 elders, the intervals of confidence may be calculated as though the profiles are normally distributed. For the mean m, the estimated standard error is $s/\sqrt{t}$, where t is the sample size; hence the 68% confidence limits are $m \pm s/\sqrt{t}$. For the standard deviation the corresponding limits are $s \pm s/\sqrt{2t}$ (Moroney 1951: 241, 245, 263). The 68% confidence limits for variability are therefore $d(1 + \frac{1}{2}t) \pm d\sqrt{(2/t)}$, where $d = s^2/m$. The confidence limits for all 50 samples are noted in Appendix I, and further ovals could be drawn for these.

12. Froggatt, Dudgeon, and Merrett (1969)–doctor consultations; Spencer and Wright (1971)—mobility and consultations with colleagues.

13. Mitchell (1959: 32–33) makes a similar point in relation to labor migration. Incidentally, this would be another potential topic to use in exploring the negative binomial series if data were available in a suitable form.

14. Fortes (1949: 72) also notes the newly won riches of chiefs and headmen—an innovation that would seem to have gathered momentum by 1967.

15. Gulliver (1955) included dead wives in his sample and this could distort the profiles for the Turkana and Jie. For this reason, I have included in Figure 4b a further analysis of Turkana that was undertaken among taxpayers in Samburu District in 1959. The manner of collecting this data was somewhat suspect, but at least it was possible to provide subsamples of adequate size, and they show a consistency with the profiles derived from Gulliver's material. For details of this census, see Spencer (1965: 319).

16. Personal communication, D. Turton, 1974.

17. The variety in polygyny rates between clans (or phratries) was linked to a previous attempt to devise a competitive-conformist scale, and here I have drawn on the same data: the more worthy clans were Lngwesi and Lorogushu, and the less worthy clans were Loimusi and Masula. The age groups in the graphs are Merisho, Kiliako, and Mekuri/Kimaniki (combined). In the earlier exercise, the term "differentiation" (following Van Gennep) referred to the social boundaries between groups. In the present exercise, it is used in a more pervasive sense to indicate degrees of difference (Spencer 1965: 290, 304).

18. Table 3 excludes seven samples for which the exercise of fitting a binomial distribution was trivial (see pp. 130–131)—their partition values in any case would have been negligible—and also the Tikar, for whom the marriage data were not available in a suitable form.

REFERENCES

Ashton, H. 1952. *The Basuto*. London: Oxford University Press.
Banton, M. P. 1957. *West African City*. London: Oxford University Press.
Barnes, J. A. 1949. Measures of divorce frequency in simple societies. *Journal of the Royal Anthropological Institute*, 79: 37–62.
———. 1951. *Marriage in a Changing Society*. Rhodes-Livingstone Paper No. 20. London: Oxford University Press.
Basutoland. 1937. *Basutoland Census 1936*. Pretoria: Government Printer.
Bohannan, P. 1954. *Tiv Farm and Settlement*. London: HMSO.
———. 1966. *African Outline*. Harmondsworth, Middlesex: Penguin African Library.
Brain, R. 1972. *Bangwa Kinship and Marriage*. Cambridge: Cambridge University Press.
Brown, G. G., and A. M. B. Hutt. 1935. *Anthropology in Action*. London: Oxford University Press.
Chapple, E. D., and C. S. Coon. 1947. *Principles of Anthropology*. London: Jonathan Cape.
Childs, G. M. 1949. *Umbundu Kinship and Character*. London: Oxford University Press.
Clignet, R. 1970. *Many Wives, Many Powers*. Evanston: Northwestern University Press.
Colson, E. 1958. *Marriage and the Family Among the Plateau Tonga*. Manchester: Manchester University Press.
Crosby, K. H. 1937. Polygamy in Mende Country. *Africa*, 10: 249–264.
Curley, R. T. 1973. *Elders, Shades and Women*. Berkeley: University of California Press.
Dorjahn, V. R. 1959. The factor of polygamy in African demography. In R. B. Bascom and M. J. Herskovits, eds., *Continuity and Change in African Cultures*, pp. 87–112. Chicago: University of Chicago Press.
Douglas, M. 1967. Primitive rationing: a study of controlled exchange. In R. Firth, ed., *Themes in Economic Anthropology*, pp. 119–147. London: Tavistock.
Durkheim, E. 1952. *Suicide*. Trans. J. A. Spaulding and G. Simpson. London: Routledge and Kegan Paul.
Elam, Y. 1973. *The Social and Sexual Roles of Hima Women*. Manchester: Manchester University Press.
Fallers, L. A. 1956. *Bantu Bureaucracy*. Chicago: University of Chicago Press.
Forde, C. D. 1941. *Marriage and Family Among the Yakö*. London: London School of Economics.
Fortes, M. 1949. *The Web of Kinship Among the Tallensi*. London: Oxford University Press.
———. 1954. A demographic field study in Ashanti. In F. Lorimer, ed., *Culture and Human Fertility*, pp. 253–339. Paris: UNESCO.
Fosbrooke, H. A. 1948. An administrative survey of the Masai social system. *Tanganyika Notes and Records*, 26: 1–50.

Froggatt, P., M. Y. Dudgeon, and J. D. Merrett. 1969. Consultation in general practice, analysis of individual frequencies. *British Journal of Preventative and Social Medicine*, 23: 1–11.

Galletti, R., K. D. S. Baldwin, and I. O. Dina. 1956. *Nigeria Cocoa Farmers*. London: Oxford University Press.

Gamble, D. P. 1957. *The Wolof of Senegambia*. Ethnographic Survey of Africa (West Africa, Part XIV). London: International African Institute.

Gluckman, M. 1950. Kinship and marriage among the Lozi and Zulu. In A. Radcliffe-Brown and D. Forde, eds., *African Systems of Kinship and Marriage*, pp. 166–206. London: Oxford University Press.

———. 1965. *Politics, Law and Ritual in Tribal Society*. Oxford: Blackwell.

Goody, E. 1973. *Contexts of Kinship*. Cambridge: Cambridge University Press.

Goody, J. 1973. Bridewealth and dowry in Africa and Eurasia. In J. R. Goody and S. J. Tambiah, *Bridewealth and Dowry*. Cambridge Papers in Social Anthropology, No. 7. Cambridge: Cambridge University Press.

Goody, J., ed. 1958. *The Developmental Cycle in Domestic Groups*. Cambridge: Cambridge University Press.

Greenwood, M., and G. U. Yule. 1920. An inquiry into the nature of frequency distributions. *Journal of the Royal Statistical Society*, 83: 255–279.

Gulliver, P. H. 1955. *The Family Herds*. London: Routledge and Kegan Paul.

Henin, R. A. 1969. Marriage patterns and trends in the nomadic and settled populations of the Sudan. *Africa*, 39: 238–259.

Johnson, N. L., and S. Kotz. 1969. *Discrete Distributions*. Boston: Houghton Mifflin.

Kuper, H. 1947. *An African Aristocracy*. London: Oxford University Press.

Legesse, A. 1973. *Gada*. London: Collier-Macmillan.

Lewis, I. M. 1961. *A Pastoral Democracy*. London: Oxford University Press.

Mair, L. P. 1953. African marriage and social change. In A. Phillips, ed., *Survey of African Marriage and Family Life*. London: Oxford University Press.

McCulloch, M., M. Littlewood, and I. Dugast. 1954. *Peoples of the Central Cameroons*. Ethnographic Survey of Africa (West Africa, Part IX). London: International African Institute.

Mead, M., ed. 1937. *Cooperation and Competition Among Primitive Peoples*. New York and London: McGraw-Hill.

Mitchell, J. C. 1959. Labour migration in Africa south of the Sahara: the causes of labour migration. *Bulletin of the Inter-African Labour Institute*, 6 (1): 12–46.

Moroney, M. J. 1951. *Facts from Figures*. Harmondsworth, Middlesex: Penguin.

Nadel, S. F. 1942. *A Black Byzantium*. London: Oxford University Press.

———. 1947. *The Nuba*. London: Oxford University Press.

Nukunya, G. K. 1969. *Kinship and Marriage Among the Anlo Ewe*. New York: Athlone Press.

Parkin, D. 1974. Congregational and interpersonal ideologies in political ethnicity. In A. Cohen, ed., *Urban Ethnicity*, pp. 119–157. London: Tavistock.

Phillips, A., ed. 1953. *Survey of African Marriage and Family Life*. London: Oxford University Press.

Richards, A. I. 1939. *Land, Labour and Diet in Northern Rhodesia*. London: Oxford University Press.

———. 1940. *Bemba Marriage and Present Economic Conditions*. Rhodes-Livingstone Paper No. 4. London: Oxford University Press.

Rigby, P. 1969. *Cattle and Kinship Among the Gogo*. Ithaca and London: Cornell University Press.

Schapera, I. 1940. *Married Life in an African Tribe*. London: Faber and Faber.

Siegel, M. 1940. *The Mackenzie Collection*. Memoir of the American Anthropological Association, No. 55. Supplement to the *American Anthropologist*, 42(4, Part 2).

Smith, M. G. 1955. *The Economy of Hausa Communities of Zaria*. London: HMSO.

Spencer, P. 1965. *The Samburu: A Study of Gerontocracy in a Nomadic Tribe*. London: Routledge and Kegan Paul.

————. 1973. *Nomads in Alliance: Symbiosis and Growth Among the Rendille and Samburu of Kenya*. London: Oxford University Press.

Spencer, P., and J. J. Wright. 1971. Consultation frequencies in general practice. In P. Spencer, *General Practice and Models of the Referral Process*. Health Report No. 6. London: Institute for Operational Research.

Tait, D. 1961. *The Konkomba of Northern Ghana*. London: Oxford University Press.

Taylor, B. K. 1969. *The Western Lacustrine Bantu*. Ethnographic Survey of Africa (East Central Africa, Part XIII). London: International African Institute.

Turner, V. W. 1957. *Schism and Continuity in an African Society*. Manchester: Manchester University Press.

Turton, D. 1973. The social organisation of the Mursi. Ph.D. dissertation. London School of Economics.

Wagner, G. 1940. The political organization of the Bantu of Kavirondo. In M. Fortes and E. E. Evans-Pritchard, eds., *African Political Systems*, pp. 197–236. London: Oxford University Press.

————. 1949. *The Bantu of North Kavirondo*. London: Oxford University Press.

Wilson, M. 1950. Nyakyusa kinship. In A. Radcliffe-Brown and D. Forde, eds., *African Systems of Kinship and Marriage*, pp. 111–139. London: Oxford University Press.

Winter. E. H. 1956. *Bwamba: A Structural Functional Analysis of a Patrilineal Society*. Cambridge: Heffer.

Part Four

GRAPH THEORETICAL PROCEDURES

Trees and Stars: Graph Theory in Southern Mexico

THOMAS CRUMP

ANTHROPOLOGY AND MATHEMATICS

The mathematical process characteristically takes place in two stages. The first is to discover some perfectly abstract property of material phenomena, out of which are created certain entities, which can then stand on their own. The second stage is to analyze the properties of these entities in terms entirely divorced from the base from which they were abstracted, endlessly combining them in original structures, with new properties open to investigation in mathematical research. There is nothing in the mathematical process that requires these structures to be in any way applicable to the essential phenomenological base, but they may be so, and indeed may be developed with precisely this end in mind: this provides the essential distinction between applied and pure mathematics. In either case, for the mathematician the second stage is much more interesting and important than the first.

The anthropologist looks to mathematics for two different kinds of contribution. The first kind consists of results that are applicable to empirical material collected in the course of field work. Here the anthropologist is similar to any natural scientist who uses applied mathematics. Statistics is the most obvious example of this first kind of mathematics, and it is not surprising that it is regarded by the anthropologist as the one essential mathematical tool. The second kind of contribution consists of mathematical models that correspond to structures developed within the local culture itself. It is characteristic of such a model that it expresses in one language structures that the primitive community expresses in another, but essentially isomorphic, language. This point was made by Leach (1954: xiii, xiv) some twenty-five years ago,[1] but not in such a way as to be illustrated in explicitly mathematical terms. It is particularly apt in kinship studies, and Weil (in Lévi-Strauss 1967: 257–265) gives a fascinating illustration of how the sophisticated methods of pure mathematics can be used to validate the rules for prescribed marriage. Here again mathematics is liable to take off on its own and develop parallel analyses of its own structures (see Barbut 1970), which can interest the anthropologist only by analogy. This second

163

kind of contribution corresponds to little that is essential in the natural sciences, which lack the intellectual structures developed within every culture.

GRAPH THEORY

Graph theory[2] is a branch of mathematics which depends on a fundamentally different type of abstraction from that of arithmetic; its own classifications into trees, stars, walks, and so on, often correspond to concepts in preliterate cultures. A graph is any collection of points, some of which may be (although none need be) joined to each other by lines. It is commonly assigned a number pair $[p, q]$, where p is the number of points and q is the number of lines; generally $[p, q]$ does not uniquely determine one particular graph, as Figure 2 illustrates. The number of points in a graph is important mainly in determining the distinct possible graphs that may be drawn connecting them. A graph that is a single point is a trivial one, requiring no further consideration. Two points offer two possibilities: they either are, or are not, joined by a line. Three points allow for four possibilities, as Figure 1 shows, and four points, eleven, as Figure 2 shows. It would be hopeless to try to illustrate the possible graphs for numbers greater than four, since if $g(N)$ is the number of possible graphs connecting N points, then it is an almost exponential function of N. In algebraic terms, no precise formula has been found for $g(N)$, although asymptotic solutions are possible; the same is true for restricted types of graphs, such as trees, which will be considered below.[3] This is a common limitation of combinatorial mathematics (of which graph theory is a part), but it hardly affects its usefulness to the social scientist.

The first two figures, particularly Figure 2, enable us to make a number of remarks. The first is that the points and lines in a graph are essentially unordered. Thus in Figure 1 graph b is the only possible one-line graph ([3, 1]), although the one line could be any one of the three possible sides of the

FIGURE 1

Possible Graphs Determined by Three Points

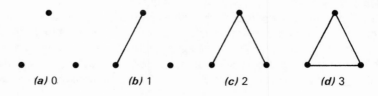

(a) 0   *(b)* 1   *(c)* 2   *(d)* 3

FIGURE 2

Possible Graphs Determined by Four Points

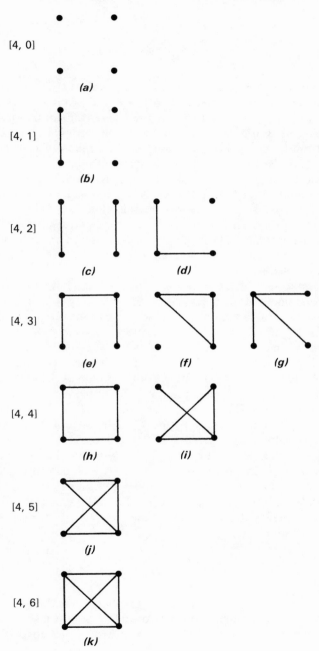

triangle. With numerous points the essential equivalence of two graphs may not be immediately evident; for example,

is not included in Figure 2, because it is equivalent to h. (One should, of course, realize that the intersection of the two diagonals is *not* a point on the graph.) We note next that certain graphs are transformations of others. One simple rule of transformation is for the new graph to have lines wherever, but only where, there are none in the original. This new graph is called the *complement*. Complementary graphs are represented symmetrically about the middle horizontal axis—that is, the fourth row—in Figure 2. For example, c (in the third row) is the complement of h (in the fifth row). On the axis itself, e is its own complement, and f and g are complements of each other. This is an elementary type of transformation, but others play an important role in graph theory. In fact, it may well be that particular propositions about a given graph can be proved by means of a prescribed transformation.[4]

The classification of graphs, or of certain features of graphs, is essential to the development of the theory. A *walk* exists between any two points on a graph whenever it is possible to go from one to the other over lines of the graph. The length of a walk is the number of lines it contains. A graph is *connected* when there is at least one walk between all possible pairs of points. It is *complete* when a line joins all such pairs, which means that the minimum length of every walk between two points is always 1. The graph is *partially disconnected* when there is at least one pair of points that cannot be joined by a walk; it is *totally disconnected* only when there are no walks at all, indeed no lines. In Figure 2, a is totally disconnected; b, c, d, and f are partially disconnected; and k is complete. The longest walk has length 3 and is in graph e. It can quite simply be proved that for N points, the graph with the longest walk will be that which can be represented by laying all the points on a single straight line (which can be done with graph e by "unfolding" it). The length of this walk will then be $N - 1$.

A useful index[5] for measuring the degree of connectedness—or density—of a graph is

$$100 \times \frac{2n}{N(N - 1)}$$

where N is the number of points in the graph and n is the number of lines. The index is clearly designed to vary from 0 for a totally disconnected graph to 100 for a complete graph. In terms of density, which might for instance relate to roads connecting a group of villages, a *tree* is the most economical type of connected graph; since a tree with N points always has $N - 1$ lines, its density is invariant at $200/N$. Any graph with lower density must be partially disconnected. The inversion, by means of a complementary graph, of the above analysis shows that a graph with a density greater than $100[(N - 2)/N]$ must be connected.

A *cycle* is a walk that begins and ends at the same point, without ever crossing any line twice. In Figure 1 graph d is the most elementary cycle in graph theory, with the minimum of three lines. (A two-line cycle is excluded by the rule that only one line can join two points: such cycles are possible with directed graphs, where the rule does not apply.)[6] In Figure 2, graphs f, h, i, j, and k contain cycles.

A tree can then be formally defined as a connected graph that has no cycles (Harary 1969: 32). In Figure 2, graphs e and g are trees. It is an elementary theorem that in a tree there is only one possible walk connecting any two points. A *star* is a connected graph that becomes totally disconnected when one particular point is removed; hence any walk in a star must include that one point. In Figure 2, g is the only star; indeed for N points there is only one possible star, constituted by setting one point apart and joining it by lines to all the others. A star, in fact, is a very specialized type of tree.[7] In Figure 3, which shows all the possible trees with seven points, k is the only star. Note that there are six lines in every one of the trees, illustrating the point that in a tree the number of points is always one more than the number of lines. It is a significant property of a complete graph that if all the lines are removed save those incident on any one of the points, the result is invariably a star. Conversely, a complete N-graph is a composite formed by the superimposition of N stars, each with $N - 1$ lines. This point will prove to be significant when we consider the political and religious organizations of Chamula and Zinacantan.[8]

A *subgraph* of a graph is any graph made up of some of the points and lines of the whole graph; a subgraph is called a *component* if it is connected. The most elementary example of components is given by graph c in Figure 2, in which each of the two lines is a component of the graph as a whole. A component may also be complete, according to the definition above, in which case it is called a *complete subgraph*.

For any practical application of graph theory, there must be a collection of separate entities, sharing some significant common characteristic, with the additional provision that a certain relationship—of interest to the researcher—exists, or may exist, between certain pairs of such entities. The hypotheses that interest the researcher must be such as to depend entirely on this common characteristic and on the prescribed relationship. Although in mathematical theory graphs are generally unlabeled[9]—that is, the different points and lines are not distinguished from each other by such an extrinsic characteristic as a particular name assigned to each of them—

FIGURE 3

All Possible Trees with Seven Points

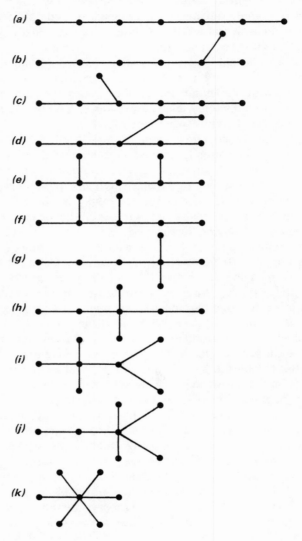

in practical application it is quite permissible to retain any such names, if only to make the whole operation intelligible in its context in the social sciences.

In many respects the anthropologist can readily adapt the work of the economic geographer. This can be done whenever the points on the graph

are fixed geographically, such as villages connected to each other in a recognized pattern of commerce. Several examples are given below for Chiapas. The adaptation becomes more difficult when individuals or groups are
substituted for places. There is a sort of transitional stage represented, say,
by fixed households, whose main interest for the anthropologist is not their
location but the identity of the family which inhabits them. In this case the
lines on a graph represent marriage alliances or ties of kinship. It is only
one stage further to dispense altogether with the geographical base; this can
lead to graph theoretical concepts of extreme elegance, which become
more interesting when they correspond to models existing within the local
culture.[10] The present applied analysis will take graphs developed from ties
of kinship and alliance merely as a starting point. But before this can be
done, some description must be given of the highlands of Chiapas and of
the communities to be found there.

THE HIGHLANDS OF CHIAPAS

Chiapas (see Map 1), one of the four Mexican states lying beyond the isth-
mus of Tehuantepec, is predominantly mountainous and is in parts subject
to volcanic activity. The highland climate is temperate rather than tropical,
with obvious consequences for agriculture and particularly agricultural
exports. The agricultural export economy depends very largely on the coffee production from the *fincas* along the Pacific coast. The central highlands, dominated by the old colonial capital of San Cristóbal Las Casas,
were until some thirty years ago accessible only by mule-train. In 1950 the
Pan-American Highway was opened and transformed the economy of the
whole area; at the present time the process is being continued by the construction of a comprehensive all-weather road system. This growth particularly favors the economic development of the Grijalva river valley, which
roughly demarcates the southern extent of the highlands. There sugar cane
and cattle are raised by the methods of modern industrial farming. Development of the infrastructure has not been neglected in the highlands, but
geophysical and demographic factors tend to frustrate agricultural progess.

The highland region is nonetheless well suited to supporting a relatively
large population of small-scale sedentary cultivators. It is not surprising,
then, that it had a large Indian population when the Spaniards first
arrived,[11] nor even that this population has increased, since none of the
factors that caused such drastic depopulation elsewhere in Mexico applied
to Chiapas.

The Spanish—or Ladino[12]—presence is largely confined to San Cristobal, a city which gives the impression that it quite rapidly achieved its present size after being founded in 1528. All the evidence—such as disused
mine shafts which were never productive—suggests that the wealth that

MAP 1

The Highlands of Chiapas

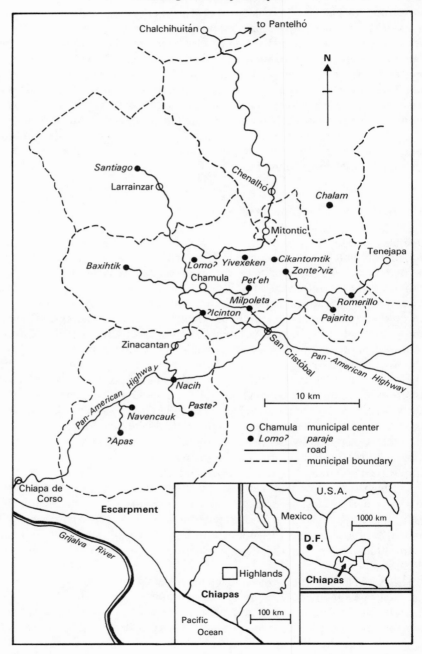

the first colonists sought was never realized. The Ladinos got by for more than four centuries simply by exploiting the Indian populations around them, employing them either as laborers or, more commonly, simply as a source of tribute to be rendered in maize, the universal Central American staple (Furtado 1970: 215). Characteristic Spanish institutions of church and state, such as the *encomienda* (Elliott 1963: 70–75), were adapted to this purpose. In the last century Indian labor was exported to meet the demands of the *fincas* on the Pacific coast, and even today economic necessity constrains many Indians to offer themselves for such work during the coffee harvest. Now San Cristóbal shows unprecedented signs of growth and prosperity (such as are characteristic of Mexico as a whole, see Yates 1961: particularly page 105, Table 43), and offers local employment to many hundreds of Indians. It stands out as the economic and political center of the entire region, and although its population is but 20,000, its preeminence is unquestionable.

The smallest political unit in Mexico is the *municipio*. The government of Chiapas has attempted to divide the highlands into *municipios* according to the Indians' own political divisions; the result is shown on Map 1. My own field work took place in the Tzotzil-speaking *municipios*, which are closely focused on San Cristóbal.[13] I was interested mainly in monetary institutions developed within the different Indian communities, particularly Chamula. This is not only the *municipio* closest to San Cristóbal, but it is also the largest in area (374 square kilometers) and population (about 35,000), and the most densely populated. It is not surprising, then, that the natural forest cover is depleted, many areas are critically eroded, and *parajes* (hamlets) tend to run into each other. The ethnographer soon discovers that the average Chamulan can only survive, and support his family, by always keeping open as many options as possible. The final resort is always a spell on the *fincas*, which is the lot, at some time or another, of the majority of the working men. But there are any number of jobs to be performed in San Cristóbal, although these tend to be beyond the commuting range of the remoter *parajes*. Commerce provides many opportunities for earning a living, and itinerant Chamula traders, sometimes traveling on foot, sometimes by bus or truck, are to be met all over the highlands, both as buyers and sellers. Few can still be regarded as traditional peasant cultivators. Although almost every household still retains its own *milpa* (cornfield) for growing maize, one seldom meets a family that can live off its own harvest for more than two months in the year. There are exceptional large-scale cultivators, with a surplus of maize for sale in the market, but Chamula as a whole could well be a net importer of maize. Wool is probably the only natural commodity of which a surplus is produced, and significantly sheep (originally a Spanish importation) are cared for only by women and children. A household would expect only a fraction of its cash income to come from this source. There is one industry in which Chamula has an

unofficial monopoly throughout the highlands. This is the sale of *pox*, a
distilled liquor made in many parts of the *municipio*, but with the greatest
concentration of producers around Zonte'viz and along the road to Tenejapa (see Map 1). Here relatively abundant woodland (which is also the
location of Chamula's charcoal industry) provides the essential fuel for the
stills, while limestone enables them to be located out of sight. (The legitimate producers, who are of course Ladinos operating on a large scale under
government license and subject to government excise taxes, call insistently
for the suppression of the Indian trade, but law enforcement officers are
hardly ever seen in Chamula. As things are, Chamula *pox* can be bought in
small stores throughout the highlands, while legitimate alcohol is hardly
seen anywhere.) It is out of the question for Chamula to produce its own
sugar cane, which in the form of a crude sugar known as *panela* provides
the essential raw material for *pox*, so this is imported from small-scale Ladino growers in the area around Las Rosas, overlooking the upper Grijalva.

THE STRUCTURE OF KINSHIP, ALLIANCE, AND RESIDENCE

This highly diversified economy is superimposed on the traditional structures of kinship, alliance, and residence, and these will provide the first
subject for graph theoretical analysis. Chamula is divided into some 100
parajes, each of which seems to be a random collection of one-room
houses, traditionally made with adobe walls and a thatch roof. The houses
are scattered across the fields, and when the maize is tall in the late summer, no more than the roofs are visible. Each house is the home of a
nuclear family, which will have a common two-part family name, of which
the first part, and as often as not the second as well, will be a common
Spanish name such as Gomez or Sanchez. The range of first names, of
which only one is ever given, is equally restricted, so there could well be
four men in one *paraje*—with a typical population of, say, 300—called
Manuel Gomez Sanchez. Although the second part of the family name
comes from the mother's family according to normal Mexican practice, the
government seems to be encouraging a trend for both names to descend in
the male line alone. In Pet'eh and Cikantomtik, the two *parajes* that provided the material for the present analysis, this practice seems to be well
established in the former, but only partially in the latter. Much the most
satisfactory analysis of census material, including records of all ties of kinship and marriage, comes therefore from Pet'eh, although nothing from
Cikantomtik contradicts the Pet'eh results. (Cikantomtik does record two
cases of bigamy, which seems to be unknown in Pet'eh.) Both *parajes* are
divided into clusters of houses, with a family name common throughout
each separate cluster. If, then, a graph is drawn, with every point representing a house and every line a marriage tie between two houses, in the

complement of this graph every house cluster becomes a maximal complete subgraph. The organization of census material, even for a *paraje* with only 100 households, so as to illustrate this result at all clearly within the scope of this article, is almost impossible. Figure 4*a* is therefore a simple analogue, derived from the ethnography, but not representing any actual case. The solid lines represent marriage alliances; the dashed lines represent four complete components of the complementary graph, each of which corresponds to one cluster. The complete complement includes any number of lines such as 1–12, 3–11, and 4–10 that have not been drawn. In ordinary anthropological terms, Figure 4*a* shows that the four separate house clusters, each with its own family name, are exogamous.

Suppose now that the clusters are consolidated to make a transformed graph, which will have but four points, as illustrated in Figure 4*b*. This graph is complete, and the census material gathered from Pet'eh shows this actually to be the case, even with sixteen separate clusters. Inevitably some links are missing, but the graph is dense (in the sense of Mitchell 1969: 18), and has, at first sight, little resemblance to a tree. In fact, some 30% of the inhabitants of Pet'eh and Cikantomtik, and almost certainly of any other Chamula *paraje*, marry outside the *paraje*. Here again one can analyze the position by graph theory, taking every *paraje* to be a point and drawing a line between any two *parajes* linked by marriage. The result is then to divide the whole of Chamula into some dozen or more components, each one of which is a near-complete subgraph, as Figure 5 illustrates. In every case the component corresponds to a cemetery group, for in Chamula some six to eight *parajes* must always share one cemetery, which every November 1 (Todos Santos) is the scene of a ritual enacted by the side of the graves of departed ancestors (see also Gossen 1974: 8–10). In normal anthropological terms, Chamula has cemetery-group endogamy.

POLITICAL AND RELIGIOUS OFFICE

Where kinship, alliance, and residence, together with traditional economic activities, combine to form a highly unnucleated structure, one aspect of which is represented in Figure 5, the political and religious life of Chamula, now supported by such recently developed economic activities as the trade in *pox* and moneylending, is strongly focused on the center. This, at first sight, is the typical vacant center of Mayan Central America. The focus of all activity is a large central square, with Chamula's only church, San Juan, prominent on the eastern side. The *cabildo* (town hall), together with a primary school and a government store, occupy the southern side. The other two sides are taken up mainly by stores, but there is a government health clinic on the northern side. A number of roads and paths radiate from the square, and along each of them are a number of typical Indian

FIGURE 4

Marriage Alliances in a Paraje

(*a*) Marriage ties between house clusters. (*b*) Consolidated graph of part *a*.

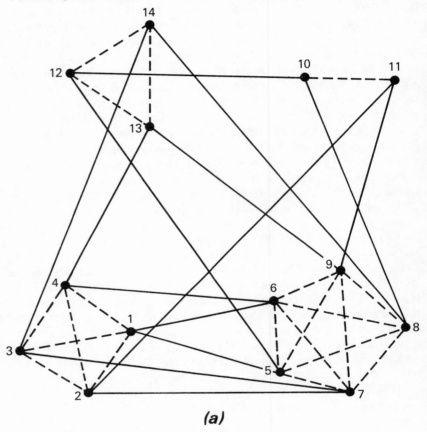

(a)

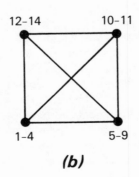

(b)

FIGURE 5

Sample Components of the Chamula Graph

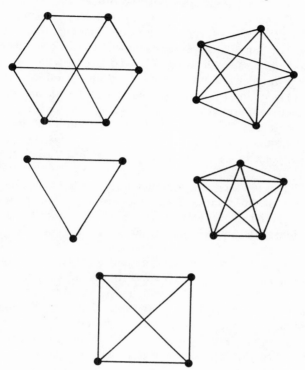

houses, in all adding up to about 220. The open spaces between the houses are *milpa* or grazing land, as in any *paraje*.

The traditional government of Chamula is so complex that anthropologists who have worked there do not completely agree on its actual composition. The only records are kept by official scribes, and are never open to inspection by outsiders. (This is a complete contrast to Zinacantan, where Cancian (1965: 110 et seq.) was able to photograph the records in order to reproduce them for publication.) The government (see Gossen 1974: 12–16) is divided into civil and religious sectors, each with representatives from all three *barrios*.[14] These officials are elected to serve for only a year at a time, and during his term in office an official rents one of the houses in the center. The political and civil sectors have their own ranked hierarchy, so that in each there are four or five classes of office. For any one class there may be several different'instances, and these sometimes go in pairs, ranked *bank-ilal/ʔitzinal*, literally older/younger brother. Every office, therefore, has its exclusive designation, e.g., ʔItzinal Martoma Anima San Pedro, literally

Junior Mayordom "Anima" (referring to a particular set of ritual responsibilities) for the *barrio* of San Pedro. The total number of all officials is about 150. There is no question of all the offices having equal power or influence; some, such as those of the *mayoletik*, or constables, are quite subordinate. In contrast, everyone knows that Bankilal Martomo San Juan for the *barrio* of San Juan is a very important office, which tends to be passed around among a small group of powerful men, who, with the holders or past holders of offices of equal rank, constitute the effective government of Chamula. (These offices are mostly religious rather than political, reflecting the complete autonomy of the local religious life, as guaranteed by the Mexican constitution. The civil offices are also traditional, in that the constitutional government of a *municipio*, the *ayuntamiento*, depends on a *presidente* supported by six counselors, or *regidores*, all elected for three-year terms.)

The meaning of government, in Indian terms, is in fact somewhat imponderable. There is little idea of executive function or policy decision; although substantial changes are taking place in Chamula, in education, communications, land improvement, and so on, the initiative, and indeed the necessary finances, must come from outside agencies of the state or federal government. If the Chamula officials have anything corresponding to departmental responsibilities, they are connected with the celebration of different religious festivities, all of which are related to each other according to a calendar that is the same every year. The coordination of the calendric ritual is structurally isomorphic to the coordination of the offices responsible for them. Thus the essential unity of the calendar is reflected in the enduring unity of the government of Chamula.

The application of graph theory to the traditional structure of civil and religious offices is somewhat problematical. At a purely formal level, two graphs could be drawn, one linking Chamula center to the individual *parajes*, according to whether an official comes from any particular one of them, and the other taking the different offices as the points, with lines drawn between them to represent some additional relationship beyond their being essential components in a unified structure. The first graph would be no more than a star, with the great majority of *parajes* as points on the periphery. (Indeed, in the course of two, or at the very most, three years, all the 100-odd *parajes* would be points of the star. There are, after all, 150 offices to be filled. Beyond this, there is simply not the material available to prove that any one *paraje* has undue over- or under-representation.) The importance of this star (in which all the lines are relatively strong) is best seen in the light of the position represented by Figures 4 and 5, which show that other local structures, based on kinship, alliance, and residence, tend to form a relatively large number of near-complete components, at the local level, which over the whole *municipio* are totally disconnected from each other.

As for the second type of elementary analysis of the office system, based on linking pairs of offices according to a prescribed relationship, the difficulty lies in finding such a relationship that would bring to light any new understanding of the way in which the system operates. The Bankilal Martoma Anima San Pedro could be joined to the ʔItzinal, or to the other Martomas, or to the other Anima officeholders, or even to all the other officeholders from the *barrio* of San Pedro, but the results would be neither new, nor very informative. It is doubtful indeed whether in the case of Chamula graph theoretical analysis could bring to light anything new about the formal structure of the office system. What is needed is an original hypothesis about how the system is used to maintain any special political or economic interests.

Clearly some rule of simplification is necessary, because the prospect of working with graphs with 150 points is simply overwhelming. Suppose, however, that the analysis is confined to those religious offices for which there is at least one case, over the last twenty years,[15] of the same man being the incumbent twice. This restriction will immediately eliminate the vast majority of offices, for which the attendant burdens are generally considered to outweigh any possible advantages. Proceeding from this point, a list could be made of all men still living who had actually held any one such office in two or more different years. A graph could then be drawn with these men as the points and with a line connecting any two of them who either had held different offices in the same year or had held the same office in different years. The hypothesis is that the graph so drawn would have surprisingly few points and would be nearly complete.[16] If the first graph drawn following the prescribed rule were too complex, the rule could be made more stringent, but this should not be necessary.

The empirical material necessary to prove—or to disprove—this hypothesis is incomplete. A critical problem in Chamula field work lies in gathering this kind of material systematically. But if the hypothesis is correct (as I believe it to be), then the empirical material does exist to suggest the names of those who will be points on the graph. That is, there is a handful of men, quite readily identifiable as entrepreneurs, each one of whom satisfies the criteria for "graph membership," and about whom one can only ask how it is that their business and political success go hand in hand. These men are not anonymous: indeed they tend to have *permanent* establishments in favored locations in Chamula center, which goes quite contrary to tradition. They clearly constitute a local oligarchy.

The significance of the relatively small, near-complete graph that links such men is that together they form an enduring political and economic elite which dominates Chamula. Their business activities extend over the whole territory, and indeed outside it. One, Salvador Lopez Castellanos, is well known for his control over the trade in *pox*;[17] most of them, in their years in office, will be involved in this trade, since the very considerable expenses of office are met by selling *pox* in Chamula center during the fiestas, when, of course, consumption is enormous. (There is, in fact, increasing competition from *frescos* (soft drinks), but this trade is also controlled by the oligarchy.) Lopez Castellanos is also established as a short-term moneylender, with high rates of interest, over the whole *municipio*. In addition, he owns the largest fleet of trucks. There are other moneylenders and truck owners, but they are all members of the oligarchy. Another type of enterprise, favored by Salvador Gomez Ozo, is to acquire land for conversion, often by means of terracing, to truck farming. This development runs counter to the rule that land cannot be bought and sold, but Gomez Ozo in fact owns land not only in many *parajes* besides his own, but also outside Chamula. There are others who operate like him, although on a smaller scale, but they do not share the advantage which he has of credit finance from the agricultural bank run by the Mexican government. They too qualify as points on the graph.

The economy of Chamula plainly allows for only a small number of such entrepreneurs. At the same time, exogenous political factors, arising out of the necessary dealings with government agencies—whether to negotiate a loan to finance the purchase of new land or to arrange that the trucks carrying *panela* to Zonte'viz are not checked on the Pan-American Highway—tend strongly to concentrate power within Chamula. The power nucleus occupies its commanding positions in the traditional system of offices, because the whole structure provides a self-maintaining communication network which extends over the entire *municipio*. It provides the means by which favors can be distributed, or new contacts made. It may well happen, for instance, that a relatively poor Chamula, constrained to remain the whole year within the *municipio* because he has been nominated for an unremunerative political office, will make up for the money which otherwise he would have earned on the *fincas* by a loan from Lopez Castellanos. Then to repay it, he may find himself having to sell off half his *milpa* to Gomez Ozo. The result is a graph such as that in Figure 6.[18] The kernel of the graph is the complete subgraph K_n, represented by the solid lines. Here the points are the members of the oligarchy. The dashed lines extend to contacts in the outlying *parajes*. Clearly, if the kernel is consolidated, the result is a star. The same result can be achieved by adding to the kernel subgraph K_n a point X, representing the corporate center of the *municipio*, thus creating a new graph, $K_n + X$. The complement of this graph is then the star $K_{1,n}$. This is an important result, for it illustrates the critical transformation of Chamula from a polity in which power was diffused around the periphery into one with a central power nucleus. It is doubtful whether it has a traditional Maya-type vacant center any more: the center is being transformed into a capital city.

Zinacantan is a complete contrast to Chamula. Its population, some 10,-000-odd, is less than a third of Chamula's, and the area of the *municipio*,

FIGURE 6

Structure of Religious and Political Offices of Chamula

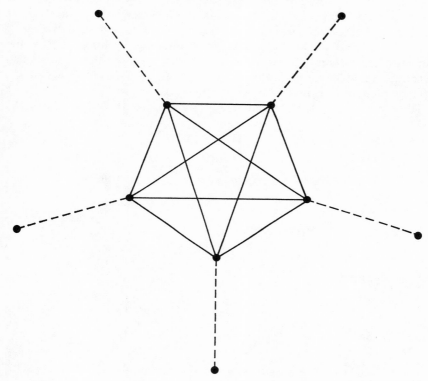

171 square kilometers, results in a significantly lower population density. The number of *parajes*, less than twenty, is smaller, so that they have substantially higher average populations. They are also less dependent on the center than are the Chamula *parajes*. Some, such as Navencauk, have their own church, supported by a local small-scale system of ritual offices. Navencauk, advantageously situated just off the Pan-American Highway, even talks of secession, taking with it a number of the surrounding *parajes*, such as ?Apas, to form a new *municipio*. This would be unthinkable in Chamula. Zinacantan is the more prosperous community; it is a net exporter of maize, and scarcely any of its members need ever resort to working on the *fincas*. The southern edge of the *municipio* is the top of the escarpment that overlooks the Grijalva valley, where substantial areas of land are rented year by year from Ladino proprietors, for the profitable cultivation of maize (an operation in which Chamulas are often employed by Zinacantecos; the reverse is never the case).

The development of the Chiapas infrastructure by the Mexican government has affected Zinacantan more than any other Indian *municipio* in the highlands. It is not only that the Pan-American Highway crosses the *municipio* along its longest axis, leaving the center in a relatively isolated corner (as Figure 7 shows), but also the new roads being built in the Grijalva valley provide unprecedented opportunities for economic development.[19] At the same time, a different structure for the system of offices threatens its disintegration, and leaves little prospect for it to develop into the nucleus of a political oligarchy, as in Chamula.

The office system for Zinacantan has been exhaustively investigated by

FIGURE 7

Zinacantan: Communications Infrastructure

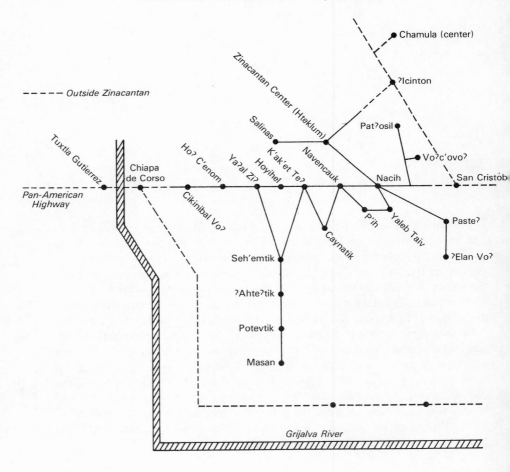

Cancian.[20] There are sixty-one offices, which is a reasonable number for a population much smaller than that of Chamula, particularly in view of the fact that in Zinacantan only the religious offices count. These are divided into four levels: *alcalde*, *regidor*, *alferez*, and *mayordomo*, in order of seniority. No office may be held more than once; no man can ever hold two offices of the same level; for an office of one level to be held, offices of every lower level must already have been held. Each official is responsible for the expenditure attendant upon the ritual associated with his own office, and certain *mayordomos*, occupying offices of the lowest level, inevitably incur the highest expenditure. Even for successful peasant farmers—and these *mayordomos*, even for Zinacantan, will be more than usually successful—the expenses of a year in office far exceed any profits that can be realized from the sale of the surplus of subsistence production. There is no question of a privileged and profitable monopoly being attached to any office, such as is the sale of *pox* in Chamula center. Within the limits of Zinacantan's traditional economy, the only possible means of finance are borrowing and calling in loans already made. The more expensive offices, which carry considerable prestige, are bespoken years in advance, so any prospective official knows that he can save for his year in office by lending his surplus funds to those actually in office. It follows, then, that an official can finance the first six months of the actual year in office by calling in loans already made, and the last six months by incurring a like indebtedness to those booked for office in later years (Cancian 1965: 100). Thus, in a graph theoretical representation, any current official can be represented as the center of a star, of which the periphery will consist—in part, at least—of past and prospective officials tied to him by debt at some time during his year of office. It does not matter in the final analysis whether in any such tie the current official is a debtor or a creditor. At the present stage of the analysis, Figure 8 illustrates how his position at the center of the star can be related to the points (or persons) on the periphery by assigning to each such point a positive or negative integer, to represent, in the case of a negative integer, not only the fact that that particular person is a debtor, but also how many years ago he served the office for which the debt was incurred, and in the case of a positive integer, the same factors, but inverted, to take into account a man who is a creditor and therefore a prospective official.

What is now needed is some way of combining the stars centered on each of a number of current officials in such a way as to produce a connected graph, to be a model of the consolidated official hierarchy, located at Zinacantan center, and showing at the same time its ties with the outlying *parajes*. This is the point already raised on page 167. Some sort of heuristic device is plainly needed. It is therefore proposed that peripheral lenders or borrowers, such as A, B, C, etc., in Figure 8, should be designated as linkmen in the case of any one of them who is tied by debt (whether as a

FIGURE 8

The Position of an Officeholder in Zinacantan

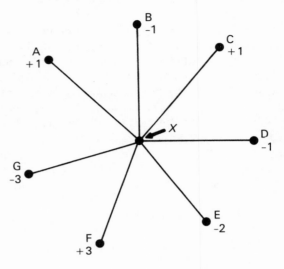

borrower or a lender) to *two* or more current officials. Thus, if A, who is a prospective official for the following year, has lent to current official Y, say, as well as to X, then he will be a link-man between X and Y, and so in the proposed new consolidated graph, X and Y will be joined together. It is doubtful whether there exist sufficient records to establish, empirically, any but a small minority of such links for any year. But if 5000 pesos may be taken as a reasonable average sum[21] for debt-finance for the ten top officials (measured in terms of requisite expenditure; Cancian 1965: 83–84) and 250 pesos (p. 101) as the average amount of all debts incurred, then strictly Figure 8 should have twenty points on the periphery. The question then is: How many of these twenty points need represent link-men, and how many link-men need there be for the consolidated graph to be complete? *Ex hypothesi* X is one of the ten star centers; if all ten are to be joined (wnich is what a complete graph requires), then there must be 36 links (this follows from Kapferer 1969: 226). At first sight each such link requires its own link-man, say A, and each such link-man is tied by debt to two star centers, say X and Y. In this case 36 link-men represent 72 debts, out of the 200 which the aggregate of the stars represent in the course of the year. The position is not as simple as this. A link-man may join together not two star centers, but three or more: A link-man may be tied by debt to X, Y, *and* Z. This would *reduce* the number of link-men. On the other hand, two link-men, say A and B, may duplicate, *redundantly*, the same link, say that between

X and Y. This would *increase* the number of link-men. Taking both these possibilities into account, we must then decide whether it is reasonable to assume that between a half and a third of the debt ties of one of the "top ten" are with link-men. To answer this question, we must first ask another: Who are the link-men likely to be? Here the answer is, in all probability, past and prospective members of the top ten, particularly those who served in the preceding year or two. Thus in Figure 8 it would be sufficient for A, B, and C to fall into this category for the half-to-a-third proportion to be met. Who then are D, E, F, and G? The answer here, quite reasonably, is that they are individuals with whom X has nonofficial ties, based, say, on kinship or proximate residence. For this to correspond to the actual situation, it is sufficient that the first loans made—in terms of time—with a view to eventual cargo service (such as *by* X *to* E and G in Figure 8) are made to individuals with whom such ties exist, and that, conversely, the last such debts incurred (such as *by* X *to* F in Figure 8) are also to such individuals. In contrast, an official close to his year in office—whether before or after— will have to become closely tied by debt to others in a functionally equivalent situation. These are more than reasonable hypotheses, and receive the strongest inferential support from the ethnography. The final result of this process is a graph that is substantially isomorphic to Figure 6, with the kernel representing the ties between current officials provided via the link-men (such as A, B, and C in Figure 8), and with the remaining dashed lines representing the ties to outlying *parajes* (such as are provided by D, E, F, and G in Figure 8).

The same line of analysis as used for Chamula then applies, although it plainly invites a number of criticisms. In the first place, it could well be said that with a like ingenuity we could have produced any number of other final results. Is the whole operation simply too contrived? The crux of the problem is that few, if any, officials serving in the same year will be making or repaying loans to their colleagues, quite clearly because each one of them needs all the money he can get for his own requisite official expenditure. One could, of course, draw a complete graph based on the principle that a tie between any two men means only that they held office in the same year, but that would merely be a tautology. But it is clear that the current offices, or at least the more prestigious of them, are supported by a continuing structure which provides the necessary finance. It is fundamental in the application of Figure 6 to Zinacantan that it is the structure which endures, while the participants change from year year; this is quite different from the case of Chamula already described. Indeed Figure 6 will be used to analyze and contrast the essentially distinct patterns of economic development in the two *municipios*.

A second possible criticism is that the actual arithmetic works out just a little bit too conveniently in the Zinacantan analysis. But as Cancian (1965: Chapters 14, 15, and 16) makes clear, the equilibrating system is the product of precisely the right arithmetical factors relating to the total population and its distribution, and to the number of offices. Indeed changes in these purely numerical factors, particularly that being brought about by population growth, threaten the whole system. Once, and indeed not so long ago, the population was much smaller: in 1900 it was less than a third of the present number (Cancian 1965: 162). At the same time there were many fewer offices. The nearly perfect articulation of the present system is itself the result of the right changes in these factors. It may be visualized mathematically as a function, $f(N)$, of population, N, which reaches its maximum when $N \simeq 10,000$.

Economic, as well as demographic factors have an important effect on the entire financial system. There is relatively little scope for increase in the costs of the more expensive offices. Any loss of interest in the official ceremonial and ritual—and this is a real possibility—will in fact decrease the expenditure. At the same time, vastly increased economic opportunities, at least for certain sectors, mean that a considerable number of officials can finance their year in office more or less out of current earnings. My own brief survey of Navencauk (in August 1972) showed that a successful flower grower there could earn in one year a sum substantially greater than the costs of even the most expensive office. For most of the *parajes* the whole economy of maize cultivation has been transformed by the vastly improved communications with the lowlands along the Grijalva. Cancian's second study (1972), which is based on these developments, has, significantly, almost nothing to say about the part played by the religious offices.

COMMUNICATIONS INFRASTRUCTURE

A useful comparison can now be made between Chamula and Zinacantan. For this a graph theoretical representation of Chamula, based on the same principles as Figure 7 (for Zinacantan), is given in Figure 9. Both figures then represent the communications infrastructure built up by the state and federal governments over the thirty odd years since the Pan-American Highway was opened. This infrastructure is the most important factor in the economic development of the whole area. For Zinacantan it substantially reduces the economic importance of the center. In the old days, when the only access to San Cristóbal from the rest of Mexico was a mule track that passed through Salinas and Zinacantan center, and the entire economic focus of Zinacantan (as of any other Indian *municipio*) was on San Cristóbal, such rudimentary infrastructure as then existed reinforced the economic primacy of the center within the *municipio*. Now, as Figure 7 makes clear, the new infrastructure, dominated as it is by the Pan-American Highway, has a pronounced eccentric bias.

FIGURE 9

Chamula: Communications Infrastructure

This graph illustrates an important tree rooted at the center of Chamula. Along one branch the important *parajes* on the road to Tenejapa can be reached by the new bypass around San Cristóbal. Another branch incorporates the eastern section of the Pan-American Highway, which is important for the import of sugar cane for the manufacture of *pox*. A third branch, incorporating the highway's western section, is important for the export of *pox* to the *parajes* of Zinacantan (cf. Figure 7). These branches also avoid San Cristóbal. There are also a number of branches leading to the *municipios*, such as Chalchihuitán, Chenalhó, Larrainzar, and Mitontic, in the hinterland of Chamula.

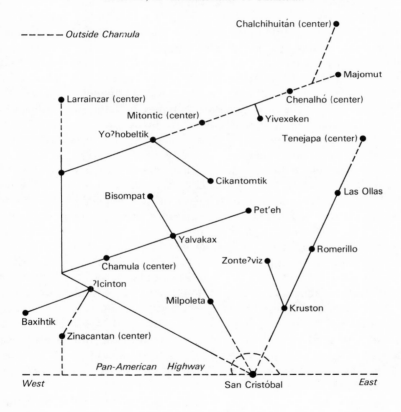

Chamula is in complete contrast. New roads give it unprecedented access to a number of outlying Indian *municipios*, such as Larrainzar, Chenalho, Chalchihuitán, Mitontic, and Tenejapa. Although certain important *parajes*, such as Las Ollas, Romerillo, Kruston, and Zonte?viz depend more directly on San Cristobal, Chamula has so reorganized its economy that its center plays an essential complementary role to that of San Cristóbal. In economic terms, Chamula is developing as an entrepôt for the *municipios* that lie beyond it. Its center is an important nodal point in a tree rooted in San Cristóbal; this is the more so in view of the development of the trade in *pox*.

CONCLUSION

The preceding graph theoretical analysis has shown that Figure 6 represents the fundamental structure of religious offices within each of the two *municipios*. Two factors are critical in the evaluation of this graph for either of them. The first is its fit with the graph that represents the respective communications infrastructure; the second is its accord with the dominant economic institutions of the *municipio*. Both these factors are positive for Chamula, and negative for Zinacantan, particularly in relation to future prospects. The traditional structures of religious and political offices for the two *municipios* are substantially the same. With the benefit of hindsight, it is clear that the fact that in Chamula a man may hold the same office more than once allowed the system as a whole to be adapted in a way that was impossible for Zinacantan, but this is far from being a complete explanation of the differential development within the two *municipios*.

The essential distinction is that in Zinacantan the bias of development was essentially conservative, whereas in Chamula it was essentially radical. In Zinacantan the system of religious offices retained its original purpose, that is, the maintenance of a highly articulated complex of religious observance, which integrated the whole *municipio* and constantly reaffirmed a common but highly traditional system of values. The financial system that developed strengthened the religious complex, but at the risk of isolating it from the mainstream of political and economic development. (It is significant that the loans made within the system are interest free, which sets them quite apart from loans made for normal business finance; Trosper 1966: Section VI.) In Chamula—a *municipio* with resources critically below the level of Zinacantan—the system of religious offices was recognized as providing an already existing structure suitable for adaptation to new political and economic ends. The way that this happened has already been described.

The graph in Figure 6, in its application to either Chamula or Zinacantan, is not a significant component of any more extended graph; this follows from the fact that in each case a quite distinct procedure, based on purely local factors, was used to construct the graph. In contrast, the graphs in Figures 7 and 9 are constituted according to the same basic rule, and are no more than localized components of a graph that extends over the whole highland area. A considerable amount of empirical material exists to analyze this extended graph, particularly in terms of local commerce (see Plattner 1969 and Siverts 1969), and the general result would be a tree rooted in San Cristóbal, at least in terms of the traditional economy of the region. So long as this graph is a tree, the essential star structures of *municipios* such as Chamula and Zinacantan are apt to be components of it. (The component of a tree defined by a given branch point, together with the points within a distance 1 from it, is always a star.) Certainly, as viewed from San Cristóbal, the dense nucleated subgraphs described above, and constituted within the respective centers of the *municipios*, counted for next to nothing. All San Cristóbal was interested in was the existence of trade routes, and these, characteristically, combine together to form a tree. The actual articulation of the tree is always liable to change when new links, such as the road joining Zinacantan center to Nacih, are opened. At first glance such a link creates a cycle, and trees have no cycles; but for economic reasons the tree tends to be maintained by the withering away of an existing branch. In the dynamic situation of the highlands of Chiapas, this is happening all the time, and the process provides the overall context for viewing the differential development, not only of Chamula and Zinacantan, but also of the other Indian *municipios*. At every stage graph theoretical analysis can usefully be applied, not only to illustrate the present state of affairs, but also to predict future developments.

In conclusion, two points, already suggested in the introductory paragraphs, need to be made. The first is positive: there is little doubt that graph theoretical representations of local structures, such as those worked out in the present study, do correspond to structures that may exist just below the surface of the local culture. To a very large extent my own reason for seeing these structures in terms of the points and lines of a graph is that this is substantially how informants have analyzed them for me, often in quite explicit terms. The second point is negative: although the whole analysis has throughout been based on precise mathematical terminology (which is not yet finally agreed upon), it has made use of none but the most elementary theorems. At this stage it is misleading to suggest that graph theory is a branch of applied mathematics, at least for social scientists. It provides, with various degrees of elaboration (such as the matrix analysis of graphs; Harary 1969: 203 et seq.), a sort of taxonomy which social scientists may adapt to their own purposes. This study is but one example.

So far the fundamental process of applied mathematics—namely, the constant interaction between the empirical material of the scientist and the abstract structures of the mathematician, each developing in essential combination with the other, and producing at every stage not only new insights into the character of the already existing corpus, but also signposts for future research—has yet to get under way. This is where to look for significant new developments, but it will be a hard search.

188   THOMAS CRUMP

ACKNOWLEDGMENT

The author wishes to acknowledge the support of the Nuffield Foundation, which
made funds available for field work expenses.

NOTES

1. The use of numbers in primitive cultures has attracted little anthropological interest, but see Gerschel (1962). On the linguistic side, Livre 1, Section 1, "Bétail et
richesse," in Benveniste (1969) is recommended.

2. The basic text for the present study is Harary (1969). The earliest systematic
study is that of Euler, dating from 1736, but the subject was hardly touched upon
for another 190 years (Harary 1969: 102). The definitions in the present study are
largely those of Harary's text.

3. For graphs in general the exponential growth of $g(N)$ is illustrated by the fact
that $g(6) = 156$, whereas $g(9) \simeq 300,000$. Even for the restricted class of trees,
enumerated by the function $t(N)$, $t(20) \simeq 1,000,000$ and $t(26) \simeq 280,000,000$.

4. A classic example of this is Ramsey's theorem that at a party of six people, there
are either three mutual acquaintances or three mutual nonacquaintances (Harary
1969: 15).

5. One does not have to be a very advanced mathematician to work out this index
for oneself. It is to be found in Kephart (1950), cited by Kapferer (1969: 226).

6. The extension of graph theory to cases in which loops and parallel lines are
permitted is dealt with by Garbett in the following article in this book.

7. It is also a very special type of complete bigraph, $K_{1,n}$. In general, a bigraph is
based on two discrete sets of m and n points, with any point of one set being joined
only to points of the other. A complete bigraph $K_{m,n}$ has all possible pairs of such
points adjacent (Harary 1969: 17).

8. See pages 173–184.

9. For labeled graphs see Harary 1969: 10.

10. This follows from the procedure of Leach (1961: 12–13). See also Malinowski
(1932: 6–24), especially for the following passage: "The method of reducing information, if possible, into charts or synoptic tables, ought to be extended to the study
of practically all aspects of native life."
    At this point the most sophisticated cases are to be found as far away as Australia:
See Lévi-Strauss (1969: Chapter 2, "Australian nominalism").

11. In 1524. under the leadership of Luís Marín, one of Cortés' lieutenants.

12. This usage is correct for Central America; in Mexico as a whole Ladino has a
different meaning (see Pitt-Rivers 1969).

13. Until 1972 this was the site of the local Centro Co-ordinador of the Instituto
Nacional Indigenista, the Mexican government agency dealing with Indian affairs.
This has now been moved some 80 kilometers to the Northeast, to Ocosingo, a
center for the Tzeltal-speaking Indians. San Cristóbal retains the headquarters of
PRODESCH (Proyecto de Desarollo Económico y Social de Chiapas), the state
agency for economic and social development.

14. A *barrio* is essentially part of a township, in appropriate cases almost a suburb. The word has no official meaning in Mexico.

15. One of the most important figures in present-day Chamula politics was first *presidente municipal* in 1940.

16. See the definition on page 166.

17. *Pox* is sold at relatively small profit margins: in 1972 a 20-liter *garrafón*, bought for 50 pesos when sold in bottles, yielded a profit of 10 pesos; at the present time these prices are probably five times as large, as the result of inflation.

18. This is also the graph in Harary (1969: Figure 9.8).

19. For a general study of this development and its consequences for Zinacantan, see Cancian (1972).

20. In Cancian (1965), which provides a substantial part of the material for the present study.

21. Inflation in the last ten years has made this sum, based on Cancian (1965), quite unrealistic; see also note 17.

REFERENCES

Barbut, M. 1970. On the meaning of the word "structure" in mathematics. In M. Lane, ed., *Structuralism, a Reader*. London: Jonathan Cape.

Benveniste, E. 1969. *Le vocabulaire des institutions indo-européennes*. Paris: Les Editions de Minuit.

Cancian, F. 1965. *Economics and Prestige in a Maya Community*. Stanford: Stanford University Press.

———. 1972. *Change and Uncertainty in a Peasant Economy*. Stanford: Stanford University Press.

Elliott, J. H. 1963. *Imperial Spain*. London: Pelican.

Furtado, C. 1970. *Economic Development of Latin America*. Cambridge: Cambridge University Press.

Gerschel, L. 1962. La conquête du nombre: des modalités du compte aux structures de la pensée. *Annales E.S.C. 17e année*, No. 4: 691–714.

Gossen, G. H. 1974. *Chamulas in the World of the Sun*. Cambridge, Mass.: Harvard University Press.

Harary, F. 1969. *Graph Theory*. Reading, Mass.: Addison-Wesley.

Kapferer, B. 1969. Norms and the manipulations of relationships in a work context. In J. C. Mitchell, ed., *Social Networks in Urban Situations*. Manchester: Manchester University Press.

Kephart, W. M. 1950. A quantitative analysis of intragroup relationships. *American Journal of Sociology*, 55: 544–549.

Leach, E. R. 1954. *Political Systems of Highland Burma*. London: London School of Economics Monographs on Social Anthropology.

———. 1961. *Rethinking Anthropology*. London: L.S.E. Monographs on Social Anthropology.

Lévi-Strauss, C. 1967. *Les structures élémentaires de la parenté*. Paris and the Hague: Mouton.

———. 1969. *Totemism*. London: Penguin.

Malinowski, B. 1932. *Argonauts of the Western Pacific*. London: Allen and Unwin.

Mitchell, J. C., ed. 1969. *Social Networks in Urban Situations*. Manchester: Man-
  chester University Press.
Pitt-Rivers, J. 1969. Mestizo or Ladino. *Race*, 10, (4): 463–477.
Plattner, S. 1969. Peddlers, pigs and profits: itinerant trading in South-East Mexico.
  Ph.D. dissertation. Stanford University.
Siverts, H. 1969. Ethnic stability and boundary dynamics in Southern Mexico. In
  F. Barth, ed. *Ethnic Groups and Boundaries*. London: Allen and Unwin.
Trosper, R. L. 1966. Lending and borrowing in ?Apas. Columbia-Cornell-Harvard-
  Illinois Summer Field Studies Program. Unpublished paper.
Yates, P. L. 1961. *El desarollo regional de México*. Mexico, D.F.: Banco de Méx-
  ico.

Graph Theory and the Analysis of Multiplex and Manifold Relationships

G. K. GARBETT

BASIC GRAPH THEORETICAL NOTIONS

Graph theory has many attractions. It provides an abstract, content-free, mathematical system (Sweetser 1967: 287) that focuses attention on the properties of relations. It leads us away from what have been termed "pure measurement systems" (cf. Abell 1968), where the concern is with measuring the properties of objects, to "structural measurement systems," where the concern is with the properties of relations between objects. It may well be that, because of these considerations, graph theory provides a mathematical structure that has many sociological applications. Here I consider first the various procedures that can be applied to complex empirical data to derive various types of abstract structures, concentrating in particular on techniques that can be utilized in the analysis of multiplex and manifold[1] relationships. As we shall observe, once a particular objective has been decided upon, the techniques of graph theory can be applied virtually mechanically to order and simplify the data. Structures that were obscured by the complexity of the data may then become apparent, and further inferences can be made from the structure of the derived graph to the empirical data. Second, by using a simple example, I illustrate a number of measures that may be applied to structures and that have relevance for the analysis of social networks. Finally, I consider a more complex example based on a series of transactions occurring among members of caste groups in an Indian village. It is at this point that I raise the problem of isomorphism and discuss the relationship between empirical reality and our representation of that reality in some analytic model, and between both of these and the mathematical structures we call graphs.

In general, topological graphs may be divided into two categories: undirected and directed. Graphs in the first category consist of points[2] (vertices) joined by undirected lines (edges) and can be applied to the study of symmetrical relationships where order is irrelevant. Graphs in the second category consist of points joined by directed lines (arcs): they can be applied to the study of asymmetrical relationships where order may be significant. Since we are reaching the stage in network studies where directionality is assuming significance (cf. Mitchell 1969: 24), I concentrate here on directed graphs.

A social network can best be represented by the most general form of directed graph,[3] a net. Formally defined, a *net* consists of a finite, nonempty set of points *P*, a finite set of directed lines *X*, and a mapping function (a "set of rules") that maps elements of *X* onto elements of *P* in such a way that each line has a first and a second point (cf. Harary, Norman, and Cartwright 1965: 6). While the set of points and the set of lines (if it contains any) must be finite, the definition of a net does not restrict the number of directed lines between any pair of points, nor does it specify that the first point of the line must be different from its second point. A net can therefore contain "parallel" lines and loops (lines whose first point is also their second point and which represent reflexive relations). For our purposes we can dispense with the loops. A net without loops is presented in Figure 1.

Such a net might have meaning for us if we distinguished among the lines and divided them into three subsets, *a*, *b*, and *c*. Subset *a* might represent, say, the relation "gives assistance to"; the subset *b*, "gives advice to"; the subset *c*, "accords prestige to." From the net we can see, for example, that of the individuals represented by the points, person 2 receives advice and assistance from person 1 and in return accords prestige to person 1. The relations in a net could be presented quite easily by means of lines of different colors or thicknesses, and so forth, but this still leaves us at the level of visual aids. If the complexity of a net is to be formally analyzed, it must first be decomposed into a series of graphs, each one of which contains the same set of points as the net but has only one relation defined on the set. This relation may represent one set of empirical relationships or, as I consider later, it may represent two or more sets of empirical relationships that have been compounded into one abstract relation for purposes of analysis. A graph that is defined in such a way that it contains no parallel lines and no loops is an irreflexive relation and is known as a directed graph or *digraph* (Harary et al. 1965: 9).

Which relationships we choose to abstract from a social network and include in a net will depend, obviously, on our objectives. There are some problems, but these are not insuperable, and we are already accustomed to separating out, for analytic purposes, the various normative components of multiplex relationships or to treating a social relationship, which is dominated by one identifiable set of norms, as uniplex and disregarding other minor contents that we as observers deem irrelevant (Mitchell 1969: 22), or to abstracting sets of relationships by some criteria according to their interactional content. Kapferer (1969), for example, explicity discusses the way in which he abstracted sets of relationships from the various face-to-face interactions he observed among the workers in part of a section of a zinc-

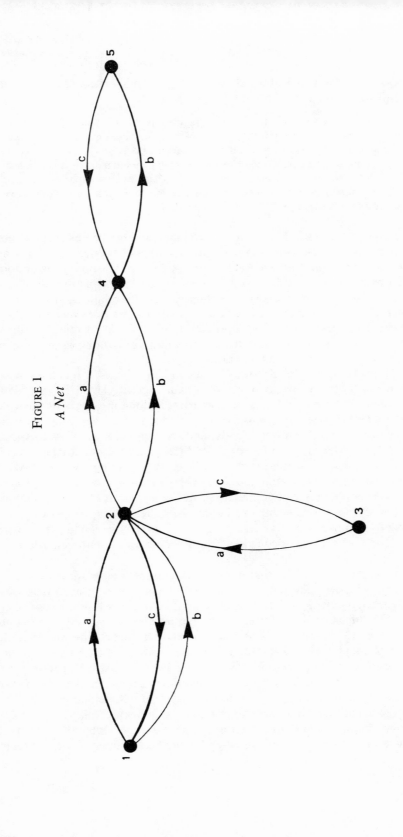

FIGURE 1

A Net

processing plant in Kabwe (Broken Hill), Zambia, according to what he terms their exchange content:

> I have extrapolated from my observations of the face-to-face interaction between the workers . . . some of the major elements which *regularly* appeared in these interactions. The exchange contents presented here are an attempt on the part of the observer to categorise the many forms of interaction which took place and are, therefore, not exhaustive; for each exchange content or element of a relationship which I isolate here can be broken down into further elements [p. 212].

He goes on to state that the five exchange contents he abstracts—conversation, joking behavior, job assistance, personal service, and cash assistance—constitute "an accurate summary" of the various types of content he observed, and he discusses in some detail the types of behavior subsumed under each category. He then represents relationships falling into each category by means of separate adjacency matrices and makes inferences from these about the "strength" of each worker's relationships with those with whom he comes into direct contact, according to the number of exchange contents in each relationship.

Marriott (1968), in his study of an Indian village—aspects of which I consider later—made two kinds of abstraction. He first recorded all exchanges of food and services occurring among members of the village. He then classified these into five folk categories: the exchange of "raw," "superior," and "inferior" foods, and the two services of the disposal of garbage and feces. Next he condensed the multitude of actual transactions occurring among members of the village by accepting the folk view that, since each villager is a member of a corporate caste group, the transactions among individuals can be regarded as representative of the five general types of transaction occurring among the caste groups. In this way he was able to summarize on five adjacency matrices the many actual transactions in food and services occurring among members of the twenty-four caste groups.

It may be, however, that in order to analyze a network of transactions adequately, we may have to move to a higher level of abstraction, compounding many apparently diverse empirical relationships into one analytic relationship. Consider, for example, the problems involved in conceptualizing A. C. Mayer's (1966) "action-sets" as nets. The significance of Mayer's material is that it demonstrates how quite long chains of social relationships, each relationship of which is often distinct in terms of normative and interactional content, stretch from the candidate to the voter. He demonstrates how the candidate is able to initiate action among some of those with whom he has direct relationships, which ultimately results in some service or aid being bartered with a remote voter, at the end of a chain of relationships, in exchange for political support. Here it would be pointless to represent the actually observed empirical relationships by digraphs since many of these would be disconnected. One would proceed by compounding various relationships as conceptually equivalent at a higher level of abstraction in terms of some relationship such as "has influence over" or "gives political support to."

Once a particular mode of abstracting from relationships has been decided on—and this will be determined by the analytic model one is employing—a digraph can be constructed. As I have indicated, a digraph is an irreflexive relation containing no loops or parallel lines. Its structure can be analyzed quite abstractly by applying digraph theory. Four concepts are basic to digraph theory: joining, reaching, connectedness, and distance.[4] After preliminary definitions of the four concepts, I consider some problems related to the concepts of reaching and distance.

In directed graph theory, one point is said to be adjacent to another if a line is directed from one to the other. In Figure 2, for example, point 2 is adjacent to point 3, point 3 to point 4, point 2 to point 1, and so forth. In general, pairs of points are said to be *joined* if, ignoring the direction of the lines, one may trace some route from one to the other. All pairs of points in Figure 2 are, in some degree, joined. Degrees of joining are specified according to whether pairs of points are *disconnected,* joined by a *semisequence* (a route that contains lines whose direction may differ, such as that between points 6 and 1 in Figure 2), a *sequence* (a route in which the lines all have the same orientation, such as the route 5—2, 2—3, 3—4, 4—2, 2—1 in Figure 2) in one direction, or a sequence in both directions. Pairs of points joined by a semisequence in which no point or line occurs more than once are said to be joined by a (strict) *semipath* (e.g., points 6 and 2 in Figure 2). Pairs of points joined by a sequence in which no point or line occurs more than once are said to be joined by a *path* (e.g., points 3 and 1 in Figure 2). The *distance* of a path from one point to another is the number of directed lines it contains. The distance from point 3 to point 1 in Figure 2 is 3. The shortest path between two points is a *geodesic.*

Joining is a symmetrical, transitive relation. In Figure 2, for example, considering the four points 6, 5, 1, and 2, point 6 is joined to 5, point 5 to 2, and point 2 to 1. Therefore, point 6 is joined to 1 and point 1 to 6. The transitivity implied by the weaker degrees of joining may need interpreting with care. If, for example, person *a* gives advice to *b* and *c* gives advice to *b* but *b* does not reciprocate to either, then in a digraph this relation would be represented by a semipath between the points representing *a* and *c*. However, there may or may not be sociological significance in the fact that *a* is "weakly joined" to *c* through *b*.

Reaching, in contrast to joining, is conceived of as a reflexive, nonsymmetrical,[5] transitive relation. In a digraph of two points, one is said to reach the other if there is a path from the initial point to the terminal point. In Figure 2, for example, point 3 can reach point 1 through points 4 and 2 but

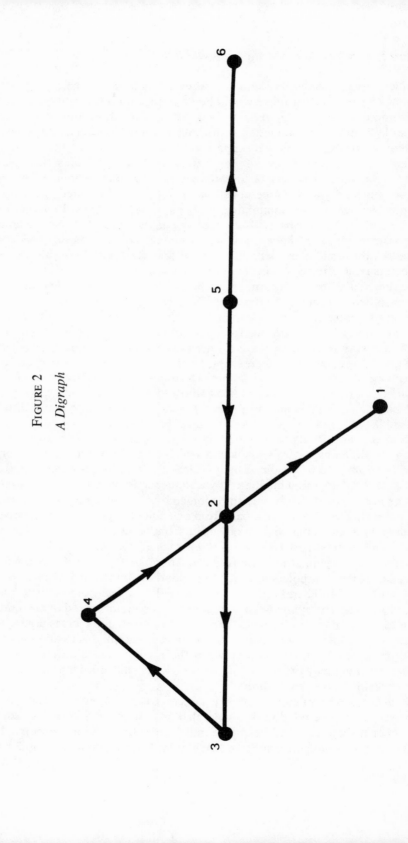

FIGURE 2
A Digraph

cannot reach point 6 because it is only weakly joined to 6 by a semipath. If there is a path in both directions, the points are said to be *mutually reachable*. Reaching is a *nonsymmetrical* relation because, if, out of any three points, *a* can reach *b* and *b* can reach *c,* then *a* can reach *c* (and by definition itself) but *there is no necessary implication* that *c* can reach *a*.

The notion of reaching has played an important part in many studies of social networks. One of the major postulates underlying analyses in terms of networks is that an individual can influence the behavior of, and have his own behavior influenced by, not only those with whom he has direct social relationships, but also others more remote, with whom he comes into relationship indirectly through one or more intermediaries. Bott (1955, 1957), Epstein (1961), P. Mayer (1961), the contributors to two recent symposia (Mitchell 1969; Boissevain and Mitchell 1973), among others, have demonstrated, or worked with the assumption, that opinions and values are transmitted through a social network. Bott's argument (1957: 60) that the role behavior of spouses is influenced by the degree of density (in her terms "connectedness") of their joint social network, which in turn influences the degree of normative consensus among network members, turns in part on the extent to which communications related to the transmission of norms and values reach the various members. However, as Mitchell (1969: 17) has indicated, reachability should not be confused with density, i.e., with the extent to which relationships that could possibly exist among members of a network do in fact exist (cf. Barnes 1968: 115 et seq.; 1969: 255 et seq.). That a network is dense may or may not mean that there is a high probability that an opinion expressed by one member will eventually reach others in the network. This will depend, as Mitchell demonstrates, on the "pattern" of the network—the way in which the various relationships are ordered and juxtaposed one with another. Nor must we assume, without empirical verification, that because, in some way, we have identified a "relationship" that can be juxtaposed with others to form some sort of interconnected "network," this type of communication actually occurs.

Similar problems arise when considering reachability in digraphs representing the transactions occurring within social networks. A. C. Mayer, as I have noted, demonstrates how a candidate in an election was able to reach distant voters and mobilize their support through quite long chains of intermediaries involved in diverse relationships. Here the fact that the candidate could reach voters was empirically established. However, caution is needed when interpreting the concept of reaching in digraphs representing, say, the flow of services of an instrumental kind among members of a network. One may be able, from some collection of individuals, to trace out the instrumental services that each provides and receives and bring them all into relationship with one another on one digraph. However, the fact that a path of some length exists across the digraph, implying that one point can reach some distant point, may have no sociological significance whatsoever. Obviously, one would first have to establish empirically that some input of services by one individual in the social network had some consequence for a more distant individual; this cannot simply be assumed.

Being a member of a network in relationship with others is obviously a necessary condition for communication and transactions to occur, but it is not in itself a sufficient condition. Mitchell (1973: 24) cites an example where, within a network, information about abortionists was transmitted only to certain of its members and not to others. These considerations have important implications for those who are exploring such hypotheses as Bott's concerning network structures and conjugal roles. It may well be that a dense network is not in itself a sufficient condition for the formation of normative consensus, as has been commonly assumed (cf. Kapferer 1973: 86).

The concepts of reaching and distance can be utilized to provide a number of interesting structural measures. Before considering these and their derivation from matrices, I comment briefly on the concept of connectedness in digraphs.

Harary and others (1965: 69) identify four categories of connectedness: C_0, C_1, C_2, C_3. As Barnes (1969: 219), in an extended treatment of connectedness, has indicated, for these authors connectedness is a property that attaches to directed graphs and subgraphs: it does not attach to pairs of points but is derived from the properties of joining and reaching, which do attach to pairs of points. A digraph in which some points are not joined to others belongs to C_0 and is said to be disconnected. A digraph consisting only of points is said to be totally disconnected. In a weak digraph belonging to C_1, any two of its points are joined by a (strict) semipath. A *unilateral* digraph, belonging to C_2, consists of a set of points arranged in an open sequence[6] such that, for any pair of points, at least one is reachable from the other. A *strong* digraph, belonging to C_3, consists of a set of mutually reachable points arranged in a closed sequence. Matrix methods have been developed for partitioning a digraph into weak, unilateral, or strong *components,* that is, subgraphs that are maximal for a particular property. Components could be used to interpret such phenomena as "cliques" (strong components), unidirectional flows of communication (unilateral components), or individuals who are, say, accorded prestige by a number of others without reciprocating (weak components).

These conceptions of connectedness in digraphs lead to considerations of their relative *vulnerability*. If we consider a social network, then we can appreciate that there will be certain individuals involved in relationships who can be considered crucial for its "morphological" properties in the sense that their removal would seriously affect, say, the flow of communication or the transmission of goods and services within it. We can approach this problem either from the point of view of specific crucial relationships or from the point of view of individuals whose total set of relationships is crucial. Intuitively, one can appreciate that the removal of an individual, particularly one involved in many relationships, will have a more weakening effect on the network than the severing of a single relationship. These various situations can be interpreted in a digraph by considering how its properties of connectedness and reachability are affected by the removal of points or lines (cf. Harary et al. 1965: 194 et seq., 225 et seq.). The points of a digraph can be classified as *strengthening, neutral,* or *weakening.* On the whole, points of high outdegree or indegree—that is, with many lines directed from or to them—are more *strengthening* than others. For example, in the digraph in Figure 3, point 1 is strengthening in that its removal, together with its associated lines, disconnects the digraph. Point 6 is weakening in that its removal places the digraph in a higher category of connectedness (C_3. strong), while point 2 is neutral since its removal does not affect the connectedness category. Lines are either strengthening or neutral. The line between points 6 and 1 in the digraph in Figure 3 is strengthening. The remaining lines are neutral. In general, a digraph is vulnerable at its strengthening lines.

The concept of vulnerability in a digraph with respect to the removal of lines is paralleled in social networks by the concept of redundancy (Frankenberg 1966: 278 et seq.). Here the basic idea is that in a multichanneled route, other channels are available should one or two fail. This can be applied either to considering, say, separate channels of communication among individuals or to conceptualizing multiplex relationships (cf. Mitchell 1969: 23). Two people involved in a multiplex relationship interact with one another in a variety of different contexts. The failure of one component of the relationship is less likely to enable them to withdraw from contact completely than is the failure of a uniplex relationship. Wheeldon (1969), in a study of voluntary associations within a colored community in Rhodesia, noted that in a dispute over policy within an association, established leaders utilized their many wide-ranging and multiplex relationships with members. They were thus eventually able to overcome opposition because the leaders could bring pressure to bear upon dissident members both directly and indirectly through a variety of channels and in a variety of contexts. Members who continued to oppose the leaders, Wheeldon noted, were those who had very small-range networks and thus remained relatively immune from the pressure of opinion since there were fewer channels through which, and fewer contexts in which, it could be applied.

In general, the more complete a digraph is—that is, the greater the extent to which there are directed lines from each point to every other point—the less vulnerable it is. Measures of vulnerability can be devised, based on such considerations as the proportion of lines that can be removed before some morphological property of the digraph is affected.

For undirected graphs Barnes (1968: 115) has derived a measure of completeness or density, as he terms it, from an earlier measure proposed by

Kephart (1950: 548). This measure has been applied by Kapferer (1969). Density is the extent to which all relationships that could possibly exist among persons do in fact exist. The measure is given by $200a/n(n - 1)$, where a refers to the actual number of relationships and n to the total number of persons involved, including ego. This measure is strictly only applicable to undirected graphs because the properties of a digraph depend on the orientation of its lines. Barnes remarks that his measure is probably best used in relation to some abstracted partial network, i.e., relationships defined in terms of one criterion, such as class, friendship, kinship, etc. I endorse this view, and would indeed go further and argue that the measures should be applied only to sets of relationships abstracted from the network in terms of some specified criterion. Two issues are involved here: the validity of the mathematical operations of addition and division performed on the relationships to compute the ratio, and the need to ensure that when comparisons between different sets of data are being made, equivalent measures are being compared. The mathematical operations performed to compute the ratio may only be performed if the relationships being examined can be considered in some way conceptually equivalent. This will depend in part on the level of abstraction. Simply computing a density measure for all identifiable relationships in a social network without distinguishing whether they are, for example, instrumental or categorical, or whether they are manifest or latent, and without specifying the level of abstraction at which they are being analyzed, is likely to produce invalid measures and to lead to meaningless comparisons. Much of the work done in attempting to test Bott's hypothesis is invalidated because these problems have not been properly considered.

Kapferer (1969), in applying the measure of density, related it to a measure of what he terms *span,* defined as the proportion of all relationships among some specified set of persons that are included in ego's primary zone. He demonstrates that there is a tendency for span to vary inversely with density. In part, as Niemeijer notes (1973), this arises because the density of an undirected graph depends on both the number of points and the *degree* of the points, that is, the number of lines from each point.

Barnes (1968: 118; 1969: 227) has suggested that in addition to measuring, for example, what Bott meant by "connectedness," and so more precisely characterizing her "close-knit" and "loose-knit" personal network, the measure can be used to identify clusters, that is, relatively dense subsets of relationships among some defined set of people. In terms of undirected graphs, a cluster is some subset of points whose subgraph is relatively dense. A complete subgraph in which every point is joined to every other will be maximally dense. We now need to specify some minimum degree of completeness that will enable us to identify a less dense subgraph. Barnes, for purposes of exposition, fixed this at 80%. For example, the total possible number of (specified) symmetrical relationships that can exist among a set of eleven persons is 55. If, of these possible relationships, 44 or more actually exist, then the set is arbitrarily defined as a cluster. Barnes classifies members of a cluster as "core" and "peripheral" according to whether or not their removal causes the density of the cluster to fall significantly. Niemeijer (1973: 54) demonstrates that this simple approach to clustering leads to contradictions and argues that "not only arbitrary thresholds, but any threshold method leads to contradictions if based on density." As he argues at length, the contradictions result from the relation between the density, size, and degree of a graph. He works toward another solution based on the criterion that a cluster has a relatively low number of external relations relative to its internal relations.

When considering a social network, one is sometimes interested in how easily some ego can mobilize an "action-set," utilizing direct and indirect relationships to achieve an objective. Other things being equal, the more "compact" the social network is, the larger the number of individuals to be mobilized at each step. Alternatively, one may be interested in how some item of information is likely to be transmitted through a social network. Here one may find individuals who both receive and transmit information to a large proportion of network members directly or through very few intermediaries. These individuals may be considered "central" to the network, at least in so far as communication is concerned. On the other hand, there may be those who receive information directly, or through few intermediaries, but who can transmit information directly to a few and only reach a high proportion of network members through long chains of intermediaries. Such individuals are, in a sense, "central" to the network for receiving information but "peripheral" to it for transmitting information. Structural measures deriving from considerations of reachability and distance can be applied to such problems and are concerned with characterizing the "compactness" of a digraph and the "centrality" and "peripherality" of its points. Such measures can be computed by inspection from a small digraph, but for large digraphs it is more convenient to derive them by matrix methods. Computers can be programmed to perform the operations or, for matrices up to 50 by 50 in size, optical coincidence cards may be used (Garbett 1968).

Consider the hypothetical digraph shown in Figure 3. It is a weak digraph and can be partitioned into two strong components: the trivial subgraph, point 6, and the strong subgraph formed by the points 1 through 5 and their associated lines. I have set out the adjacency, reachability, and distance matrices for the digraph. The adjacency matrix (Matrix 1), which is square, contains an entry of 1 in a cell if the point at the head of the row is adjacent to the point at the head of the column. The entry of 1 in the cell formed by the intersection of row 3 and column 5, for example, indicates that there is a directed line from point 3 to point 5. An adjacency matrix is a most useful way of representing a digraph. Indeed, large digraphs may be impossible to

FIGURE 3
A Digraph

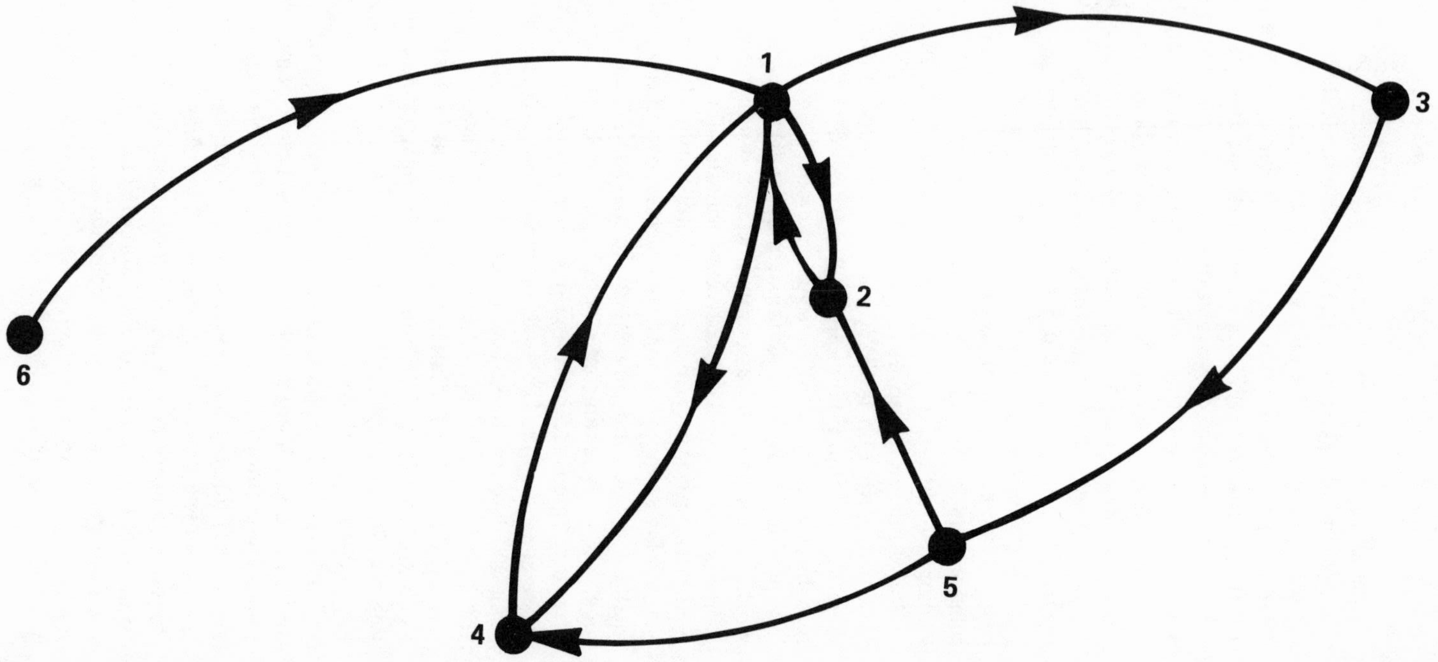

MATRIX 1

Adjacency Matrix of Digraph (Figure 3)

	1	2	3	4	5	6
1	0	1	1	1	0	0
2	1	0	0	0	0	0
3	0	0	0	0	1	0
4	1	0	0	0	0	0
5	0	1	0	1	0	0
6	1	0	0	0	0	0

draw intelligibly and can only be satisfactorily represented by matrices.[7] The row and column totals from the adjacency matrix give what is termed the "outdegree" and "indegree" of the points, that is, the number of lines directed from and to a point. Point 4, for example, has an outdegree of 1 and an indegree of 2. For certain purposes points may be classified according to their degrees.

The reachability matrix (Matrix 2) contains an entry of 1 in a cell if the point at the head of the row can reach the point at the head of the column. Point 6, for example, can reach point 5 by a path of length 3, hence there is an entry of 1 in the cell formed by the intersection of row 6 and column 5.

MATRIX 2

Reachability Matrix of Digraph (Figure 3)

	1	2	3	4	5	6
1	1	1	1	1	1	0
2	1	1	1	1	1	0
3	1	1	1	1	1	0
4	1	1	1	1	1	0
5	1	1	1	1	1	0
6	1	1	1	1	1	1

Conversely, point 5 cannot reach point 6 by a path of any length, and this is signified by an entry of 0 in the relevant cell. The row entries of the reachability matrix give those sets of points that are ultimately reachable from the points at the head of the rows. The column entries give those antecedent points that ultimately reach the point at the head of the column. These notions of reachable and antecedent sets are useful ones. It is possible to construct matrices whose row entries give sets of points that are reachable within various specified distances from the points at the head of the row. These 1, 2, 3, . . . , reachable sets correspond to Barnes' first-, second-, third-order, etc., stars in a segment of a social network defined in relation to some "alpha" (Barnes 1968: 112 et seq.). Taking some alpha as root, Barnes defined his first-order star as comprising alpha and those with whom he has direct contact, ignoring the relationships among the latter. Alpha's second-order star comprises the first-order star together with those who are two steps removed from alpha with whom he comes into indirect contact through members of the first-order star, other relationships being ignored. Alpha's first-order zone consists of the members of the first-order star together with all relationships existing among them. Alpha's second-order zone consists of members of his second-order star and all relationships existing among them. Higher-order zones can be defined similarly. In directed graphs, where all relationships may not be symmetrical, we have to take into account not only those who can be contacted from some ego within 1, 2, or more steps (and may not themselves be able to reciprocate) but also those who can contact ego within 1, 2, or more steps (and may not themselves be reached). This is why one must specify antecedent sets as well as reachable sets. For directed graphs the first-, second-, third-order, etc., zones are given by the 1, 2, 3, . . . , reachable and antecedent sets together with their associated lines.

Consider now the distance matrix (Matrix 3). A cell entry here gives the distance of the shortest path from the point at the head of the row to the point at the head of the column. The entry of 3, for example, in the cell formed by the intersection of row 4 and column 5 means that there is at least one path of length 3 from point 4 to point 5. The infinity symbols given in column 6 mean that point 6 cannot be reached from any other point by any finite path. It is from the distance matrix that we can begin to derive various measures.

The compactness of a digraph can be expressed in terms of its *diameter* and its *radius* (cf. Harary et al. 1965: 160 et seq.). The measure of diameter is only applicable to strong digraphs or subgraphs; the measure of radius is more widely applicable. The diameter of a strong digraph is simply the greatest distance between any pair of its points. The larger the diameter, the less "compact" the digraph is. The diameter may be obtained from the largest cell entry of the distance matrix. The diameter of the strong component of the digraph in Figure 3, formed by the points 1 through 5, is 3.

MATRIX 3

Distance Matrix of Digraph (Figure 3)

	1	2	3	4	5	6	Out-number	Dis-tance sum
1	0	1	1	1	2	∞	∞	5
2	1	0	2	2	3	∞	∞	8
3	3	2	0	2	1	∞	∞	8
4	1	2	2	0	3	∞	∞	8
5	2	1	3	1	0	∞	∞	7
6	1	2	2	2	3	0	3	10
Innumber	3	2	3	2	3	∞		46

The largest cell entry in each row of the distance matrix is termed the *out-number* of a point, and the largest cell entry in each column, the *innumber*. Points that have a high outnumber or a high innumber can be thought of as being peripheral to a digraph. If we are considering communication, for example, persons represented by points with high outnumbers will have to transmit messages over larger distances, through more intermediaries, than persons represented by points with low outnumbers. Similarly, persons represented by points with high innumbers will receive messages over longer distances, through more intermediaries, than persons represented by points with low innumbers. Since the diameter of a strong digraph represents the greatest distance between any pair of its points, the most peripheral points are those whose outnumber or innumber equals the diameter; such points are referred to as *outperipheral* and *inperipheral,* respectively. In the strong component of the digraph in Figure 3, points 2, 3, 4, and 5 are *outperipheral,* and points 1, 3, and 5 are *inperipheral.* Note that here peripherality is based on considerations of reachability and distance and does not have the same meaning as peripherality when used to refer to marginal members of clusters (cf. Barnes 1968).

Having identified sets of points that are, in the sense defined, peripheral, we can now proceed to identify points that are "central." Logically, one would identify "central" points as those which could reach others within some minimum distance or, alternatively, which could be reached within some minimum distance. These minimum distances are given by measures

termed the *outradius* and the *inradius,* respectively. For any digraph, the
outradius is the smallest finite outnumber in the distance matrix, and the
inradius, the smallest finite innumber. From the distance matrix, the outradius of the digraph shown in Figure 3 is 3 and the inradius is 2. Points
whose outnumber equals the outradius are called *outcentral,* and points
whose innumber equals the inradius are called *incentral.* For the digraph,
point 6 is *outcentral* and points 2 and 4 are *incentral.* This means that an
individual represented by point 6 could contact all persons represented by
the other points in, at the most, three steps, while the individuals represented by points 2 and 4 could be contacted by individuals represented by
the other points in, at the most, two steps.

Other indices of centrality have made use of the notion of the "total
distance" in a graph (Bavelas 1960; Harary 1959; both cited in Harary et
al. 1965: 188). Bavelas' index of relative centrality for a point, for example,
is computed by dividing the total distance in a graph by the distance sum
from a point. The distance sum from a point is given by the sum of the
finite row entries in the distance matrix, and the total distance is simply the
total of these sums. The total distance in the digraph in Figure 3 is 46. The
centrality indices for each point are as follows: point 1: 9.2 (46/5); point 2:
5.75 (46/8); point 3: 5.75 (46/8); point 4: 5.75 (46/8); point 5: 6.57 (46/7); and
point 6: 4.6 (46/10). Note that using this index, point 1 is now the most
"central" rather than point 6 (originally identified above as outcentral),
which is now the least central. This is because point 1 can reach separately
more points in cumulatively fewer steps than point 6. This measure is
related to situations in which one is considering, in terms of unit time or
unit cost, the total time or cost for an individual to transmit *separate* messages to each person he can reach directly or through intermediaries. Bavelas, in working with small experimental groups, was able to predict that
persons with high centrality indices were likely to emerge as leaders.

Bavelas's work on centrality stimulated a number of others to develop
more refined measures (e.g., Beauchamp 1965; Sabidussi 1966). However,
as Freeman (1977) has indicated, the problem with such measures is that
they cannot be applied to unconnected graphs. Freeman develops general
measures of centrality by extending the graph theoretical concept of
betweenness to include "partial betweenness." His measures are limited,
however, to symmetrical relations. Freeman begins with the intuitive
notion that in the graph of a communication network a point, p_k, which is
on a geodesic—a shortest path—between any two other points (such as the
central point of a star graph) is central, since the individual represented by
it may control the flow of information to all other individuals. He then treats
the situation in which there are alternative geodesics between any two
points, p_i and p_j, but where p_k may not be located on all of them. Freeman
derives an expression for the probability that p_k will fall on a randomly
selected geodesic joining p_i and p_j. This is simply the reciprocal of the

number of geodesics joining p_i and p_j on which p_k actually falls.[8] Summing these probabilities for each point in relation to all geodesics joining pairs of points, Freeman obtains an idea of "partial betweenness" or overall centrality.[9] By demonstrating that the central point of a star graph has a maximum centrality index and by deriving an expression for it, he is able to obtain a relative measure of centrality by relating the summed probabilities for each point to this maximum.[10] This enables the centrality of points of graphs of different sizes to be meaningfully compared. Finally, Freeman derives a centrality index for a graph as a whole based on the intuitive notion that a communication network has a high degree of centrality to the extent that an individual controls the flow of communications within it: the index is the average difference in centrality between the most central point and all others.

Mitchell (1969: 16) has argued that there are two distinct dimensions in the compactness of a social network: the proportion of people who can ever be contacted by each person in the network and the number of intermediaries that must be used to contact others. He suggests that a single measure for the compactness of a network represented as a digraph, which takes account of these two dimensions, may be obtained by calculating the mean number of points reached over all theoretically possible steps. He demonstrates that his measure discriminates among three digraphs which have the same number of points but different structures.

APPLICATION TO AN EMPIRICAL PROBLEM

In general, those who have used structural measures and matrix procedures in their analyses of social networks, while stimulated directly or indirectly by the theory of graphs, have made little use of deductions from the theory itself. In the following example, drawn from Marriott's (1968) work on transactions among caste groups in an Indian village, I use deductions from the theory of directed graphs, specifically from those parts of the theory concerned with acyclic graphs and level assignments, to derive the structures of digraphs obtained from a net representing five types of transaction. I then develop procedures for bringing the separate structures into relation with one another and thus obtain a ranking of the caste groups. Finally, I consider the correspondence between the folk model that Marriott discusses, the analytic model that he presents, and the graph theoretical procedures that I apply. This leads me to a discussion of the important problem of isomorphism.

In the predominantly Hindu village of Kishan Garhi in the Aligarh District of Uttar Pradesh, Marriott obtained two types of data: opinions about the ranking of castes, which he formalized by the method of paired comparisons, and observed transactions in food and services between the twenty-four caste groups.[11] The observed transactions consisted of the giving of "raw" foodstuffs, of "superior" and "inferior" cooked food, and the performance of the services of garbage disposal and feces removal.[12]

Marriott's aim was to "connect local ideas and opinions about caste rank with a model of this hierarchy as a system of symbolic interaction, also local" (Marriott 1968: 133) and to construct an index "which would accurately predict the caste rank of a locality while revealing the values by which highness and lowness of castes are locally judged" (Marriott 1968: 137). He argued convincingly that any attempt to construct an attributional index of caste rank based on occupational criteria, or considerations of diet, or notions of pollution, or combinations of these, is fraught with both logical and practical difficulties and is unlikely to be achieved. Observation, and discussion with villagers, finally led him to the conclusion that generally held opinions of caste rank derived from publicly observed intercaste transactions in food and services. Marriott then proceeded to construct a model based on the following assumptions. He argued that any publicly exhibited transaction which involves the transfer of food from a member of one caste group to a member of another, or the provision of a service by the member of one caste group for the member of another, is also a symbolic transaction expressing rank, in which the giver of food, or the receiver of a service, always ranks higher.

Given that caste rank is a corporate property of the whole membership of a caste group, the multitude of actual transactions occurring between members of any pair of caste groups can be summarized simply in terms of whether the transactions are symmetrical or asymmetrical. If the transactions are symmetrical, i.e., members of each caste group both give and receive, then the caste groups are of equivalent rank; if they are asymmetrical, i.e., members of one caste group give while the members of the other always receive, the caste groups are of unequal rank, the giving caste group always ranking higher than the receiving one. (To simplify matters, we use the term "giving" to mean either supplying food or providing feces or garbage to be removed by the "receiver.") Where members of the two caste groups do not engage in transactions with one another, but members of each engage in transactions with members of a number of caste groups, the rank order of the two is determined by the balance of transactions with these other caste groups. The model assumes that caste rank is transitive, that it constitutes a partial order, and, finally, that transactions symbolically convey different degrees of rank according to the type of service performed or food transferred; in descending order, the transactions are ranked, "raw" food, "superior" cooked food, and "inferior" cooked food exchange; garbage and feces removal.

The procedures that Marriott used to analyze the complex series of transactions occurring among the twenty-four caste groups in the village are not derived from the theory of graphs. His analysis of binary matrices depends on the fact that the five types of transactions constitute a Guttman scale and are therefore additive (Marriott 1968: 156). This may be valid for the transactions among caste groups that he analyzes, but it would not be true in general for other types of transactions. My attempt to apply graph theory to Marriott's material, however, should not be taken as a criticism of his pioneering method of analysis, but rather seen as an attempt to achieve a similar objective by different procedures that may be more widely applicable to the analysis of other types of multiplex and manifold relationships.

Marriott presents the types of transactions that occurred among the caste groups by means of five adjacency matrices. Since raw foodstuffs are given and received by all but two caste groups and feces disposal is performed for all caste groups by members of only one, Marriott concentrated his analysis on three transactions: in superior and inferior cooked food, and in garbage disposal. He computed net scores for each caste by subtracting the column sums from the row sums of the three adjacency matrices, where the row sums represent the number of transactions in which the caste group at the end of the row was the giver and the column sums represent the number of transactions in which the caste group at the head of the column was the receiver. He then summed the net scores for each caste group over the five transactions to obtain a final rank order. The rank order that he obtained is given in Table 1. Finally, he compared the rank order that he derived by these procedures with a rank order that he obtained from villagers by the method of paired comparison. This involved asking villagers of different castes to rank caste groups by means of a set of cards, each card representing a caste. Each card was "played" against every other card to ascertain if it was ranked "higher" or "lower." To obtain a final rank order of opinions about caste rank, Marriott applied a two-thirds majority rule to eliminate ties and inconsistencies. He then demonstrated that there was a high measure of agreement between the two rank orders (see Table 1), showing that the transactional model he constructed goes a long way toward explaining the underlying processes by which rank is accorded to caste.

Since the procedures which I apply do not depend on the computation of net scores to which the transactions in raw foodstuffs and in feces make no significant difference, but depend on the differentiation of transactions, I work with all five transactions. Essentially, the operations to be performed on the sets of transactions are those of union and intersection rather than the arithmetic operations of addition and subtraction, multiplication and division. Instead of working with five separate adjacency matrices, I have presented the five types of transaction in a multidimensional adjacency matrix whose cells, formed by the intersection of rows and columns, each contain five entries ranging from 11111 to 00000 (Matrix 4).[13] This is essentially the adjacency matrix of a net. In general, the entry 11111 in a cell c_{ij} signifies that there are five lines in the net directed from i to j, representing

MATRIX 4

Adjacency Matrix of Net of Transactional Relations

	24	11	1	27	33	36	30	3	14	20	25	2
24	00000	10000	10000	10000	11100	11111	10000	10000	10000	10000	11000	10000
11	11110	00000	11000	11110	11110	11111	11110	11000	11110	11110	11110	11000
1	11110	11110	00000	11110	11110	11111	11110	11110	11110	11110	11110	11110
27	10000	10000	10000	00000	10000	11111	11110	10000	10000	10000	10000	10000
33	10000	10000	10000	10000	00000	11111	10000	10000	10000	10000	10000	10000
36	00000	00000	00000	00000	00000	00000	00000	00000	00000	00000	00000	00000
30	10000	10000	10000	11110	10000	11111	00000	10000	10000	10000	10000	10000
3	11110	11010	11000	11110	11110	11111	11110	00000	11110	11110	11110	11100
14	11010	11000	11000	11110	11110	11111	11110	11000	00000	11010	11010	11000
20	10000	10000	10000	10000	11100	11111	10000	10000	10000	00000	11000	10000
25	10000	10000	10000	10000	11100	11111	10000	10000	10000	10000	00000	10000
2	11110	11010	11000	11110	11110	11111	11110	11100	11110	11110	11110	00000
29	10000	10000	10000	11110	10000	11111	11110	10000	10000	10000	10000	10000
21	10000	10000	10000	10000	11100	11111	10000	10000	10000	10000	11000	10000
35	00000	00000	00000	00000	00000	11000	00000	00000	00000	00000	00000	00000
26	10000	10000	10000	11110	10000	11111	11110	10000	10000	10000	10000	10000
34	10000	10000	10000	10000	10000	11111	10000	10000	10000	10000	10000	10000
4	11110	11010	11000	11110	11110	11111	11110	11000	11110	11110	11110	11000
15	11110	11000	11000	11110	11110	11111	11110	11000	11100	11110	11110	11000
6	11110	11010	10000	11110	11110	11111	11110	11000	11110	11110	11110	11000
19	10000	10000	10000	10000	11100	11111	10000	10000	10000	10000	11000	10000
9	11110	11000	11000	11110	11110	11111	11110	11000	11110	11110	11110	11000
13	11110	11000	11000	11110	11110	11111	11110	11000	11110	11110	11110	11000
12	11110	11000	11000	11110	11110	11111	11110	11000	11110	11110	11110	11000

Indegree												
Raw food	21	21	21	21	21	23	21	21	21	21	21	21
Superior food	11	10	9	14	16	23	14	10	10	11	15	10
Inferior food	10	1	0	14	16	22	14	2	10	10	10	2
Garbage	11	5	0	14	11	22	14	1	9	11	11	1
Feces	0	0	0	0	0	22	0	0	0	0	0	0
Total	53	37	30	63	64	112	63	34	50	53	57	34

29	21	35	26	34	4	15	6	19	9	13	12	Raw food	Superior food	Inferior food	Garbage	Feces	Total
0000	10000	11100	10000	11100	10000	10000	10000	10000	10000	10000	10000	23	5	4	1	1	34
1110	11110	11110	11110	11110	11000	11110	11000	11110	11000	11000	11000	23	23	15	15	1	77
1110	11110	11110	11110	11110	11110	11110	10000	11110	11110	11110	11110	23	22	22	22	1	90
1110	10000	11100	11110	10000	10000	10000	10000	10000	10000	10000	10000	23	5	5	4	1	38
0000	10000	11101	10000	10000	10000	10000	10000	10000	10000	10000	10000	23	2	2	1	1	29
0000	00000	11000	00000	00000	00000	00000	00000	00000	00000	00000	00000	1	1	0	0	0	2
1110	10000	11100	11110	10000	10000	10000	10000	10000	10000	10000	10000	23	5	5	4	1	38
1110	11110	11110	11110	11110	11000	11110	11000	11110	11010	11010	11010	23	23	16	19	1	82
1110	11010	11110	11110	11110	11000	11100	11000	11010	11000	11000	11000	23	23	9	13	1	69
0000	10000	11100	10000	11100	10000	10000	10000	10000	10000	10000	10000	23	5	4	1	1	34
0000	10000	11100	10000	11100	10000	10000	10000	10000	10000	10000	10000	23	4	4	1	1	33
1110	11110	11110	11110	11110	11000	11110	11000	11110	11010	11010	11010	23	23	16	19	1	82
0000	10000	11100	11110	10000	10000	10000	10000	10000	10000	10000	10000	23	5	5	4	1	38
0000	00000	11100	10000	11100	10000	10000	10000	10000	10000	10000	10000	23	5	4	1	1	34
0000	00000	00000	00000	00000	00000	00000	00000	00000	00000	00000	00000	1	1	0	0	0	2
1110	10000	11100	00000	10000	10000	10000	10000	10000	10000	10000	10000	23	5	5	4	1	38
0000	10000	11100	10000	00000	10000	10000	10000	10000	10000	10000	10000	23	2	2	1	1	29
1110	11110	11110	11110	11110	00000	11110	11000	11110	11010	11010	11010	23	23	15	19	1	81
1110	11110	11110	11110	11110	11000	00000	11000	11110	11000	11000	11000	23	23	14	13	1	74
1110	11110	11110	11110	11110	11000	11110	00000	11110	11010	11010	11010	23	22	15	19	1	80
0000	10000	11100	10000	11100	10000	10000	10000	00000	10000	10000	10000	23	5	4	1	1	34
1110	11110	11110	11110	11110	11000	11110	11000	11110	00000	11000	11000	23	23	15	15	1	77
1110	11110	11110	11110	11110	11000	11110	11000	11110	11000	00000	11000	23	23	15	15	1	77
1110	11110	11110	11110	11110	11000	11110	11000	11110	11000	11000	00000	23	23	15	15	1	77
	21	23	21	21	21	21	21	21	21	21	21	508					
14	11	23	14	16	10	10	9	11	10	10	10	301					
14	10	22	14	16	1	10	0	10	1	1	1			211			
14	11	11	14	11	1	9	0	11	5	5	5				207		
0	0	0	0	0	0	0	0	0	0	0	0					22	
63	53	79	63	64	33	50	30	53	37	37	36						1249

the giving of all five items by caste group i to caste group j (e.g., cell $c_{24,36}$ in Matrix 4). The entry 00000 in a cell c_{ij} signifies that no lines in the net are directed from i to j, and therefore that caste group i gives none of the items to caste group j (e.g., cell $c_{35,24}$ in Matrix 4). Using only the symbols 0 and 1, there are thirty-two possible combinations of entry for each cell. Given that transactions may or may not be symmetrical, and thus that it is possible for cell c_{ij} to have a different entry from cell c_{ji} (e.g., in Matrix 4, cell $c_{11,1}$ has an entry of 11000 but cell $c_{1,11}$ has an entry of 11110), the number of ways in which two adjacent points may be joined in terms of the five relations defined over the net is 1024 (that is, 32^2).

Such complexity cannot be analyzed directly, and we must first examine the structure of each relation separately before developing a procedure to bring the separate structures into juxtaposition within the net. If reachability matrices are computed for each of the five digraphs constituting the net, it is readily apparent that of any two points of which at least one can reach the other, none requires more than a distance of 1 to achieve this. In this particular example, the reachability matrices would therefore be identical with the adjacency matrices, save for an additional entry of 1 in each cell of the main upper-left/lower-right diagonal, signifying that each point could reach itself by a path of length 0 (since reaching is reflexive). Connectedness matrices can be computed from the reachability matrices. We need not show here the reachability matrices, but the connectedness matrix for the net that is computed from them is presented as Matrix 5.[14] From the connectedness matrix we can immediately identify, for each relation, those sets of points that are weakly (1−), unilaterally (2−), and strongly (3−) connected. It is readily apparent from the matrix that many points are unilaterally connected, in terms of each relation, and some are weakly connected, but the structure of the strongly connected points is not easy to perceive. The strong components of each relation in the net can be identified from the row entries of Matrix 5: each point j with which the point i at the head of the row is strongly connected in the ath relation has an entry of 3 in the ath element of the cell c_{ij}. If we take, for example, the first relation defined over the net, representing the transactions in raw foodstuffs, we can identify two strongly connected sets of points: [24, 11, 1, 27, 33, 30, 3, 14, 20, 25, 2, 29, 21, 26, 34, 4, 15, 6, 19, 9, 13, 12] and [35, 36]. These two strong components represent the two sets of caste groups engaged in symmetrical transactions in raw foods. For the relation representing the transactions in superior foods, three strong components can be identified: [11, 1, 3, 14, 2, 4, 15, 6, 9, 13, 12], [27, 30, 29, 26], and [36, 35]. For the relation representing the transactions in inferior food, three sets of strong components can be identified: [3, 2], [14, 15], [27, 30, 29, 26]; and for that representing garbage disposal, one set: [27, 20, 29, 26].

When we consider the intersection of the sets of points that form strong components in each relation, it is apparent that the sets (1, 2) and (35, 36) are strongly connected in terms of two relations—those representing trans-actions in raw and superior foods. The set (14, 15) is strongly connected in terms of the three relations representing transactions in raw, superior, and inferior foods, while the set (27, 30, 29, 26) is strongly connected in terms of the four relations representing the three transactions in food and the transaction in garbage disposal. While it would be a relatively simple matter to rewrite the matrix to bring such sets of strongly connected points together into blocks (as in the ordered Matrix 6), in general, the ordering of the strongly connected points in relation to one another and the ordering of the remaining points would still be undetermined.

We need to explore procedures for discovering what this order is, bear-ing in mind that the sets of points that are strongly connected in each rela-tion will have an equivalent order. Here we can make use of the theory of acyclic digraphs and its related procedures for assigning an order or level to each point in a graph. An acyclic digraph, as its name implies, contains no cycles, no sets of points that are mutually reachable, and no pairs of points whose connectedness index is 3. Any acyclic digraph can be ordered; this order will be either partial or complete. The adjacency matrix of an acyclic digraph can be ordered so that all its cell entries are in the upper-right triangle of the matrix. If all the cells in the upper-right triangle have an entry of 1, then the order is complete. Any digraph can be made acyclic by simply condensing its strong components and representing them in a condensed digraph as single points. The matrix of the condensed graph of the relation representing transactions in raw foodstuffs, for example, would contain only two points representing the two strong components, already identified: the set (here reordered) [1, . . . , 34] and the set [35, 36].

Acyclic digraphs can be ordered quite simply by utilizing the indegree and outdegree of their points. One of the simplest forms of acyclic digraph, with which readers will be familiar, is the formal bifurcating lineage dia-gram which is a structure that graph theorists call a "tree-from-a-point." The point, constituting the "head" of the tree, is a unique source and has an indegree of 0. Such a tree-from-a-point constitutes a partial order. If the point constituting the unique source is eliminated, the indegree of the points immediately below it falls to 0.[15] If these points are then eliminated, the indegree of the points to which they are joined similarly falls to 0. This process can be repeated until all the levels have been determined. If one were to start at the bottom of the tree, as it were, and work in terms of outdegree, then the points at the "lowest" level would be those that had an outdegree of 0. These would then be eliminated to obtain the next level and the process repeated until the unique source was obtained. For a tree-from-a-point having a unique source, whether levels were obtained by utilizing the indegree or the outdegree of the points would be immaterial, for the same number of levels would be obtained. However, for more complex acyclic digraphs, this would not be true in general. In terms of caste groups,

Unordered Connectedness Matrix of Net of Transactional Relations

	24	11	1	27	33	36	30	3	14	20	25	2
24	33333	32221	32221	31111	32221	22222	31111	32221	32221	31111	32111	32221
11	32221	33333	33221	32221	32221	22222	32221	33121	33221	32221	32221	33121
1	32221	33221	33333	32221	32221	22222	32221	33221	33221	32221	32221	33221
27	31111	32221	32221	33333	31111	22222	33331	32221	32221	31111	31111	32221
33	32211	32221	32221	31111	33333	22222	31111	32221	32221	32211	32211	32221
36	22222	22222	22222	22222	22222	33333	22222	22222	22222	22222	22222	22222
30	31111	32221	32221	33331	31111	22222	33333	32222	32221	31111	31111	32221
3	32221	33121	33221	32221	32221	22222	32221	33333	33221	32221	32221	33311
14	32221	33221	33221	32221	32221	22222	32221	33221	33333	32221	32221	33221
20	31111	32221	32221	31111	32211	22222	31111	32221	32221	33333	32111	32221
25	32111	32221	32221	31111	32211	22222	31111	32221	32221	32111	33333	32221
2	32221	33121	33221	32221	32221	22222	32221	33311	33221	32221	32221	33333
29	31111	32221	32221	33331	31111	22222	33331	32221	32221	31111	31111	32221
21	32221	32221	32221	31111	32211	22222	31111	32221	32221	31111	32111	32221
35	22210	22220	22220	22210	22210	33110	22210	22220	22220	22210	22210	22220
26	31111	32221	32221	33331	31111	22222	33331	32221	32221	31111	31111	32221
34	32211	32221	32221	31111	31111	22222	31111	32221	32221	32211	32211	32221
4	32221	33121	32221	32221	32221	22222	32221	33111	33221	32221	32221	33111
15	32221	33221	33221	32221	32221	22222	32221	33221	33311	32221	32221	33221
6	32221	33121	33111	32221	32221	22222	32221	33111	33221	32221	32221	33111
19	31111	32221	32221	31111	322Γ1	22222	31111	32221	32221	31111	32111	32221
9	32221	33111	33221	32221	32221	22222	32221	33121	33221	32221	32221	33121
13	32221	33111	33221	32221	32221	22222	32221	33121	33221	32221	32221	33121
12	32221	33111	33221	32221	32221	22222	32221	33121	33221	32221	32221	33121

29	21	35	26	34	4	15	6	19	9	13	12	
31111	31111	22210	31111	32211	32221	32221	32221	31111	32221	32221	32221	24
32221	32221	22220	32221	32221	33121	33221	33121	32221	33111	33111	33111	11
32221	32221	22220	32221	32221	33221	33221	33111	32221	33221	33221	33221	1
33331	31111	22210	33331	31111	32221	32221	32221	31111	32221	32221	32221	27
31111	32211	22210	31111	31111	32221	32221	32221	32221	32221	32221	32221	33
22222	22222	33110	22222	22222	22222	22222	22222	22222	22222	22222	22222	36
33331	31111	22210	33331	31111	32221	32221	32221	31111	32221	32221	32221	30
32221	32221	22220	32221	32221	33111	33221	33111	32221	33121	33121	33121	3
32221	32221	22220	32221	32221	33221	33311	33221	32221	33221	33221	33221	14
31111	31111	22210	31111	32211	32221	32221	32221	31111	32221	32221	32221	20
32211	32111	22210	31111	32211	32221	32221	32221	32111	32221	32221	32221	25
32221	32221	22220	32221	32221	33111	33221	33111	32221	33121	33121	33121	2
33333	31111	22210	33331	31111	32221	32221	32221	31111	32221	32221	32221	29
31111	33333	22210	31111	32211	32221	32221	32221	31111	32221	32221	32221	21
22210	22210	33333	22210	22210	22220	22220	22220	22210	22220	22220	22220	35
33331	31111	22210	33333	31111	32221	32221	32221	31111	32221	32221	32221	26
31111	32221	22210	31111	33333	32221	32221	32221	32211	32221	32221	32221	34
32221	32221	22220	32221	32221	33333	33221	33111	32221	33121	33121	33121	4
32221	32221	22220	32221	32221	33221	33333	33221	32221	33221	33221	33221	15
32221	32221	22220	32221	32221	33111	33221	33333	32221	33121	33121	33121	6
31111	31111	22210	31111	32221	32221	32221	32221	33333	32221	32221	32221	19
32221	32221	22220	32221	32221	33121	33221	33121	32221	33333	33111	33111	9
32221	32221	22220	32221	32221	33121	33221	33121	32221	33111	33333	33111	13
32221	32221	22220	32221	32221	33121	33221	33121	32221	33111	33111	33333	12

MATRIX 6

Ordered Connectedness Matrix of Net of Transactional Relations

	1	6	2	3	4	9	11	12	13	15	14	19
1	33333	33111	33221	33221	33221	33221	33221	33221	33221	33221	33221	32221
6	33111	33333	33111	33111	33111	33121	33121	33121	33121	33221	33221	32221
2	33221	33111	33333	33311	33111	33121	33121	33121	33121	33221	33221	32221
3	33221	33111	33311	33333	33111	33121	33121	33121	33121	33221	33221	32221
4	33221	33111	33111	33111	33333	33123	33121	33121	33121	33221	33221	32221
9	33221	33121	33121	33121	33121	33333	33111	33111	33111	33221	33221	32221
11	33221	33121	33121	33121	33121	33111	33333	33111	33111	33221	33221	32221
12	33221	33121	33121	33121	33121	33111	33111	33333	33111	33221	33221	32221
13	33221	33121	33121	33121	33121	33111	33111	33111	33333	33221	33221	32221
15	33221	33221	33221	33221	33221	33221	33221	33221	33221	33333	33311	32221
14	33221	33221	33221	33221	33221	33221	33221	33221	33221	33311	33333	32221
19	32221	32221	32221	32221	32221	32221	32221	32221	32221	32221	32221	33333
20	32221	32221	32221	32221	32221	32221	32221	32221	32221	32221	32221	31111
21	32221	32221	32221	32221	32221	32221	32221	32221	32221	32221	32221	31111
24	32221	32221	32221	32221	32221	32221	32221	32221	32221	32221	32221	31111
25	32221	32221	32221	32221	32221	32221	32221	32221	32221	32221	32221	32111
26	32221	32221	32221	32221	32221	32221	32221	32221	32221	32221	32221	31111
27	32221	32221	32221	32221	32221	32221	32221	32221	32221	32221	32221	31111
30	32221	32221	32221	32221	32221	32221	32221	32221	32221	32221	32221	31111
29	32221	32221	32221	32221	32221	32221	32221	32221	32221	32221	32221	31111
33	32221	32221	32221	32221	32221	32221	32221	32221	32221	32221	32221	32211
34	32221	32221	32221	32221	32221	32221	32221	32221	32221	32221	32221	32211
35	22220	22220	22220	22220	22220	22220	22220	22220	22220	22220	22220	22210
36	22222	22222	22222	22222	22222	22222	22222	22222	22222	22222	22222	22222

20	21	24	25	26	27	30	29	33	34	35	36	
32221	32221	32221	32221	32221	32221	32221	32221	32221	32221	22220	22222	1
32221	32221	32221	32221	32221	32221	32221	32221	32221	32221	22220	22222	6
32221	32221	32221	32221	32221	32221	32221	32221	32221	32221	22220	22222	2
32221	32221	32221	32221	32221	32221	32221	32221	32221	32221	22220	22222	3
32221	32221	32221	32221	32221	32221	32221	32221	32221	32221	22220	22222	4
32221	32221	32221	32221	32221	32221	32221	32221	32221	32221	22220	22222	9
32221	32221	32221	32221	32221	32221	32221	32221	32221	32221	22220	22222	11
32221	32221	32221	32221	32221	32221	32221	32221	32221	32221	22220	22222	12
32221	32221	32221	32221	32221	32221	32221	32221	32221	32221	22220	22222	13
32221	32221	32221	32221	32221	32221	32221	32221	32221	32221	22220	22222	15
32221	32221	32221	32221	32221	32221	32221	32221	32221	32221	22220	22222	14
31111	31111	31111	32111	31111	31111	31111	31111	32211	32211	22210	22222	19
33333	31111	31111	32111	31111	31111	31111	31111	32211	32211	22210	22222	20
31111	33333	31111	32111	31111	31111	31111	31111	32211	32211	22210	22222	21
31111	31111	33333	32111	31111	31111	31111	31111	32211	32211	22210	22222	24
32111	32111	32111	33333	31111	31111	31111	31111	32211	32211	22210	22222	25
31111	31111	31111	31111	33333	33331	33331	33331	31111	31111	22210	22222	26
31111	31111	31111	31111	33331	33333	33331	33331	31111	31111	22210	22222	27
31111	31111	31111	31111	33331	33331	33333	33331	31111	31111	22210	22222	30
31111	31111	31111	31111	33331	33331	33331	33333	31111	31111	22210	22222	29
32211	32211	32211	32211	31111	31111	31111	31111	33333	31111	22210	22222	33
32211	32211	32211	32211	31111	31111	31111	31111	31111	33333	22210	22222	34
22210	22210	22210	22210	22210	22210	22210	22210	22210	22210	33333	33110	35
22222	22222	22222	22222	22222	22222	22222	22222	22222	22222	33110	33333	36

this simply means that two caste groups ranked at the same level because they give to the same number of other caste groups may be differently ranked in terms of receiving. In determining the order of the points in the net, therefore, we must work with both outdegree and indegree and later develop a procedure for relating these two sets of orderings together for all five relations.[16]

Because none of the relations defined over the net representing the transactions forms an acyclic digraph except for that representing transactions in feces, we must form condensed graphs.[17] Once this has been done, we can begin to order the sets of points. As I have noted, the condensed graph representing the transactions in raw foodstuffs will consist of only two points, one representing the strong component[18] formed by the set [1, . . . , 34] and the other representing the strong component formed by the set [35, 36]. The outdegree of a point representing a strong component in a condensed graph is found from the union of the sets of lines directed from each point in the strong component of the uncondensed graph to other points not in the strong component. Similarly, the indegree of a point representing a strong component in the condensed graph is found from the union of the sets of lines directed to each point in the strong component of the uncondensed graph from other points not in the strong component. In the case of the strong components [1, . . . , 34] and [35, 36], the first will be represented by a point in the condensed graph with outdegree 1 and indegree 0 and the second, by a point with outdegree 0 and indegree 1. In terms of both indegree and outdegree, only two levels can be distinguished. These levels have been entered in Table 1.

In the condensed graph of the relation representing transactions in superior food, the strong components [1, . . . , 15], [26, 27, 29, 30], and [35, 36] are each represented by one point, while (19), (21), (24), (33), and (34) remain as separate points. In terms of the outdegree of the points in the condensed graph, five levels can be distinguished; they are, in order, {[1, . . . , 15]}, {(19), (20), (21), (24)}, {(25)}, {[26, . . . , 30], (33), (34)}, and {[35, 36]}. These levels are obtained in the following way. When the condensed graph is formed, the strong component [35, 36] becomes a single point having no outdegree. Eliminating this point from the condensed graph causes the outdegree of the points representing (33), (34), and the strong component [26, . . . , 30] to fall to 0. Eliminating these, we obtain (25) at the next level. By iterating the procedure successively, we obtain two further levels from the sets of points (19), (20), (21), (24), and [1, . . . , 15]. If we now consider the indegree of the points in the condensed graph, we find that the point representing the strong component [1, . . . , 15] has no indegree. This must be the unique source of the condensed graph. When this point is eliminated, the indegree of the points representing (19), (20), (21), (24), and the strong component [26, . . . , 30] fall to 0. Iterating the procedures we find in order the sets {[1, . . . , 15]}, {(19), (20), (21), (24), [26, . . . , 30]}, {(25)}, {(33) (34)}, {[35, 36]}. These procedures are then repeated for the condensed graphs of the digraphs representing the other three transactions. The orders obtained in terms of both indegree and outdegree have been entered in Table 1. Note that rank I in terms of outdegree (i.e., giving) means that points so ranked have a higher outdegree than all other points, while rank I in terms of indegree (i.e., receiving) means that points so ranked have a lower indegree than all other points. In terms of caste groups, this simply means that those that give to *more* other caste groups rank higher in terms of giving, and those that receive from *fewer* caste groups rank higher in terms of receiving.

When the points have been ordered for all relations in terms of both their indegree and outdegree, it becomes possible to derive a combined rank order for the set of points that constitute the net. The simplest way to do this is to classify as of equal rank those sets of points that have the same set of levels, in terms of their indegree and outdegree, for all relations in the net. Taking (1) and (6), for example, we observe from Table 1 that (1) is ranked I for all relations in terms of both indegree and outdegree. While (6) is ranked I in terms of indegree in all relations, it is only ranked I in terms of outdegree in the relations representing the transactions in raw and superior food and feces removal; it is ranked II in terms of the relations representing the transactions in inferior food and garbage disposal. This differentiates its set of ranks from that of (1) and makes it second in the combined rank order. If these procedures are iterated for all points and all relations, eleven ranks can be distinguished, as shown in Table 1. Caste groups of equal rank have been bracketed. There is no way of differentiating them.[19]

THE GRAPH OF INCLUSION

The ranked sets of caste groups given in Table 1 can be presented in a different form by means of what I have termed a "graph of inclusion." This brings out more clearly the structure of the transactions among caste groups and enables anomalies to be perceived. The graph of inclusion is presented in Figure 4; it is acyclic and can be assigned levels. In some respects it is similar to a semilattice (cf. Dubisch 1963), but since it represents the operations of intersection as well as union, has a horizontal as well as a vertical order, and has certain sets repeated at a number of levels, it is not a strict semilattice.

The unique source of the graph of inclusion is level A, and the directed lines from it indicate those subsets of which it is composed. A directed line from a point *i* to a point *j* can be read as "*i* includes *j*." The sets of caste groups have been indicated, together with the criteria which generated

TABLE 1 Rank Order of Caste Groups in Kishan Garhi by (1) Combined Level Assignments, (2) Net Scores (Marriott 1968), (3) Opinions (Marriott 1968)

Caste Group	Caste Code Number	Level Assignment										Rank		
		Outdegree (giving)					Indegree (receiving)					By Combined Level Assignment	By Net Scores	By Opinion
		Raw Food	Superior Food	Inferior Food	Garbage	Feces	Raw Food	Superior Food	Inferior Food	Garbage	Feces			
Sanadhya Brahman	1	I	I	I	I	I	I	I	I	I	I	I	I	I
Maithil Carpenter	6	I	I	I	I	I	I	I	I	I	I	II	II	II
Jat Cultivator	2	I	I	II	II	I	I		II	II	I	III	III	II
Barahseni Merchant	3	I	I	II	II	I	I		II	II	I	III	III	II
Kulasrestha Scribe	4	I	I	II	II	I	I		II	II	I	III	IV	II
Jogi Devotee	9	I	I	II	II	I	I		II	III	I	IV	IV	III
Phulmali Gardener	11	I	I	II	III	I	I		II	III	I	IV	IV	III
Kachi Cultivator	12	I	I	II	III	I	I		III	III	I	IV	IV	IV
Baghele Goatherd	13	I	I	II	III	I	I		III	IV	I	IV	IV	V
Thakur Barber	15	I	I	III	IV	I	I		III	IV	I	V	V	V
Turai Waterman	14	I	I	III	IV	I	I		IV	IV	I	V	V	VI
Gola Potter	19	I	II	IV	V	I	I	II	IV	V	I	VI	VI	VI
Darzi Tailor	20	I	II	IV	V	I	I	II	IV	V	I	VI	VII	VI
Karhera Cottoncarder	21	I	II	IV	V	I	I	II	IV	V	I	VI	VII	VII
Kali Weaver	24	I	II	IV	V	I	I	II	IV	V	I	VI	VII	VIII
Khatik Cultivator	25	I	III	V	V	I	I	III	IV	V	I	VII	VIII	VIII
Muslim Faqir Devotee	26	I	IV	V	V	I	I	II	IV	V	I	VIII	IX	IX
Muslim Mirasi Singer	27	I	IV	V	V	I	I	II	IV	V	I	VIII	IX	IX
Muslim Manihar Bangleman	30	I	IV	V	V	I	I	II	IV	V	I	VIII	IX	X
Muslim Teli Oilman	29	I	IV	V	V	I	I	II	IV	V	I	VIII	IX	X
Jatav Leatherworker	33	I	IV	V	V	I	I	IV	IV	V	I	IX	X	XI
Mathuriya Washerman	34	I	IV	V	V	I	I	IV	V	V	I	IX	X	XI
Kanjar Hunter	35	II	V	VI	VI	II	II	V	VI	V	I	X	XI	XII
Bhangi Sweeper	36	II	V	VI	VI	II	II	V	VI	VI	II	XI	XII	XIII

FIGURE 4

Graph of Inclusion

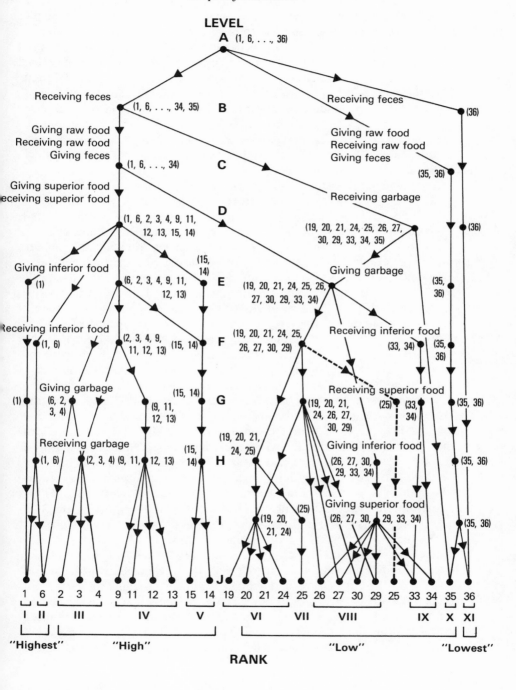

LEVEL

A (1, 6, . . ., 36)

Receiving feces   Receiving feces
(1, 6, . . ., 34, 35) B   (36)

Giving raw food   Giving raw food
Receiving raw food   Receiving raw food
Giving feces   Giving feces
(1, 6, . . ., 34) C   (35, 36)

Giving superior food
Receiving superior food   Receiving garbage
D
(1, 6, 2, 3, 4, 9, 11,   (19, 20, 21, 24, 25, 26, 27,   (36)
12, 13, 15, 14)   30, 29, 33, 34, 35)

Giving inferior food   (15,   Giving garbage   (35,
(1)   14)   E   (19, 20, 21, 24, 25, 26,   36)
     (6, 2, 3, 4, 9, 11,   27, 30, 29, 33, 34)
     12, 13)

Receiving inferior food   Receiving inferior food
(1, 6)   (2, 3, 4, 9,   (15, 14) F (19, 20, 21, 24, 25,   (33, 34) (35,
              11, 12, 13)   26, 27, 30, 29)   36)

(1)   Giving garbage   (15, 14) G   Receiving superior food   (25) (33,   (35, 36)
             (6, 2,   (9, 11,   (19, 20, 21,   34)
             3, 4)   12, 13)   24, 26, 27,
                                               30, 29)

             Receiving garbage (15,   (19, 20, 21,   Giving inferior food
(1, 6)   (2, 3, 4)(9, 11, 12, 13) 14) H 24, 25)   (26, 27, 30,   (35, 36)
                                                           29, 33, 34)

                                                 (25) Giving superior food
                                              (19, 20,   (26, 27, 30, 29, 33, 34)
                                          I   21, 24)   (35, 36)

1 6   2 3 4   9 11 12 13   15 14   J 19 20 21 24 25 26 27 30 29 25 33 34 35 36

I II   III   IV   V   VI   VII   VIII   IX   X   XI

"Highest"   "High"   "Low"   "Lowest"

RANK

them. Below level A, each point represents a subset of caste groups of equivalent rank in terms of the stated transactional criterion. By tracing the path from a point at a given level to points at a lower level, one is able to observe how the set it represents is decomposed into subsets as the transactional criteria vary. Note that at certain levels the criteria of differentiation among those caste groups ranked "high" (1, 6, . . . , 14) are different from those ranked "low" (19, 20, . . . , 36). In addition, those caste groups ranked "high" generate one less level (A through H) than those ranked "low" (A through I). This reflects the fact that transactions among caste groups ranked "low" generate one more rank than those among caste groups ranked "high." The procedures applied in constructing the graph of inclusion are given in the appendix.

Beginning at the source of the graph, we see that the set of caste groups (1, 6, . . . , 36) is differentiated into two subsets, (1, 6, . . . , 34, 35) and (36), at level B, the Bhangi Sweeper caste group (36) being differentiated from all others in terms of the receiving of feces. At level C, three criteria, the giving and receiving of raw food and the giving of feces, differentiate the Kanjar Hunters[20] (35), who now form a subset with the Bhangi Sweepers (36). At level D, a significant differentiation occurs when the subset (1, 6, . . . , 14) is formed by the criteria of the giving and receiving of superior food. It is at this level that caste groups categorized by villagers as "high" are differentiated from the rest. Among those caste groups categorized as "low," the criteria of differentiation change at this level. Here it is the receiving of garbage that differentiates the subset (19, . . . , 35) from the Bhangi Sweeper caste group. At level E, the giving of inferior food differentiates the high castes into three sets, the Sanadhya Brahmans (1) being differentiated for the first time from the Thakur Barber and the Turai Waterman caste groups (15, 14) and from the subset (6, 2, . . . , 13). Among low castes at the same level, the subset (19, . . . , 34) is differentiated from the subset formed by the Bhangi Sweeper and Kanjar Hunter caste groups in terms of the giving of garbage. It is at this level, therefore, in terms of these two transactional criteria, that those caste groups categorized as "high" (1, . . . , 14), as "low" (19, . . . , 34), and as "lowest" (35, 36) are clearly differentiated. At the next level (F), among the high castes, the Sanadhya Brahmans (1) form a subset with the Maithil Carpenters (6) in terms of the receiving of inferior food, while the subset (2, 3, . . . , 13) is also differentiated. Among high castes at level G, the Sanadhya Brahmans are once more differentiated in terms of the giving of garbage, as is the subset formed by the Jogi Devotee, Phulmali Gardener, Kachi Cultivator, and Baghele Goatherd caste groups (9, . . . , 13). This differentiation is repeated for the latter subset at level H in terms of the receiving of garbage, to place it fourth in the final rank order. In addition, at level H, by the same criterion, the Jat Cultivator, Barahseni Merchant, and the Kulasrestha Scribe caste groups (2, 3, 4) are finally differentiated and placed third in rank. The Thakur Barber and Turai Waterman caste groups (15, 14), differentiated at level G, are placed fifth in rank. Note that the Maithil Carpenters (6) are differentiated and paired with the Sanadhya Brahmans at level F in terms of the receiving of inferior food and at level H in terms of the receiving of garbage, which places them in the category of highest rank. However, they do not form a set with the Sanadhya Brahmans at levels E or G and are thus ranked second.

Among low castes from level F onward, the position is more complex than among high castes. At level F the Kanjar Hunter and Bhangi Sweeper caste groups (35, 36) are once more differentiated, and this differentiation is repeated at all subsequent levels. The Jatav Leatherworker and Mathuriya Washerman caste groups (33, 34), however, while differentiated at levels F and G by the receiving of inferior and superior food, respectively (differentiations which place them ninth in the final rank order), form subsets at levels H and I with the Muslim caste groups (26, 27, 30, 29). The formation of these subsets in terms of the giving of inferior food at level H and superior food at level I brings the Muslim caste groups into eighth position in the rank order.

The Gala Potter, Darzi Tailor, Karhera Cottoncarder, and Khali Weaver caste groups (19, . . . , 24) are differentiated from the Muslim caste groups (26, 27, 30, 29) at level I by the giving of superior food and, at level H, from the subset formed by the Muslim and Khatik Cultivator caste groups by the giving of inferior food, to place them in sixth position in the rank order. The anomalous position of the Khatik Cultivator caste group (25) appears clearly at levels G and I. At level G, in terms of the receiving of superior food, it is differentiated from, and ranked above, the Jatav Leatherworker and Muthuriya Washerman caste groups (33, 34). However, at level I, the Khatik Cultivator caste group is ranked above the Muslim caste groups in terms of the giving of superior food, and it has been assigned seventh position in the rank order, the giving relationship being weighted higher than the receiving one.

It is clear from the graph of inclusion that, among high caste groups (1, . . . , 14), the transactions in inferior food and garbage provide the most significant criteria for differentiating among them. Among the low caste groups (19, . . . , 36), however, the most important criteria of differentiation are the transactions in inferior and superior food. For both high and low caste groups, the transactions in inferior food are the most discriminating, producing eight differentiated subsets. Further deductions could be made from the analysis, such as the significance which the transactions of the middle range of caste groups have for differentiating the rank order and so forth, but this would be to repeat points that Marriott ably makes in his analysis.

THE PROBLEM OF ISOMORPHISM

If we consider now the elements of the analytic model that Marriott (1968) constructed, we see that they were derived by a number of acts of abstraction. From the observed behavior of villagers and from their statements about their behavior, Marriott constructed what Barnes (1968) would term "partial networks" of transactions. He then inferred that these partial networks could be abstracted further and interpreted as relations holding between corporate caste groups. The mechanism, or explanatory principle, of his model was that transactions among caste groups were also symbolic statements about rank in which, for those in food, the giver ranks higher than the receiver and, for those in services, the receiver ranks higher than the provider.

In reanalyzing his data, I first assumed an isomorphism between his analytic model and the structure of a net, the points of the net representing the caste groups and its lines representing the five transactional relations. I then decomposed the net into five digraphs, each representing a single relation. The mechanism of Marriott's model was then assumed to be isomorphic with the operation of assigning levels to an acyclic graph. Four of the digraphs were not acyclic, however. In order to make them so, I constructed condensed graphs for each, in which sets of points representing the caste groups that engaged in symmetrical transactions among themselves but in asymmetrical transactions with others were treated as strong components and condensed to single points. For each condensed graph, each point was then assigned two levels: an ascending one in terms of the union of the sets of lines directed *to* each of the points of the set forming the strong component, and a descending one, similarly, in terms of the union of the sets of lines directed *from* each of the points in the set. This procedure appears to have created difficulties only in the case of the points representing caste groups 14 and 15. These groups were accorded equal rank in terms of their level assignments in the condensed graphs, but in fact they differ in terms of their outdegree in the relation representing transactions in inferior food. Hence the graph theoretical procedures yield eleven ranks compared with the twelve ranks Marriott derived using net scores. Finally, having determined levels for each relation, I ordered the points of the net by combining descending and ascending levels for all five relations. This order was then assumed to be isomorphic with the order which the mechanism of Marriott's model would logically generate.

The application of graph theory to the analysis of manifold and multiplex relationships raises the problem of isomorphism particularly acutely, although it is an issue whenever mathematical procedures are applied to analytic models (cf. Cicourel 1964; Abell 1968). Isomorphism concerns us at three levels: between the analytic model and reality, between the analytic model and some mathematical structure of graph theory, and between the mechanism of the analytic model and the mathematical operations performed on the graph. Unless, in some definable sense, these isomorphisms exist, one cannot make meaningful inferences from the structure of a graph to an analytic model and from this to reality.

In constructing analytic models we abstract, condense, and simplify, hoping thereby to produce a structure whose elements can be manipulated to enable us to understand better relationships among phenomena deemed to be of significance in reality. The degree of isomorphism between the model and reality depends on the correspondence between the properties of the model's elements and the properties of the phenomena they represent. In general, the higher the level of abstraction, the less is the correspondence and the greater the difficulty in making inferences from the model to reality. Models constructed of elements at high levels of abstraction are elegant structures but often difficult to apply to any specific set of social phenomena. A balance has to be struck, therefore, between producing an elegant structure at a high level of abstraction and producing a model that is so little removed from the phenomena it seeks to represent that its very complexity defeats the object of its construction: the meaningful manipulation of its elements.

In addition to depending on the level of abstraction, the explanatory power of a model depends on the mechanism or explanatory principle employed in it. Given that most models used in social anthropology and sociology are iconic (cf. Willer 1967: 37), their mechanisms are derived directly from the behavior of the phenomena they represent. In Marriott's (1968) model, for example, the mechanism was the transaction. This was assumed to generate the differentiation in rank among caste groups. Those who have employed the concept of social network in analytic models have, in the main, relied on one of three mechanisms: communication of norms and values leading to normative consensus (e.g., Bott 1964), transactions involving the exchange of goods and services for political support (e.g., A. C. Mayer 1961; Kapferer 1969), or processes of alliance and opposition leading to the periodic restructuring of relationships (e.g., Jongmans 1973).

Models can be manipulated logically and verbally, and in certain cases mathematical procedures can be employed to perform certain manipulative operations. It is clear from my reanalysis of Marriott's data that different mathematical procedures may produce different results for the same model. In this case, the differences were trivial, but in other cases they could be considerable. The only tests ultimately of which procedures have the most utility are in terms of logical consistency, explanatory adequacy, and generality of application.

In applying graphs to analytic models, one must take great care in defining relationships that are to be manipulated. In general, the minimum requirements for applying graph theory are that relationships can be classified and ordered. This seems initially attractive, but even these minimal

requirements raise difficulties. Basically, they require one to be able to
state that all relationships in a set that one has chosen to abstract are logically equivalent. This requires particular care in ascertaining the level of
abstraction at which one is working. There is no utility in attempting to
analyze by graph theoretical procedures relationships which are not conceptually equivalent. The widely used two-dimensional topographic representation of a social network by means of points and lines is, I suspect, a
prime source of error in this regard. Operations are performed on this structure as if all the relationships it contained were conceptually equivalent.
Density measures, for example, are computed for relationships of different
types and different orders of abstraction. That is why I have suggested that
a net—a multirelational structure—with each of its relationships precisely
defined, is the correct graph theoretical structure to apply to the analysis of
the multiplex and manifold relationships that occur in such models.

Finally, and perhaps most critically, there is the question of isomorphism
between the mechanism of the analytic model and the mathematical operations performed on a graph to simulate its operation. In the reanalysis of
Marriott's data, the issue was raised when I assumed an isomorphism
between the operations of assigning levels to an acyclic graph and the rank
conferred by transactions among caste groups. Earlier I indicated problems
that are likely to arise when one assumes an isomorphism between reachability in a graph and communication of norms and values in a social network. Here the central issue is that while in a graph some point may be
reachable from another by a path of a certain length, the inference cannot
be made that such communication actually occurs in a social network
between the two individuals represented by the points. It follows, therefore, that the further inference that the more complete a graph the greater
is the normative consensus in the social network is also invalid. Reachability in a graph is a necessary condition for such communications to occur
but not a sufficient condition.

Graph theory offers a wide choice of procedures that may be suitable
isomorphs for the mechanisms of analytic models. In terms of the problems
discussed in this paper, the graph theoretical procedures employing such
concepts as joining, reaching, connectedness, vulnerability, and level
assignment have obvious relevance. For other types of problems there are
more powerful procedures, such as the concept of balance in signed graphs
and the possibility of analyzing stochastic models by applying concepts
from the theory of networks.[21] The procedures for each category of graph
raise their own specific set of problems in interpretation and application. In
general, as one moves from the application of undirected to directed
graphs, from signed graphs to networks, the level of abstraction is raised
and the demands on one's theoretical understanding and the nature of the
data collected grow. I have restricted myself in this paper to areas where I

think, given the problems with which we are at present concerned and the levels of measurement and abstraction at which we work, graph theory may have applications. Graph theory provides a quite exciting set of mathematical structures, many of which are compatible with the analytic models that social anthropologists construct and the types of data they collect. It will come, one hopes, to be more widely applied.

APPENDIX: PROCEDURES FOR THE CONSTRUCTION OF THE GRAPH OF INCLUSION

The graph of inclusion (Figure 4) is constructed by applying the following procedures.

1. The universal set of all caste groups being considered (1, 6, . . . , 36) is represented by a point as the unique source of the graph.

2. From Table 1, the ranked subsets of caste groups are listed in order of size and a note made of their rank and of the transactional criteria which generate them. (For example, (1, 6, . . . , 35), I, receiving feces; (1, 6, . . . , 34), I, giving raw food; . . . ; (2, 3, . . . , 13), II, receiving inferior food; . . . ; (2, 3, 4), II, receiving garbage; . . . ; (35, 36), II, giving raw food; etc.)

3. To assign levels to the points of the graph, take the universal set (1, 6, . . . , 36). Identify the largest subset listed. Delete those caste groups from the universal set of which this subset is composed. Examine the remaining caste groups of the universal set. Identify from the list the largest subset into which the remainder can be formed. Delete those caste groups from the universal set of which this subset is composed. Iterate the procedures until all caste groups have been allocated to subsets. Assign each subset a point. Arrange the points at the same level according to the designated rank order of the subsets they represent, such that points representing subsets of caste groups designated "high" are to the left of the graph and those designated "low" are to the right.

4. (a) Record the criterion or criteria that generated the subsets.

   (b) When more than one criterion generates the same set of subsets (e.g., level C, where the subsets (1, 6, . . . , 36) and (35, 36) are generated by three criteria: the giving and receiving of raw food and the giving of feces), the subsets are held to have the same level assignment and are each represented by only one point.

   (c) Where more than one criterion generates one or more subsets, only those subsets that are generated by the least number of criteria being applied at that level are represented by points.

For example, if the subsets of caste groups used in the construction of level E, together with the criteria that generate them, are listed (assuming that subsets and their associated criteria used in the construction of superior levels have been deleted), one obtains the following table.

Subsets	Transactional criteria
(19, 20, . . . , 34)	Giving garbage.
(6, 2, . . . , 13)	Giving inferior food.
(15, 14)	Giving inferior food, receiving inferior food, giving garbage, receiving garbage.
(35, 36)	Giving superior food, receiving superior food, receiving inferior food, giving garbage.
(1)	Giving inferior food, giving garbage.

Inspection shows that of the transactions that generate the subsets (15, 14,), (35, 36), and (1), giving inferior food and giving garbage are common to all three, while giving garbage alone generates the subset (19, 20, . . . , 34) and giving inferior food alone generates the subset (6, 2, . . . , 13). Arbitrarily, but following the general principle of parsimony, the subsets (1) and (15, 14), generated by the giving of inferior food, have been grouped with the subset (6, 2, . . . , 13), generated by the same criterion, and, similarly, the subset (35, 36), generated by the giving of garbage, has been grouped with the subset (19, 20, . . . , 34).

5. Delete from the list all subsets that are generated by transactional criteria used in the construction of the level.

6. To construct the next level, take the universal set and identify the largest subset remaining in the list. Repeat the procedures given in steps 3 and 4 above.

7. (a) When all levels have been constructed and all subsets of caste groups have been represented by points, join the points by directed lines such that a point j of an inferior level is joined by a line directed from a point i of a superior level and the statement "j represents a proper subset of i" holds.

   (b) Delete all redundant directed lines until the minimum number compatible with step (a) remains and no point is disconnected.

ACKNOWLEDGMENTS

An earlier version of this paper was presented to a seminar on Network Approaches at the Afrika-Studie Centrum, Leiden, in 1969. A revised version was presented to a staff seminar in the Department of Sociology, Keele University, Staffordshire, in 1970. I thank the members of these seminars for their helpful comments. I am most grateful to Professor John Barnes, who made detailed comments on a later draft, and also to Dr. J. Clyde Mitchell and Professor Bruce Kapferer, who, at various times, have commented on the argument and encouraged its development. Needless to say, the responsibility for the argument and for any remaining errors and omissions remains entirely mine.

NOTES

1. "Manifold" is a useful term suggested to me by the late Professor Max Gluckman. It enables a multiplex relationship, based on different *normative* contents, to be distinguished from a relationship containing a number of *instrumental* or *transactional* contents. Of course, a relationship can, and usually will be, both manifold and multiplex.

2. Throughout I write in terms of lines, directed and undirected, and of points, rather than in terms of the edges, arcs, vertices, and nodes of the mathematician.

3. In general, I have written of representing social networks, or abstractions from them, as graphs. No complex system containing many different types of relationships can be graphed adequately. Each abstracted relationship is best represented by means of an adjacency matrix. I discuss the adjacency matrix below.

4. For an extended account of directed graphs, see Harary et al. (1965). I have relied heavily on their treatment of directed graphs in my discussion. For other treatments of graphs, see particularly Berge (1962), Busacker and Saaty (1965), Flament (1963), and Ore (1962). For bibliographies consult Abell (1968), Barnes (1969), and in particular Fiedler (1964).

5. Harary et al. (1965) do not distinguish between *asymmetrical* and *nonsymmetrical* relations. The distinction between them is important.

6. A sequence is *open* if its initial and terminal points differ and *closed* if they are the same (Harary et al. 1965: 409).

7. Adjacency matrices are also useful for systematically recording data about social networks. It is surprising that they are not more widely employed, and their use should be encouraged.

8. $b_{ij}(p_k) = (1/g_{ij}) [g_{ij}(p_k)]$, where $b_{ij}(p_k)$ is the probability that p_k falls on a randomly selected geodesic joining p_i and p_j.

9. The expression is
$$C_B(p_k) = \sum_{i<j}^{n} \sum^{n} b_{ij}(p_k)$$
where $C_B(p_k)$ is the index of overall centrality and n is the number of points in the graph.

10. max $C_B(p_k) = (n^2 - 3n + 2)/2$, and hence
$$C_B^1(p_k) = \frac{C_B(p_k)}{(n^2 - 3n + 2)/2} = \frac{2C_B(p_k)}{n^2 - 3n + 2}$$
where max $C_B(p_k)$ is the upper limit of $C_B(p_k)$ and $C_B^1(p_k)$ is the relative centrality index of any point in the graph.

11. In fact, he was not able to observe all types of transactions among all caste groups but, to complete the cells in his matrices, he ascertained from village members what generally occurred in the cases in which his observations were deficient.

12. Raw food *(sidhā)* comprises such foods as flour, sugar, ghee, and whole fruit; superior cooked food *(pakkā)* comprises foods prepared with ghee and expensive vegetables such as red squash and potatoes; inferior cooked food *(kaccā)* comprises such foods as dry-baked barley cakes, certain types of pickles, the cheaper curries, and dried pulses. Garbage *(juthā)* is food left on plates after eating, which is considered to have been polluted by the saliva from the mouth of the eater (Marriott 1968: 142–144).

13. The caste code numbers in the matrices have been taken from Table 1 of Marriott's paper. The numerical order is not complete. The key is given in Table 1. I

have randomized the order of the castes in Marriott's adjacency matrices, so there is no direct correspondence between the order of the castes in Matrix 4 and the order of the castes in the adjacency matrices he presents.

14. The reachability matrix is obtained by performing the operation $(A + I)^{P-1\#}$, where I is the identity matrix, A the adjacency matrix, P the number of points, and the symbol # indicates that the rules of Boolean arithmetic apply. The connectedness index for each pair of points in each relation is obtained from $R_a + R'_a + J$, where R_a is the reachability matrix of the ath relation, R'_a is its transpose, and J is the universal matrix (each of whose cell entries is 1). For each relation, the connectedness index for the ath relation for each cell, therefore, is given by $r_{a_{ij}} + r_{a_{ji}} + 1$.

For example, if two caste groups i and j engage in symmetrical transactions in, say, raw food, the cells $r_{a_{ij}}$ and $r_{a_{ji}}$ in the reachability matrix of the digraph representing these transactions will each contain an entry of 1. The connectedness index given by the sum $r_{a_{ij}} + r_{a_{ji}} + 1$ will be 3. If caste group i engages in an asymmetrical transaction with caste group j, then, if the entry in the cell $r_{a_{ij}}$ is 1, the entry in the cell $r_{a_{ji}}$ will be 0. The connectedness index will be 2. If neither caste group engages in transactions (but both are engaged in transactions with others), then the cell entries $r_{a_{ij}}$ and $r_{a_{ji}}$ will both be 0, giving a connectedness index of 1. In order to establish that no points of a digraph are disconnected (and therefore have a connectedness index of 0), its adjacency matrix is examined to see if there are any points with an outdegree and an indegree of 0 which would signify that they are not joined to any other points. In the case considered, only the digraph representing transactions in feces contains a disconnected point, (35), since this point has no indegree or outdegree.

15. In terms ot the analogy, if one removes the first ancestor from a lineage diagram, his immediate descendants then become "first ancestors."

16. Here I depart from the method which Harary et al. (1965) develop for deriving levels from an acyclic digraph that constitutes a partial order. Their method, essentially, assigns a level to a point in terms of its longest path from the source of the graph (cf. Harary et al. 1965: 270 et seq., Theorem 10.2 and its corollaries).

17. The connectedness matrix of an acyclic digraph can be ordered so that it will have cell entries in the upper-right triangle of either 2 or 1, except for the entries of 3 in the main diagonal. Any pair of points that is 3-connected will form a cycle. Strictly speaking, the graph representing transactions in feces is disconnected since caste group 35 is 0-connected to all other points (see Matrix 6). This creates a slight problem of ordering since, while the other points, treated as forming an acyclic subgraph, can be assigned levels, the order of caste group 35 is indeterminate. For this one relation, I have ranked caste group 35 according to its indegree and outdegree. In terms of receiving feces, caste group 35 has been ranked with caste groups 1, . . . , 34 since they, like it, do not receive, and in terms of giving, it has been ranked with caste group 36, since neither gives to any other caste groups.

18. Sets of points that constitute strong components are enclosed in square brackets: [35, 36]; other sets (and single points not representing strong components in condensed graphs) are enclosed in parentheses: (19, 20), (21), (24); sets of points constituting an assigned level are represented by braces: {[35, 36], (19), (20)}.

19. The Khatik Cultivator caste group (25) is anomalous. The reason for assigning it rank VII is considered during the discussion of the graph of inclusion in the following section.

20. The anomalous position of the Kanjar Hunter caste group in this one relation has already been noted in footnote 17.

21. Signed graphs have positive and negative values attached to their lines and can be used for interpreting such logically opposite relations as liking and disliking, alliance and opposition. For an interesting application of signed graphs to the interpretation of relationships of alliance and opposition, see Jongmans (1973). Networks or valued graphs have values attached to their lines. They can be used to interpret flows through structures and can be applied to the study of such phenomena as marriage connubia, migration, occupational mobility, and so forth (cf. Busacker and Saaty 1965).

REFERENCES

Abell, P. 1968. Measurement in sociology. *Sociology*, 2: 1–20.
Barnes, J. A. 1968. Networks and political process. In M. J. Swartz, ed. *Local Level Politics*, pp. 107–130. Chicago: Aldine. Republished in J. C. Mitchell, ed., 1969, *Social Networks in Urban Situations*, pp. 57–76. Manchester: Manchester University Press.
———. 1969. Graph theory and social networks: a technical comment on connectedness and connectivity. *Sociology*, 3: 215–232.
Bavelas, A. 1960. Communication patterns in task oriented groups. In D. Cartwright and A. Zander, eds., *Group Dynamics: Research and Theory*, Vol. 3, pp. 669–682. Evanston: Row Peterson.
Beauchamp, M. A. 1965. An improved index of centrality. *Behavioural Sciences*, 10: 161–163.
Berge, C. 1962. *The Theory of Graphs and Its Applications*. London: Methuen.
Boissevain, J. F., and J. C. Mitchell, eds. 1973. *Network Analysis: Studies in Human Interaction*. The Hague: Mouton.
Bott, E. J. 1955. Urban families: conjugal roles and social networks. *Human Relations*, 8: 345–384.
———. 1957. *Family and Social Network: Roles, Norms and External Relations in Ordinary Urban Families*. London: Tavistock.
———. 1964. Family, kinship and marriage. In M. Douglas, G. Barry, J. Bronowski, J. Fisher, and J. Huxley, eds., *Man in Society: Patterns of Human Organisation*, pp. 82–103. London: Macdonald.
Busacker, R. G., and T. L. Saaty. 1965. *Finite Graphs and Networks: An Introduction with Applications*. New York: McGraw-Hill.
Cicourel, A. V. 1964. *Method and Measurement in Sociology*. Toronto: Collier-Macmillan.
Dubisch, R. 1963. *Lattices to Logic*. New York: Blaisdell.
Epstein, A. L. 1961. The network and urban social organisation. *Rhodes-Livingstone Journal*, 29: 29–62.
Fiedler, M., ed. 1964. *Theory of Graphs and Its Applications: Proceedings of the Symposium held in Smolence in June, 1963*. Prague: Czechoslovak Academy of Sciences.
Flament, C. 1963. *Applications of Graph Theory to Group Structure*. Englewood Cliffs, N.J.: Prentice-Hall.
Frankenberg, R. J. 1966. *Communities in Britain: Social Life in Town and Country*. Harmondsworth: Penguin Books.
Freeman, L. C. 1977. A set of measures of centrality based on betweenness. *Sociometry*, 40: 35–41.
Garbett, G. K. 1968. The application of optical coincidence cards to matrices of digraphs of social networks. *Sociology*, 2: 313–331.

232   G. K. GARBETT

Harary, F. 1959. Status and contrastatus. *Sociometry,* 22: 23–43.
Harary, F., R. Z. Norman, and D. Cartwright. 1965. *Structural Models: An Intro-
duction to the Theory of Directed Graphs.* New York: John Wiley and Sons.
Jongmans, D. G. 1973. Politics on the village level. In J. F. Boissevain and J. C.
Mitchell, eds., *Network Analysis: Studies in Human Interaction,* pp. 167–217.
The Hague: Mouton.
Kapferer, B. 1969. Norms and the manipulation of relationships in a work context.
In J. C. Mitchell, ed., *Social Networks in Urban Situations,* pp. 181–244. Man-
chester: Manchester University Press.
———. 1973. Social network and conjugal role in urban Zambia: towards a refor-
mulation of the Bott hypothesis. In J. F. Boissevain and J. C. Mitchell, eds.,
Network Analysis: Studies in Human Interaction, pp. 83–110. The Hague:
Mouton.
Kephart, W. M. 1950. Quantitative analysis of intragroup relationships. *American
Journal of Sociology,* 55: 544–549.
Marriott, M. 1968. Caste ranking and food transactions: a matrix analysis. In M.
Singer and B. Cohn, eds., *Structure and Change in Indian Society,* pp. 133–
172. Chicago: Aldine.
Mayer, A. C. 1966. The significance of quasi-groups in the study of complex soci-
eties. In M. Banton, ed., *The Social Anthropology of Complex Societies,* pp.
97–122. ASA Monograph No. 4. London: Tavistock.
Mayer, P. 1961. *Tribesmen or Townsmen: Conservatism and the Process of Urban-
isation in a South African City.* Capetown: Oxford University Press.
Mitchell, J. C. 1973. Networks, norms and institutions. In J. F. Boissevain and J.
C. Mitchell, eds., *Network Analysis: Studies in Human Interaction,* pp. 15–35.
The Hague: Mouton.
———, ed. 1969. *Social Networks in Urban Situations.* Manchester: Manchester
University Press.
Niemeijer, R. 1973. Some applications of the notion of density. In J. F. Boissevain
and J. C. Mitchell, eds., *Network Analysis: Studies in Human Interaction,* pp.
45–64. The Hague: Mouton.
Ore, O. 1962. *Theory of Graphs.* Colloquium Publications, Vol. 38. Providence:
American Mathematical Society.
Sabidussi, G. 1966. The centrality index of a graph. *Psychometrika,* 31: 581–603.
Singer, M., and B. Cohn, eds. 1968. *Structure and Change in Indian Society.* Chi-
cago: Aldine.
Sweetser, D. A. 1967. Path consistency in directed graphs and social structure.
American Journal of Sociology, 73: 287–293.
Wheeldon, P. D. 1969. The operation of voluntary associations and personal net-
works in the political processes of an inter-ethnic community. In J. C. Mitchell,
ed., *Social Networks in Urban Situations,* pp. 128–180. Manchester: Manches-
ter University Press.
Willer, D. 1967. *Scientific Sociology: Theory and Method.* Englewood Cliffs, N.J.:
Prentice-Hall.

Part Five

CATASTROPHE THEORY

The Geometry of Confidence: An Analysis of the *Enga* te and *Hagen* moka, a Complex System of Ceremonial Pig Giving in the New Guinea Highlands

MICHAEL THOMPSON

Fain would I climb yet fear I to fall. [Sir Walter Raleigh]

If thy heart fails thee, climb not at all. [Queen Elizabeth's reply]

Natural and physical scientists are fortunate in knowing what should be put together and what should be kept apart: dogs with dogs, cats with cats, never dogs with cats; inert gases with inert gases, halogens with halogens, never inert gases with halogens. Anthropology, by contrast, is beset by false starts: some dogs lumped with some cats, some inert gases lumped with some halogens; and discussion, far from starting from an agreed base, is almost entirely concerned with what that base should be. It is for this embarrassing reason that catastrophe theory is likely to give its largest payoffs in the so-called soft sciences, for it provides a qualitative technique for discovering hitherto unsuspected connections, identities, and family resemblances.

The connection investigated here is that between the trade cycle of the industrial West and the cyclical ceremonial exchange of pigs in the New Guinea Highlands. These phenomena are not usually bracketed together. The trade cycle, the periodic alternation of boom and slump normally seen as resulting from advanced industrialization, is convincingly annexed by economics. By contrast, ceremonial exchange is one of the delights of anthropology. It is something of which we in the industrial West have very little but of which primitive societies tend to have a lot. Both economics and anthropology stand to gain from the eradication of this invalid distinction between the West and the Rest, between Us and Them.

A similar version of this chapter appears in a book by the author, *Rubbish Theory: The Creation and Destruction of Value* (London and New York: Oxford University Press, 1979).

THE PIG CYCLE AND ECONOMIC THEORY

The phenomenon that I call the pig cycle is an elaborate system of ceremonial exchange in the Central Highlands of New Guinea. Gold-lip shells,
feathers, stone axes, and the like feature in the exchanges, but their main
component is pigs (and to a lesser extent pork). The system extends over
150 miles of mountainous terrain and so passes through several different
cultures. Thus parts of the system have been described by anthropologists,
insofar as they relate to particular peoples, but there is no comprehensive
account of the total system.[1] The view which the various peoples involved
in the system have of the system is as restricted as that of their ethnographers. The Enga call the system the *te* and see it as a linear system, with
exchanges coming into and going out of their area. The Kyaka, who are at
one end of the system, call it the *moka* and see it rather differently from
the Enga since, while it is open at one end, for them it is closed at the other.
Map 1 shows the geographic extent of the system, and Figure 1, more sche-
matically, demonstrates the linear sequence and its various branches. I will
refer to the Kyaka area as the Hagen end of the system.

Probably the most striking feature of this extraordinary exchange system
is its periodicity. It is not a steady flow; nor is it a seasonal flow. Every
four years or so it builds up to a tremendous climax. (Elkin, by chance,
arrived in the Wabag area just as one of these climaxes occurred and found
the landing strip covered with thousands of pigs all tethered to neat lines of
stakes.) This creates further problems in observation, since a full account
would require the anthropologist's field work to extend over four years.
But even this would not be adequate, since in the subsequent four-year
period all the exchanges flow in the opposite direction; hence observation
of a truly complete cycle would require eight years.

When looked at in more detail, the pig cycle can be divided into a number
of distinct phases (distinct both to the observer and to the people involved).
The cycle, of course, is continuous, but the description must start somewhere, and it is convenient to begin just after the climax in which the thousands of pigs have been exchanged and most of them eaten, leaving only a
minimal population of pigs to start breeding from again.

Phase A.   Solicitory gifts *(kenju)*—legs of pork, live pigs, pearl shells, and
axes—are passed from partner to partner in the direction of the main prestations in the previous half of the cycle. This phase lasts from several
months to over a year.

Phase B.   The main prestations, *maku pilyanin* ("true moka"), come in
the opposite direction. These are much more substantial gifts, on the order
of eight or ten pigs per solicitory unit. This phase takes place consecutively
in each clan along the sequence, and two types of festivals may be distin-

MAP 1

Approximate Line of the Enga Te *and Hagen* Moka

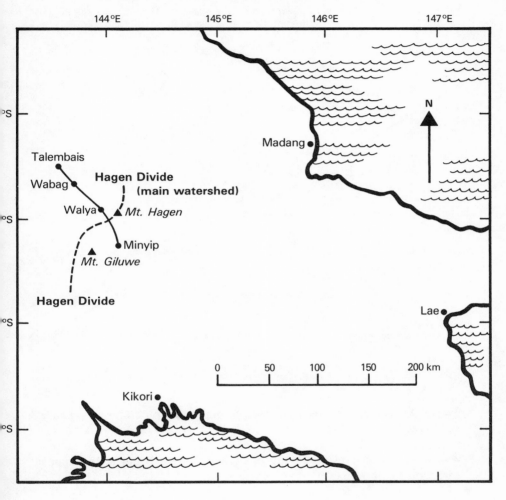

guished: the internal *moka* among members of one clan, and the much more spectacular external *moka* among members of different clans.

Phase C. This phase starts when the main festivals have reached the last clans in the chain. The pigs, or the majority of them, are killed and cooked, and the pork is passed back once more from partner to partner, leaving in its wake an epidemic of gastric disorders.

FIGURE 1

The Flow of Exchanges in the Pig Cycle

The arrows show the directions of flow during phase B. At each subsequent phase
the directions are reversed.

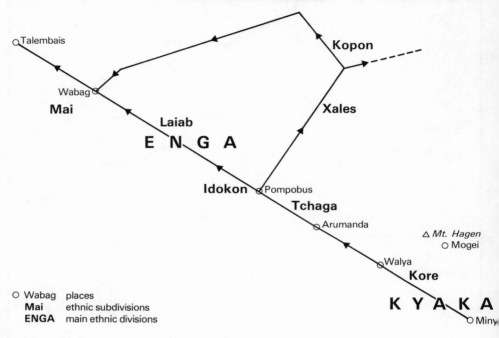

Phase D.   Solicitory gifts are passed from partner to partner as in phase A
but in the opposite direction.

Phase E.   Main prestations are made as in phase B but in the opposite
direction.

Phase F.   Cooked pork is passed along as in phase C but in the opposite
direction.

The cycle is now complete, the seventh phase being identical to phase A.
Although the *telmoka* appears to be a unique phenomenon, the various
cultures through which it passes seem to be fairly similar and fairly typical
of the New Guinea Highlands in general. These peoples are settled agriculturalists with economies based mainly on sweet potato cultivation and pig
breeding. They are territorially and politically organized on the basis of a

segmentary type of lineage framework, including in its widest span anywhere from about 1000 to 5000 persons. There is considerable variation in
the rigidity with which territorial and political organization are tied to the
segmentary lineage system, and also in the extent to which ancestors may
be "fiddled." Attempts to relate the rigidity/flexibility of the segmentary
lineage system to variations in the density of population, the pressure on
land, or land available for sweet potato cultivation have met with little success, and it has been suggested that, within any one lineage, there is a fairly
regular and predictable variation in these properties over time, deriving
from the effects of that celebrated New Guinea political figure, the Big Man
(Meggitt 1967).

New Guinea Highlands society is highly individualistic, competitive, and
materialistic. The competition is normally conducted in terms of shell
money, elaborate dress and ornaments, and, most of all, pigs. The breeding
of pigs requires, first, the services of wives and, second, the support of
followers, the securing of which depends on the personal qualities and drive
of the aspiring Big Man. Most men never achieve the status of Big Man,
and those who do can sustain it only during their prime. No man who
reaches a ripe old age can hope to die a Big Man.

The *te/moka* ceremonial exchange system is cyclical in that there are
periodic destructions of pigs, but it also conforms to a pattern of linear
oscillation between the two extremities, Talembais and Minyip. Elsewhere
in the New Guinea Highlands the cycle exists without the linear oscillation.
Further afield, the *kula* ring in the islands off southeastern New Guinea
(Malinowski 1922; Thompson 1968) and the *kulu* among aborigines of
northern Australia (Stanner 1934; Falkenberg 1962; Thompson 1968) provide examples of exchange systems that are linear but not associated with
either a cycle or an oscillation.

The Enga *te* or Hagen *moka* is thus the most complex of these exchange
systems and presents three separate problems: the cycle, the linearity, and
the oscillation.

The linear flow of goods such that an individual or group is simply one
link in a chain of exchanges or partnerships often extending for hundreds
of miles is a familiar phenomenon in economic anthropology and may readily be understood as resulting from an evenly spread demand for goods
from localized centers of production. For example, in the *kulu* exchanges
European goods, such as calico, which originate in the Darwin area tend to
flow southward in exchange for stone spearheads, pearl shells, and boom-
erangs, which are produced far to the south. By contrast, *churinga* (sacred
carved wooden boards), which are not produced in localized centers, pass
in either direction. Thus linearity is to be expected in any exchange situation in which raw materials and/or special skills are localized. Topographi-
cal features that dictate lines of communication and settlement patterns will
merely serve to accentuate this linear nature of the exchange sequences.

In the *kula* ring exchanges there is an opposed flow resulting from the separation of localized centers of production for the *kula* valuables, but, unlike the flow for the *kulu* exchanges, this linear flow eventually bends around and joins up with itself. This inevitably imposes a "coals to Newcastle" quality upon one-half of the ring. Such systems may appear to both the ethnographer and the native, both of whom can see only a small segment of the total system, to be essentially similar. But it is what happens to the ends of the linear sequence, beyond these limits of observation, that determines the crucial property of the system, its behavior over time.

There are three possibilities concerning the ends: a linear sequence can come to a dead end, it can feed into a larger and more complex system of exchanges, or it can bend around and eventually join up with its other end to form a ring. Thus any system, however complex, can be reduced to linear sequences (with either open or closed ends) and annular sequences. (The open end is, of course, simply an heuristic device and must ultimately reduce to closed ends and annuli.)

The *kulu* is an example of an open-ended linear sequence, the *te/moka* is a closed-ended linear sequence, and the *kula* is an annular sequence. In the case of the *kulu*, any surplus that arises at the open ends is readily absorbed by the larger and more complex systems with which they connect, so the volume of flow will normally remain fairly constant over time: it is a steady-state system. In the case of the *kula*, the steady state exists only with one specific set of parameters, which are not those given by a gradually extending linear system that happens to link up with its other end—the likeliest form of evolution for an annular sequence.[2] Thus an annular system is almost certainly not steady state, but regenerative, giving rise to an ever-increasing volume of flow, even with an input that is steady or even diminishing.

In the case of the *te/moka*, the volume of flow at any point in the sequence will remain constant, but the system as a whole will not be steady state but regenerative, since there will be a steadily increasing pile-up of goods at the two closed ends, except with one particular set of parameters, which would provide a steady state but which are extremely unlikely to be met in practice. For a closed-ended system to conform to these parameters, it would be necessary for the people involved to be aware of the parameters, for them to have a perfect knowledge of the market, and for them to be able to adjust their own stock to the desired stock, *without* any time lag. Such conditions are certainly not met in the case of the *te/moka* and, as the theory predicts, the *te/moka* is regenerative, giving rise to pile-ups of pigs at the extremities, Talembais and Minyip. Such a regenerative system, left to itself, would eventually either break down or transform itself, since only a steady-state system can hope to survive unchanged over time. However, there are two possible modifications that can be applied to a closed-ended linear system, which, even if they do not transform the system to a steady state, can at least contain its fluctuations within a steady-state envelope. First, if instead of being exchanged in a steady flow, the goods were transmitted periodically in "packets," then when the pile-up occurred at one end, it would be possible to reverse the direction of flow to drain away the accumulated goods. Such oscillating systems are common in electronics, and there is no reason why they should not also occur in the communication of goods. Such a system, once it has been set in oscillation, will continue to oscillate with a constant period and amplitude so long as the reversed flow from one end does not reach the other end, thereby progressively increasing the size of the pile-ups. This condition is met by the *tel moka,* where the cooked pork never passes all the way from one end to the other. The transformation of the pile-up of live, comparatively durable pigs into dead and autodestructive cooked pork may be seen as a secondary modification for ensuring that the envelope containing the pig cycle remains steady state.

Moreover, the odd number of phases—the three types of prestation (solicitory gifts, main prestations, cooked pork) each being the signal for initiating the reciprocal phase in the opposite direction—ensures the regular reversal of flow direction. An even number of phases could never provide the switching mechanism for reversing the flow directions, and so could never give rise to an oscillating system.

Thus some exchange systems in primitive societies are undoubtedly generative phenomena and can never be adequately accounted for by steady-state theory. The trouble is that, at present, this vital distinction is not recognized. Economic anthropologists, whether they follow Firth in believing that classical economic theory (suitably modified) is applicable to primitive societies or whether they follow Polanyi in rejecting such an approach on the grounds that the economic relationships are of a totally different order, are all agreed on one point (and one point only!): that Keynesian economic theory is quite inapplicable in primitive societies. In holding to this view they stand out like living fossils beside the community of economists who are "all Keynesians now" (or post-Keynesians), and it is here, at the divide between pre-Keynesian and post-Keynesian theory, that the gap between anthropology and economics is located.

Economists are all Keynesians now, not in the sense that they all subscribe to specific concepts such as the multiplier (many emphatically do not), but in the sense that they subscribe to a body of theory which can handle steady-state *and* generative phenomena. Classical economists saw the trade cycle as a steady-state phenomenon. Admittedly there was an alternation, an upswing and a downswing, but the whole was contained within a steady-state envelope, and the possibility of a regenerative or degenerative trend was not entertained (a view which Keynes scathingly criticized as predicting that once the storm has passed the sea will be calm once more). Keynes' general theory of employment, interest, and money did not assume a steady state. It started out by accepting that economic phenomena are likely to be generative, and that only with one specific set of parameters will they be steady state and so appear to fit the classical model.

But even those who try to transcend the differences between the neo-classicists and the substantivists agree that Keynesian analysis is irrelevant: "Keynesian economics . . . has little relevance for the study of traditional peasant economics. . . . In fact, most economic analysis of this kind has been devised to solve certain intellectual puzzles or practical problems which do not arise for the anthropologist" (Cohen 1967: 103). The intellectual puzzles and practical problems are certainly there in the case of the pig cycle; it is just that anthropologists, by this carving up of convenience (primitive society and classical theory versus industrialized society and Keynesian and post-Keynesian theory), have avoided being confronted by them. Another scholar put the argument in this fashion: "There can be no doubt that the conventional textbook economics models commonly relate to the explanation of phenomena that do not occur in primitive economics. . . . Money, interest, employment, boom and slump are convenient examples" (Joy 1967: 32).

The substantivists actually use this inapplicability of Keynesian theory as a stick with which to beat the neoclassicists: "If it is thought that Western price theory is relevant to primitive economy, why not other branches of Western theory—say Keynesian income and employment theory—as well? The answer, perhaps, is that in the attempt to apply Keynesian theory to primitive economy it would become evident that the assumption of functional similarity of economic organisation between the primitive and the West is empirically indefensible. In a word, it cannot be done" (Dalton 1961: 16). The neoclassicist reply to this supposed *reductio ad absurdum* is: "Precisely, but then no one said it could" (Frankenberg 1967: 66). But this challenge of Dalton's, to apply Keynesian theory to primitive society, is not a *reductio ad absurdum;* it is a perfectly reasonable and proper step to take. In short, it can be done.

PIGS, CREDIT, AND CONFIDENCE

Before meeting this theoretical challenge, we should look more closely at some characteristics of the exchange system. The curve for the pig cycle, with total pig population plotted against time, can be deduced in qualitative terms from invariants of New Guinea pig husbandry such as average litter size, the availability of lactating women for the supplementary suckling of runts, and the porcine gestation period. Without going into these fascinating but technical and time-consuming details, we note that the curve turns out to be something like the one in Figure 2.

Leaving aside, for a few moments, various other possible explanations, I will boldly state that the only wholly satisfactory account must be in terms of the causal relationship between the pig cycle and the aggregate level of credit.

In addition to the visible, tangible, cyclical fluctuations in pig population, there is a parallel invisible, intangible credit cycle. To appreciate the nature of this cycle, we need to break into what is in fact a continuous process. During the preceding phase of the cycle successive Big Men along the line have been receiving increasingly larger and larger prestations of pigs as each Big Man in turn adds more pigs to those he has received from the external *moka,* in order to pass on an even larger prestation to his recipient. In this way recipients incur increasingly larger obligations to their donors right down the line. Big Men acquire the pigs to make these gifts through the internal *moka* from local followers to whom they had previously given pigs so that these followers could build up their stock of pigs.

The enormous growth in the pig population during the early part of the cycle thus coincides with the period during which aspiring Big Men are building up their followings, using their energy, dynamism, and rhetoric to inspire confidence among their fellow men. Once this confidence is created, they can convert their fellow men into followers by the extension of credit. The extension of credit creates a larger following, the size of the Big Man's following promotes confidence in him among those who are still uncommitted, and they in turn become his followers. This tremendous upsurge in confidence results in an enormous increase in the pig population. Similarly, a decay of confidence will lead to the calling in of debts and, at the very least, a rapid falling off in the growth rate of the pig population. If this turning point also involves ruthless competition in which some men are ruined by bankruptcy while others, presiding first over the presentation of thousands of pigs and then over the feasts in which these pigs are consumed, survive triumphantly, then there will actually be a sharp *drop* in the total pig population.

This hypothetical credit cycle would be of the same period as the pig cycle, but its turning points would be displaced in such a way as to anticipate the turning points in the total pig population. This displacement would be due, at the lower turning point, to the time it takes to convert the gaining of confidence and the granting of credit into live pigs, and, at the upper turning point, to the time it takes to convert a loss of confidence and a calling in of credit into cooked pork. The two curves, the pig cycle (expressed in real pigs) and the credit cycle (expressed in promised pigs), will look like those in Figure 3.

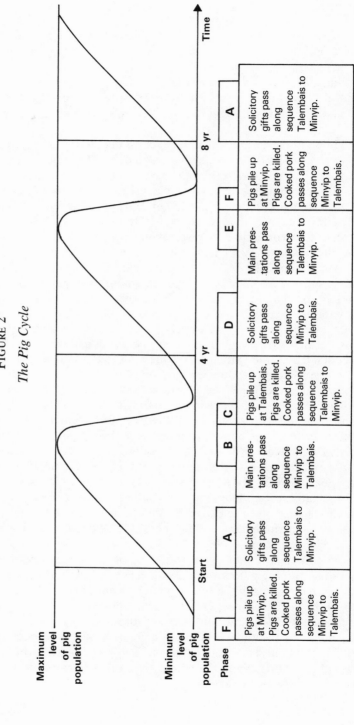

FIGURE 2

The Pig Cycle

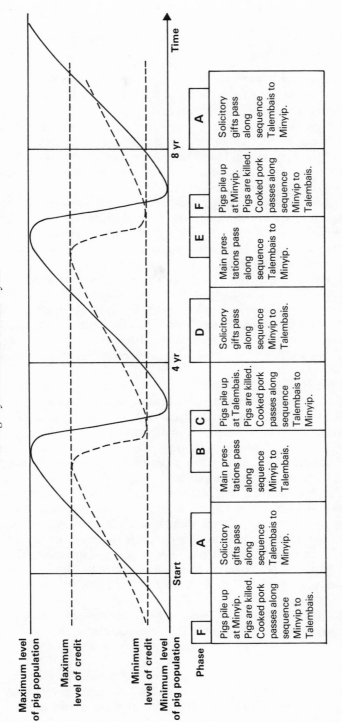

FIGURE 3

The Pig Cycle and the Credit Cycle

POSSIBLE EXPLANATIONS

How is it that the hypothesis contained in the relationship between these two curves provides an explanation of the pig cycle, and how is it that this explanation is essentially Keynesian?

In the New Guinea Highlands pigs are a scarce resource. The pig cycle consists of regular fluctuations in the pig population, and the level of the pig population depends on individual decisions concerning pig breeding. It is thus an economic cycle, so it is reasonable to look to economic theory for an explanation.

Cyclical fluctuations have been familiar to economists since the birth of their discipline, and the development of economic theory has, to a considerable extent, derived from successive attempts to explain these fluctuations. The fluctuations have come to be known as the trade cycle or the business cycle, and the body of theory seeking to explain the fluctuations is called trade cycle theory. The trade cycle fluctuations were first noticed (or, at any rate, considered worthy of explanation) in the nineteenth century. From then until comparatively recently the trade cycle and the problem of its explanation have been central to economic theory. In particular, Keynesian theory derives largely from problems of the trade cycle, and provides an explanation where classical economic theory was inadequate.

Since the economic revolution, which came with the adoption, particularly by the United States and Great Britain, of economic policies based on Keynesian theory, both the trade cycle and its theory seem to have become of less interest to economists. It could be too optimistic to say that this is because Keynes has provided the first adequate explanation of the trade cycle. However, the adoption of policies based on his theory has helped to tame the trade cycle itself, in particular the violent alternations of booms and slumps and the recurring periods of heavy unemployment.

The first nineteenth-century explanation for the trade cycle was that its cause lay in some other environmental cycle, in some regular fluctuations in nature. In this case it was the sunspot cycle (seven years approximately), which has been observed to coincide with a thunderstorm cycle. This climatic cycle might be expected to affect the crop yields, and hence, since agriculture was at that time the main component of the economy, would give rise to an economic cycle. This most elegant explanation had to be discarded when it was discovered that the lengths of the trade cycle and the sunspot cycle were not quite the same, and also that the trade cycle fluctuations *increased* as agriculture *decreased* as a component in the economy.

The fact that the period of the pig cycle is between six and eight years suggests that it is not caused by any natural cycle in the environment, and this conclusion is confirmed when we find that the period of the cycle has changed over the years and that there are similar cycles elsewhere in the New Guinea Highlands, some with longer and some with shorter periods.

The next likely explanation is the cobweb cycle or hog cycle, as it is called in America. The cobweb cycle results from the lagged adjustment of supply to demand and is commonly advanced as a model of fluctuations for particular agricultural commodities. Briefly, a man goes to market with ten pigs and the dealer says, "Only ten? Why, I would buy a hundred if you had them." The dealer, of course, says this to every breeder, with the result that they all go away and some months later return with a hundred pigs each. The market is swamped, prices plummet, and the breeder loses heavily. He learns by his mistake, and on his next visit to market he has only ten pigs, and so on. A necessary condition for the cobweb cycle is that the demand for pigs is not perfectly elastic, so that their price varies inversely with the number offered for sale.

It is difficult to discover the variations in pig prices in the New Guinea Highlands since, for a start, pigs are themselves monetary units. Elsewhere in New Guinea (e.g., Siuai and in some sense Kapauku) prices (in terms of shell money) do not fluctuate, a fact which indicates that demand may be perfectly elastic, and this indication receives support from the decisions of individual Enga pig breeders. The individual pig breeder strives at all times to increase his stock of pigs as fast as possible, suggesting that demand is insatiable. At the moment when the level of supply is at its maximum (during the main prestations), the level of demand is also at its maximum, as shown by the fact that each producer gets rid of almost his entire stock of pigs.

Thus there would appear to be no fluctuation in prices, perfect elasticity of demand, and no decisions to be made about the number of pigs to raise (since the main aim *at all times* is to raise as many pigs as possible). Hence the cobweb cycle cannot possibly provide an explanation of the pig cycle.

Recently there has been a resurgence of explanations in terms of the intervention of some external, natural constraint. Rappaport (1967) has advanced an ecological explanation for another pig cycle in New Guinea in terms of the homeostasis between the pig and its environment and the pig parasite and its environment (the pig). It is difficult to know what to say about such ecological explanations since they are concerned primarily with delineating the natural limits to human activities and not with understanding the possible forms which these human activities can take. Provided there are no flaws in such ecological arguments, I have no quarrel with them; they are simply irrelevant to my concern in the sense that if the human activities I wish to study were not ecologically possible they would not be there.

Most economic explanations that have been advanced for the trade cycle have been of this type, based on the idea that people pursue their cultural values until collectively they come up against some natural limit. These theories rely on buffers: sometimes two buffers with the variable bouncing back and forth between them, sometimes just one, a ceiling or a floor with either a balloon- or ball-like variable. But there is one explanation—the Hansen-Samuelson model of the trade cycle (see Matthews 1959)—which shows how economic fluctuations will occur even in the total absence of natural limits or restraints. In this model the cycle is derived solely from the interaction of those two Keynesian concepts, the multiplier and the accelerator.

Fortunately there is no need to go into the technicalities of the Hansen-Samuelson model. It is sufficient for my present purpose to explain that the multiplier involved Keynes in propounding his celebrated fundamental psychological law "that men are disposed, as a rule and on the average, to increase their consumption as their income increases, but not by as much as the increase in their income" (1936: 96). Thus Keynes found it necessary to take individual motivation into economic account but conveniently, and alas erroneously, was able to treat it as a constant.

The accelerator is more technical. It is based on the notion that in a representative industry there is a ratio between the value of capital and annual output. More simply, it is the idea that there is a ratio between the number of machines in a factory and the number of goods produced by that factory. Of course, you can overuse or underuse machines, but the ratio is taken to be that optimum state of affairs where the machines are neither so overused that they and their operators are subjected to undue strain nor so underused that a proportion of the capital tied up in them is in effect lying idle. The next step in the accelerator is the idea that as the level of demand for the products of the factory varies, as inevitably it will, the factory owner strives continuously to adjust his stock of capital, by buying more machines, or postponing the buying of more machines, or *in extremis* selling off machines, so as always to remain as close as possible to this optimum ratio. This he will do by seeing how things are going, which actually means seeing how things have gone, for this feedback of information as to how well or badly his products are selling is inevitably subject to a time lag. Stripped to its essentials, the accelerator is based on the lagged relationship between plant and product, and is applicable to any process in which the production of one sort of good is governed by the production of another sort of good. Pig husbandry is one such process: the production of what we may call *disposable* pigs is governed by the production of *breeding* pigs. The accelerator is a formalized description of the rational decision-making process that determines why this little piggy goes to market and this little piggy stays home.

The Hansen-Samuelson model of the trade cycle incorporates this very simple feedback mechanism—inevitably time-lagged feedback of information concerning levels of demand—and gives rise to cycles even in the absence of buffers. These cycles will, in general, be generative—either damped (settling down and dying away) or antidamped (getting worse and worse)—and only with one specific set of parameters will they be of constant amplitude. The Hansen-Samuelson model, incidentally, provides a neat condensation of the Keynesian spirit: the insistence that economic phenomena are in general generative and only steady state in the special case, the focusing of attention on real world processes such as the factory with its machines and its products, and, above all, the conviction that the totality must be understood as the aggregation of individual contributions each in itself rational in terms of that individual's situation.

The way in which cyclical fluctuations result from these lagged adjustments is most easily explained by a famous mechanical example of exactly the same sort of process. Imagine a rather badly designed central heating system in which the supply of fuel to the boiler is regulated by a thermostat in one of the rooms. If the temperature of the room falls below the desired level, the thermostat causes more fuel to be fed into the boiler but, of course, the benefit of this is not felt immediately since it takes some time for the additional fuel to raise the temperature of the room. So the thermostat causes more fuel to be fed into the boiler even though that which it is already receiving would be sufficient, given time, to raise the room temperature to the desired level. The room overheats and the thermostat then reacts by cutting down the supply of fuel to the boiler. But, of course, it takes some time for this cutback of fuel to affect the temperature of the room, so the thermostat cuts back the fuel further, with the result that the room becomes too cold, the thermostat overreacts, and away the cycle goes again. If the system is really badly designed, these cycles may be antidamped and the boiler will eventually explode. If it is not so badly designed, the cycle will be damped down until it oscillates between more or less tolerable extremes of temperature.

If we were to plot, on the same graph, the variation with time of both the fuel added to the boiler and the temperature of the room, we would obtain two oscillating curves that remained in step with one another but with the peaks and troughs of the fuel curve always anticipating those of the temperature curve—the anticipation at the trough reflecting the time taken for an addition of fuel to be converted into an increase in room temperature, and the anticipation at the peak reflecting the time taken for a reduction of fuel to be converted into a drop in room temperature.

It is not too difficult to deduce qualitatively what the curves for the *disposable* pig population and the *breeding* pig population must be in the case of the pig cycle, and they turn out to be something like those in Figure 4. "Aha" or even "eureka," one cries: curves with *exactly* the same characteristics as those for the central heating system. It is just a matter of playing around with the parameters until one obtains a near-perfect fit

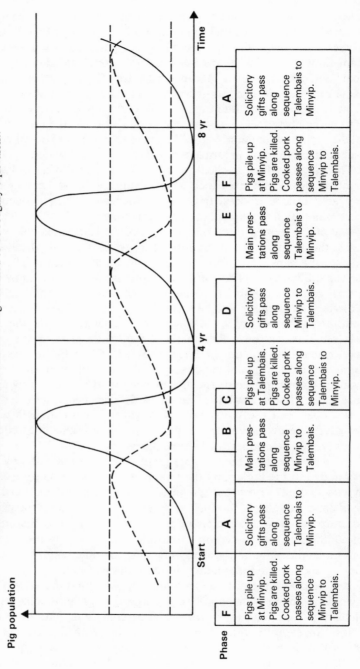

FIGURE 4

Curves for the Disposable Pig and Breeding Pig Populations

These two curves added together give the total pig population curve. The exact shapes of these curves have been deduced by using the data on pig husbandry among the Mae-Enga (Meggitt 1957a,b, 1958, 1959, 1965, 1967, 1970), augmented by data on pig husbandry in the early nineteenth century in Britain (Wilson n.d.), the states of the art in these two contexts being assumed to be roughly equivalent.

Pig population

Phase

F	A	B	C	D	E	F	A
Pigs pile up at Minyip. Pigs are killed. Cooked pork passes along sequence Minyip to Talembais.	Solicitory gifts pass along sequence Talembais to Minyip.	Main prestations pass along sequence Minyip to Talembais.	Pigs pile up at Talembais. Pigs are killed. Cooked pork passes along sequence Talembais to Minyip.	Solicitory gifts pass along sequence Minyip to Talembais.	Main prestations pass along sequence Talembais to Minyip.	Pigs pile up at Minyip. Pigs are killed. Cooked pork passes along sequence Minyip to Talembais.	Solicitory gifts pass along sequence Talembais to Minyip.

Start   4 yr   8 yr   Time

- - - - - - *Breeding pigs*

between the pig cycle and the Hansen-Samuelson model. But there is a snag, and a serious snag at that!

A pig breeder will, at any moment in time, mentally divide his herd into those pigs that he reserves for breeding and those that he regards as disposable, but this division is not fixed (except in the case of castrated male pigs), and he can if he likes convert a breeding pig into a disposable pig or vice versa simply by changing his mind. Now in the pig cycle this is what happens. Near the top of the upswing individual pig breeders are faced with critical and difficult decisions about just when to start converting into disposable pigs those breeding pigs that will not have time to produce a mature litter in time for the main prestations. The decision is critical because the breeder must have as many mature disposable pigs as possible available for the main prestations, and difficult because, although he knows the time of the main prestations is approaching, he cannot tell exactly when it will arrive.

Now this sort of thing is not reconcilable with a feedback mechanism. To return to the mechanical analogy of the feedback system in which the temperature of the room governs the amount of fuel added to the boiler via the mediating device of a thermostat, we find that converting breeding pigs to disposable pigs is equivalent to converting the excess heat in the room directly into unburnt fuel—an impossible process that would completely do away with the need for any thermostat. Feedback mechanisms are based on the feedback of *information*—of temperature in the case of the room and boiler, and of knowledge about changes in levels of investment in the case of the trade cycle. The thermostat is the device that does this in the first case; the entrepreneur adjusting his actual stock of capital to his desired stock of capital is the device in the second case. The feedback mechanism will function only so long as the two parts of the system between which it mediates are mutually nonconvertible. This is certainly so in the case of the room and boiler, but certainly not so in the case of the breeding pig and the disposable pig.

What we have is something that looks just like an oscillating and feedback system but is not one. What then *is* the fuel that drives the pig cycle? It is the aggregated confidence of the individual pig breeders. If their confidence is high, they will be eager to extend credit, if they are aspiring Big Men, and to accept credit, if they are the followers of the Big Men. If their confidence falls, they will respectively be eager to call in this credit and to pay off these alarming debts.

CONFIDENCE AND CERTAINTY: A TOPOLOGICAL HYPOTHESIS

It is now clear why it is that the only wholly satisfactory explanation must be one in terms of the causal relationship between the pig cycle and the aggregate level of credit. Turning back to the hypothetical diagram of this relationship (Figure 3), we can see that the curves are exactly of the type associated with an oscillating system deriving from a feedback mechanism. In this case, credit can only be converted into pigs via the pig husbandry process, the time scale of which is determined by invariants associated with the human breeding cycle, the pig breeding cycle, the sweet potato growth rate, the cycle of the seasons, and so on, that is, invariants deriving from the ecosystem. Thus the credit-into-pigs transformation can be effected only through this mechanism, and with this time lag, and so, if it can be shown that the credit cycle must be of this form, then the form of the pig cycle is also determined.

The expansive style of operation of the Big Man would seem to validate the upswing of this hypothetical credit cycle, but what of the turning point and the downswing? A faint clue to the explanation of the turning point is provided by one of the parting shots in the fruitless debate on the rigidity/flexibility of New Guinea lineage systems.

Meggitt (1967), in discussing political aspects of Enga organization, has suggested that, within any lineage, a cyclical pattern is generated by the interaction of the Big Man system and the segmentary lineage structure: "Only a diachronic analysis of the data reveals the full complexity of the pattern. Within the life history of any given clan, and its subordinate segments, we must recognize that there is a more or less regular and predictable alternation of conditions defining the form of leadership at any time" (p. 33).

I do not wish to suggest that the cyclical alternations of the pig cycle and the cyclical alternations of lineage fortunes proposed by Meggitt are one and the same. Rather they should be seen as two possibilities that can be generated by the relationship between two partially conflicting ideologies, that deriving from the Big Man and that deriving from the segmentary lineage structure (hereafter referred to as SLS). The conflict between these two coexisting ideologies resides in the simple distinction that the Big Man ideology is ego-focused while the SLS ideology is not. The former provides an admirable validating framework for the maximization of individual advantage but can furnish no basis for cooperation for the benefit of the whole. The Big Man ideology is basically that of "might is right."

The SLS ideology similarly provides a validating framework for the maximization of individual advantage but *within certain limits*. Exactly what these limits are cannot be decided, for the rigidity/flexibility of the lineage framework varies spatially (that is, from one society to another) and temporally (that is, within any given society, over time). These variations are most pronounced in the New Guinea Highlands, but there is no justification for assuming them to be absent in other societies so long as the possibility of "fiddling" exists (e.g., Tiv genealogies and Tiv politics, the Big Man in the form of market pact holders, whose "might is right" ideology is, admittedly, severely curtailed by witchcraft accusations).

Ideally the lineage framework provides a ranking of claims for support between any one man and all his fellows, this ranking being a function of the genealogical distances between him and his fellows. In practice, however, this rating is never absolute since frequently there exists the possibility of restructuring the lineage framework in such a manner that a linkage particularly desired for the maximization of some individual advantage is promoted to the top.position in the ranking. Nevertheless, the simple fact that the SLS, although continually transformed, persists through time is proof that not all such possible restructurings are equally probable; considerable constraints exist upon the avenues whereby individual advantage may be maximized.[3]

These same conditions apply to the social systems involved in the pig cycle. The Big Man is always there, sometimes riding flamboyantly on the crest of a wave, whipped up by his own exuberance, at other times shortening sail, calling in his loans and wondering how he can weather the storm which his rapid translation from wave crest to wave trough has precipitated. And throughout all these ups and downs, there persists in some form or other, at times practically submerged, the lineage framework that the Big Man has so forcefully used and abused in his single-minded pursuit of pig power.

The problem now is to obtain a description of the range of possibilities which the relationship between these two coexisting and partially conflicting ideologies can generate. Such a description can be expressed in terms of person-to-person credit relationships, both those within a discrete section of the system and those crossing from that section to the rest of the system. By taking as this section the clan, which is the widest grouping encompassed by the segmentary lineage framework, we can be sure that all those credit links that are forged between the section and the rest of the system must be validated *only* by the Big Man ideology, since they extend beyond the widest scope of the SLS ideology.

During the course of the pig cycle there are significant aggregate variations in credit relationships, in terms of both their density (reflected in the total number of such relationships both within and across the boundary of the clan) and their intensity (reflected in the total credit load imposed on these relationships).

All credit relationships are forged in response to the perceived advantages of the participants, but only some are, in addition, validated by the SLS ideology (they represent the Big Man's use of the SLS ideology). Other relationships (including all those across the clan boundary) are formed in spite of the SLS ideology (they represent the Big Man's abuse of the SLS ideology).

Three variables can be isolated:

1. The level of credit
2. The number of credit relationships validated by the SLS ideology
3. The number of credit relationships forged despite the SLS ideology

These variables can be rearranged as follows:

1a. The level of credit
2a. The total number of credit relationships
3a. The ratio of the total amount of credit extended through relation-
    ships created despite the SLS ideology to the total amount of
    credit extended through relationships validated by SLS ideology

A three-dimensional graph in terms of these variables will provide the
description we are seeking: the manner in which the credit cycle (1a), the
entrepreneurial activities of the Big Man (2a), and the partial contradiction
of the two ideologies (3a) are related.

The first two variables are self-explanatory, but the third requires some
elaboration. The assumption here is that the degree of conflict depends on
the relative credit load between validating and nonvalidating relationships.
(This would seem to be a reasonable assumption since the Big Man who
has, say, half his relationships despite the SLS ideology but only, say, one-
quarter of his credit is surely creating less confusion than another who has,
say, three-quarters of his credit extended through the same proportion of
relationships.)

The significance of this variable expressing the degree of ideological conflict resides in the fact that the Big Man ideology, being ego-focused, con-
firms the world view characterized by Hobbes' notion of a war of all against
all, while the SLS ideology insists that this war is confined only to certain
areas of the world—that there are regions to which it can never spread and
which, in consequence, stand out as fixed islands of certainty in the turbu-
lent sea of unpredictability. If one is prepared to accept this philosophical
position, then the rate of change of this third variable becomes an expression of the degree to which certainty is being destroyed (or, if its value is
negative, the degree to which certainty is being created).

Such profound speculations apart, and despite the total absence of quantitative data, it is still possible to state some geometrical properties concerning these three variables.

1. The relationship must be contained in a three-dimensional space, with
x = total number of relationships, y = ratio of invalidating relationships to
validating relationships, and z = level of credit, as shown in Figure 5.

FIGURE 5

The Axes of a Three-Dimensional Space Defining the Pig Cycle

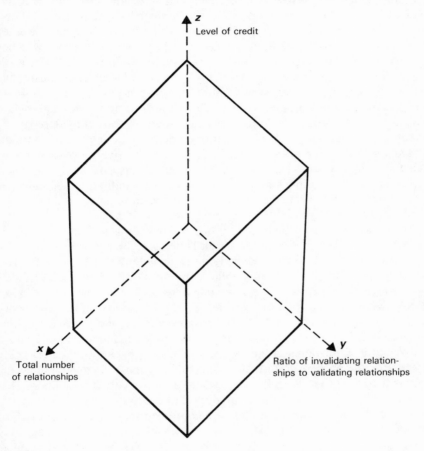

2. In terms of x and y in Figure 5, at any moment in time there are four logical possibilities:

(a) neither x nor y is increasing;
(b) x is increasing but y remains constant;
(c) y is increasing but x remains constant;
(d) both x and y are increasing.

We can draw a (qualitative) probability distribution for the desired levels of credit for each of these types of situation.

In the case in which neither x nor y is increasing, the most likely outcome is that there will be no change in the desired level of credit, as indicated in Figure 6A. When x is increasing but y remains constant, we have a situation in which more credit links are being forged but there is no erosion of certainty. That is, the gulf between people's expectations, based on their references to the SLS, and what actually happens is neither widened nor narrowed. In such a situation the most likely outcome is an increase in the desired level of credit, as shown in Figure 6B. When y is increasing but x remains constant we have a situation in which no more links are being forged but there is a progressive transfer of credit from those relationships validated by the SLS ideology to those created despite this ideology. In other words, certainty is being steadily eroded and people's expectations, based on their references to the SLS, are progressively confounded by what actually happens. Increasingly that which seems least likely to happen happens. Such situations of increasing uncertainty and unpredictability are not conducive to expansive optimism, and the most likely outcome is a decrease in the desired level of credit (see Figure 6C).

In the situation in which both x and y are increasing, more links are being forged and therefore more credit is being extended, but at the same time these new links are increasingly made despite the SLS. Here the two ideologies are increasingly in conflict, the Big Man ideology constantly encouraging the forging of new relationships and the lavish extension of credit, while at the same time eroding certainty at an ever-quickening pace and increasing unpredictability so as progressively to encourage the calling in of credit. There can be no justification for assuming any kind of balance between the extension and the calling in of credit (except in the very early stages); as the process continues, so increasingly must the pendulum swing one way or the other, as in Figure 6D, and progressively the likelihood that there will be no change in the desired level of credit decreases.

In the absence of any quantitative data it is not possible to say anything about the exact shape and size of these probability distributions, and any description derived from them must be based solely on qualitative facts such as whether the curve has one or two maxima, one or no minima; whether these indicate no change, an increase, or a decrease in the level of credit; and their positions relative to earlier or later situations.

Consider the following examples.

1. As the rates of increase of x and y change in Figures 6B and 6C, the maxima will be displaced to give greater increases and decreases, respectively, in the level of credit; moreover, although the relationship is probably not linear, it is certainly smooth and continuous: gradual changes in the rates give rise to gradual shifts in the positions of the maxima.

2. Similarly, there is a continuous sequence of changes linking Figures 6A and 6B from no change in both x and y through a steady increase in both rates; as this occurs the single maximum in Figure 6A will become

progressively flattened and will then form a shallow minimum which, as the sequence proceeds, is gradually deepened, while the maxima which it separates become more and more laterally displaced.

3. In the same way, a gradual variation in the mix of the rates of change of x and y in Figure 6D will result in progressive asymmetry in the probability distribution, with one or the other maximum becoming smaller, with their being displaced increasingly unequal amounts from the neutral position, and with a corresponding displacement of the minimum until, at some point along these sequences, the minimum will disappear and at the limits, where the rate of increase of y approaches zero and that of x approaches zero, the distribution will become congruent with one of the configurations of Figures 6B and 6C, respectively.

These different effects on the level of credit, given steady changes in the number of debt relationships established and the proportion of these relationships that are contracted outside the SLS, may all be derived from a surface linking all three variables—a surface that has the peculiar characteristic of an overhanging fold occupying part of its extent. The projection of this overhanging fold onto the base of the three-dimensional space in which the surface is contained takes a particular shape known as a *cusp*. The surface and its projection will appear something like the diagram in Figure 7.

All the minima and maxima described in examples 1, 2, and 3 above will lie on this single smooth continuous surface, and it has been the great achievement of the French mathematician René Thom to show that this must be so.[4] Thom gave the name of "catastrophe theory" to that branch of topology dealing with surfaces of this sort, where the value of one of the variables is likely to exhibit dramatic changes when the values of the other variables are changing regularly and smoothly.

The next questions are as follows: First, how is the change in the actual level of credit, indicated by the difference in the most desired credit level between initial and final values of x and y, effected? Second, what happens in case (d), where two opposite changes are indicated? These changes, the realignment of the actual levels of credit with the desired ones, will only occur if there is a *dynamic*, that is, some process that effectively maximizes credit at all times.[5]

Credit is extended through myriad relationships between credit givers (and callers-in)—the Big Men—and credit receivers (and repayers)—the Big Men's followers. The level of credit within the society is the aggregation of individual borrowings. Each individual will, at any moment, have an idea of his desired level of borrowing; the optimists will wish to increase the level, the pessimists to decrease the level. The probability distributions depict this range of individually desired borrowing.

The Big Men (the credit givers and callers-in) strive at all times to maximize their followers, which means that they constantly adjust their exten-

FIGURE 6

*Probability Distributions of Desired Credit Levels
at Two Points in Time* (t_1, t_2)

(*A*) When total number of relationships (*x*) and ratio of invalidating to validating
relationships (*y*) remain constant. (*B*) When total number of relationships is
increasing but ratio of invalidating to validating relationships remains constant.

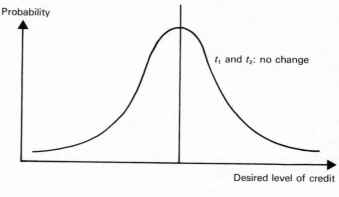

(A)

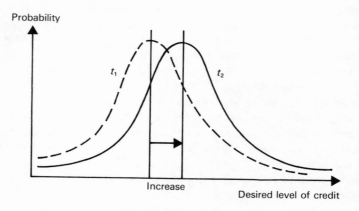

(B)

FIGURE 6 (CONTINUED)

(*C*) When total number of relationships remains constant but ratio of invalidating to validating relationships is increasing. (*D*) When total number of relationships and ratio of invalidating to validating relationships are increasing.

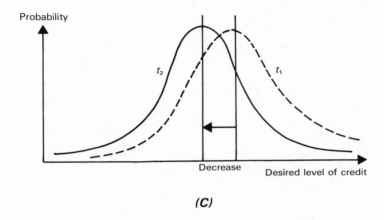

(C)

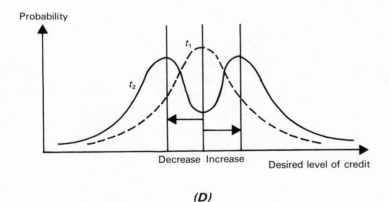

(D)

sion of credit so that it accords more closely with the most popularly desired level among the receivers. Now, of course, the granting of this credit and the activities of the Big Men influence individual receivers and cause them to revise their desired levels of borrowing. In consequence, the probability distribution changes shape again, and the Big Men extend or call in credit so as to maximize their followings by adjusting to the new position of the peak.

FIGURE 7

The Catastrophe Surface

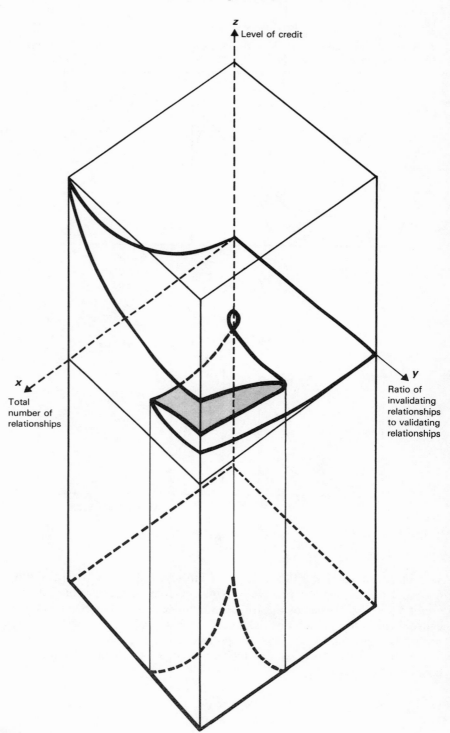

In this way, the relationship between the Big Man and his followers provides the dynamic that constantly maximizes the behavior dimension, the
level of credit. The dynamic ensures the continuous smooth process
whereby the Big Man constantly strives to position himself at the maximum: to extend (or call in) credit by an amount that will give him access to
the largest number of followers. His behavior is thus very *local*—chasing
his peak as it changes position—and he has to ignore the *global* situation,
what is happening elsewhere along the distribution. But the pack does not
just change position: it changes *shape* as well, and in certain circumstances
it disappears completely. What happens then?

The Big Man continuously adjusts to his local maximum, and so is una-
ware that this is becoming less pronounced and that another peak has
appeared at a very much lower level of credit. If this new peak grows while
his local peak declines, then there will come a moment when the local peak
flattens out. In this situation there is no longer a local maximum for the Big
Man to adjust to and he has no option but to make the sudden and discontinuous jump to the new maximum at the much lower level of credit. For
instance, the sequence of changes described by the curve in the control
space shown in Figure 8 will result in the sequence of curves shown in
Figure 9. This means that, where two opposite changes are indicated by

FIGURE 8

*A Hypothetical Sequence of the Position of a Big Man with Respect to the
Total Number of His Relationships and the Ratio of Invalidating to
Validating Relationships*

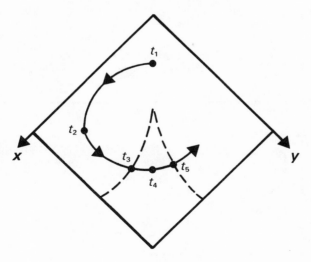

FIGURE 9

The Changes in the Level of Credit Related to the Position of the Big Man
in the Control Space of Figure 8

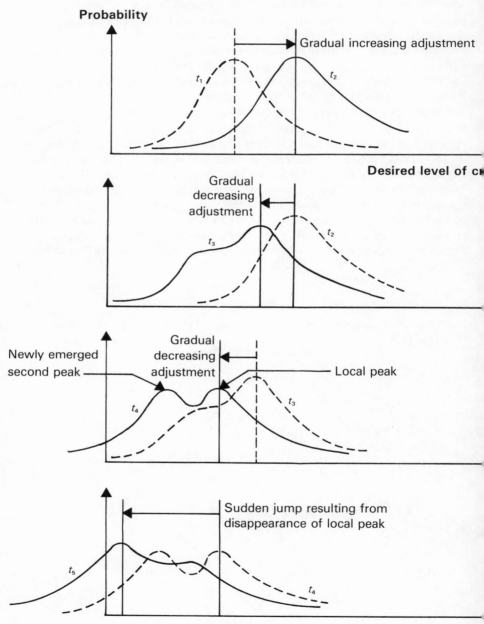

the probability distribution, the choice is determined by the *history* of the system. If credit has been at the high level, it will stay there until that higher peak disappears, and only then will it jump to the lower level, and vice versa. This is the *delay convention*.[6]

THE HYPOTHESIS AND THE PIG CYCLE

The question now is: What are the probabilities in the pig cycle? What changes in the values of x and y are happening there?

Once again, despite the absence of quantitative data, it is still possible to say something about the qualitative changes that will occur. First, there is a finite, and indeed quite small, number of potential relationships that are validated by the SLS ideology, while there is, in theory, an infinite, and in practice a very large, number of potential relationships that are not validated by the SLS ideology. Second, it would seem reasonable that a man who is trying to maximize his control over pigs will, in the first instance, try to activate those potential relationships that are validated by the SLS ideology, and only when he has done this will he seek to activate those that are, to some extent, disputed and then those that are not validated at all. The ethnographies tend to support this assumption.

Third, a consequence of these two qualitative factors is that, as the pig cycle develops, the relationship between x and y *must* be of the type reflected in Figure 10. This amounts to saying that as the density and inten-

FIGURE 10

The Relationship of the Ratio of Invalidating to Validating Relationships to the Density and Intensity of Credit Relationships

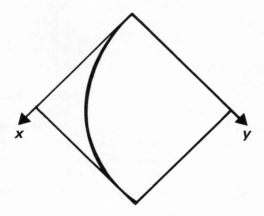

sity of credit relationships increase, so increasingly will this growth be among those relationships that are not validated by the SLS ideology. This means that inevitably the situation will move into the cusp. Here we can expect sudden discontinuous change, in this case a sudden reduction in the level of credit such as occurs during the main prestation phase of the cycle. If we assume that unactivated credit relationships, like talents, atrophy, then this sudden reduction in the level of credit will be followed by a rapid diminution in the density and intensity of relationships, especially those that are not validated by the SLS ideology. It is in such gloomy unpredictable times that one discovers who one's friends really are, and it is in the nature of these things that, blood being thicker than water, they turn out to be those whose closeness to oneself is enshrined by the kinship ideology. As a result the total number of credit relationships diminishes, and increasingly those that remain are validated by the SLS ideology. The situation returns to its starting point. In terms of x and y, the situation follows a cyclical career, as shown in Figure 11. For the total picture of this career, we must go into three dimensions, projecting this two-dimensional cycle upward until it cuts the surface of the three-dimensional graph, as illustrated in Figure 12.

If we plot the level of credit against time, we obtain an oscillating graph containing the fold catastrophe,[7] as shown in Figure 13. This is the graph for the level of credit within *one* clan; for the total picture it is necessary to sum all the clans. The main prestations occur sequentially over a period of several months. This means that the graph of credit level against time for the entire system will be somewhat softened and, in particular, the extraordinary ingredient, the fold catastrophe zone, will disappear and be replaced by an ordinary ingredient, a steep slope linking peak and valley; that is, we will obtain the curve for the credit cycle, as in Figure 3.

The existence of the turning point is now explained without recourse to external intervention. The actions of individual pig breeders, in aggregate, transform the system to which each belongs, yet which is nothing other than the totality of such individual contributions. This transformation propels the system into, *and through,* the cusp, and in consequence the most likely outcome, before the system leaves the cusp, is a sudden catastrophic collapse in the level of credit, and the least likely outcome is that there will be no such change.

The protagonists of catastrophe theory place great emphasis on the way in which, with a single simple picture, one can describe something that would require pages and pages of verbal description. The claim goes even further, for with the appropriate picture one can describe clearly, concisely, and without contradiction something that either cannot be adequately described in words at all or else requires a verbal description that is full of seeming contradictions and tautologies. One such apparent tautol-

FIGURE 11

*The Cyclical Pattern of Increase and Decrease of Validating and
Invalidating Relationships*

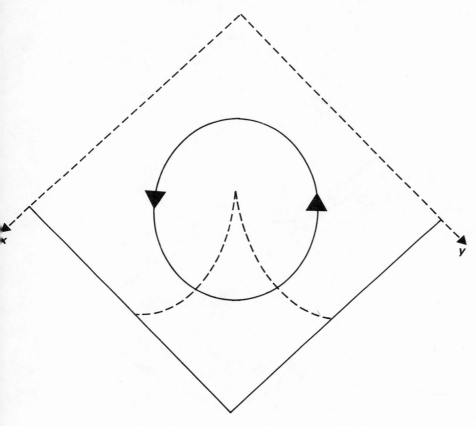

ogy is the very Keynesian statement I have just made about the totality
being nothing other than the sum of its parts. But when one looks instead
to the catastrophe picture, of which this is so inadequate a verbal description, the tautology disappears and the normally intractable problem of the
relationship between micro (the individual) and macro (the totality) is
resolved. This is why the catastrophe theory part of the explanation is so
crucial; equipped with this topological formulation, we can now move
smoothly, without recourse to any conventions and without sinking into
tautologies, from the individual pig breeder to the total system of which he
is but one element.

FIGURE 12

Representation of the Catastrophe Surface Linking the Total Number of Relationships (x), *the Ratio of Invalidating to Validating Relationships* (y), *and the Level of Credit* (z)

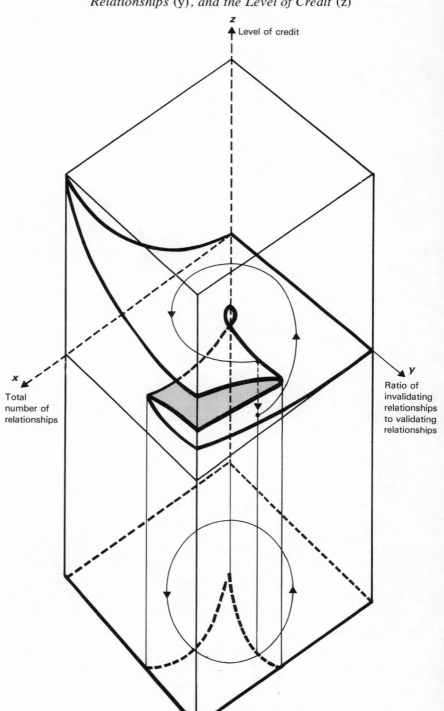

FIGURE 13

The Level of Credit Through Time

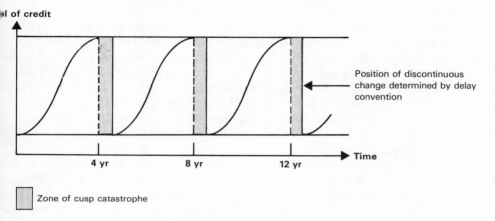

Zone of cusp catastrophe

CONCLUSION

Two tasks remain: first, to try to dispel some of the mysticism that at present surrounds explanations in terms of catastrophe geometry;[8] second, to ask what, if anything, the significance of all this is.

In W. H. Auden's expedition ("The Quest") the members were:

. . . sound on Expectation
Had there been situations to be in;
Unluckily they were their situations. . . .

The same is true of the New Guinea pig breeder. The cyclical career traced over the three-dimensional graph is a convenient, clear, and concise way of describing just this sort of relationship between observer and observed, between actor and situation. The graph, with its cusp catastrophe, provides a way of depicting the probabilities of certain social phenomena—these phenomena being, in general, social actions in relation to which there exist partially contradictory ideologies. The cyclical career traces out a particular sequence of such probabilities, each of which, so far as any pig breeder is concerned, defines his situation. It follows, therefore, that the answer to the question "What forces constrain the situation to pass through the particular sequence of probabilities described by this career?" is "the rational maximizing behavior of the individual pig breeders."

A simple transaction theory approach will describe this rational behavior throughout the upswing, until it enters the cusp, and throughout the downswing, once it has left the cusp. The SLS ideology insists that there are, in the formation of relationships, certain rules that should be adhered to. The Big Man ideology urges that the way to get on is, if need be, to ignore the rules. The problem for the rational pig breeder lies in deciding which of these partially contradictory counsels he should heed. During the upswing, if he heeds the former he will find his expectations confounded, while if he heeds the latter he will find his expectations confirmed. Being a rational man he soon adopts the ideology that most closely relates expectation and actuality. Thus, during the upswing, the Big Man ideology becomes dominant and the SLS ideology becomes submerged. During the downswing, the converse applies and the SLS ideology becomes dominant and the Big Man ideology is submerged.

Within the cusp rational behavior becomes more difficult. The Big Man ideology which has served the breeder so well during the upswing still urges expansive confidence, while all around he sees the desirability of such behavior negated by bankruptcies and gathering uncertainty. This contradiction and uncertainty is the direct result of the two-humped probability distributions that define the cusp. The level of credit will either rise or fall, but he cannot know which; the only thing he can be sure of is that the worst thing he can do is to do nothing. Of course, the situations of two individuals are never identical, and one may still be cheerfully extending credit while another is glumly trying to call it in.

The basic assumption of transaction theory—that the dialectical relationship between values and behavior ensures that values (ideologies) are continually modified in the direction of consistency, integration, and systematization—is not valid within the cusp, where no such direction exists.[9] The cusp is a geometrical representation of the irreducible contradiction of coexisting ideologies.

In trying to assess what, if anything, the significance of all this is (apart from the sheer delight involved in trying to solve difficult problems), it occurs to me that although this catastrophe theory approach succeeds where even the Hansen-Samuelson model fails, it is nevertheless wholly in the spirit of Keynes. Thus, if it has any implications, they should have the effect of improving upon Keynes rather than rejecting him (which, with our post-Keynesian ills, is the popular trend at present).

Keynes quite deliberately entitled his great work *The General Theory of Employment, Interest and Money* so as to parallel Einstein's "General Theory of Relativity," for he saw his theory as subsuming classical economics as a special case in the same way that Einstein's theory subsumed Newtonian mechanics. Catastrophe theory holds out the prospect of doing a Keynes on Keynes. Keynes made an expedient assumption—his famous fundamental psychological law—concerning the point at which economic theory must take note of social considerations and chose to regard that input as a constant. As the pig cycle goes through its violent ups and downs, it is all too evident that the Enga pig breeders are not "disposed by and large and on the average" to save a constant proportion of any increase in income that they may receive. The marginal propensity to consume is a constant *only in the special case*. In general, it varies as a result, not of economic forces, but of the social and cultural forces related to changes in the amount of certainty within the system—the tug-of-Hobbesian-war. Anthropologists have been remiss in not trying very hard to discover what these forces might be, but now, rather belatedly, it looks as though catastrophe theory will allow us to write the general equation of which Keynesian theory, with its social constant, is the special case. This, it seems, is what we stand to gain by bringing together the West and the Rest, economics and anthropology.

NOTES

1. The account that follows has therefore been pieced together from a great many different (and sometimes conflicting) sources. Difficulties are compounded by the need to see the pig cycle as a dynamic and changing process, which means that it is not possible to fall back on that convenient fiction, the ethnographic present. The most important of these sources are Oliver (1949, 1955), Newman (1965), Meggitt (1957a,b, 1958, 1959, 1965, 1967, 1970), Williams (1937), Ross (1936), Strathern (1966–1967, 1974), Lepervanche (1965), Langress (1964), Salisbury (1962), Pouwer (1961), Bus (1951), Ryan (1955, 1959), Glasse (1959a,b,), Read (1951, 1952, 1966), Brown and Brookfield (1959), Elkin (1953), Gitlow (1947), Bulmer (1960), and Rappaport (1967).

2. An open-ended linear system will remain steady state if the rate at which new goods are fed into the system is equal to the rate at which goods are being lost along the sequence *plus* the rate at which goods are flowing out of its open ends. If those open ends become connected to one another, then the goods passing out of them are no longer lost to the system—they are fed back into it. For such an annular system to become steady state, the rate at which new goods are fed into the system will have to be drastically reduced until it equals only the rate at which goods are being lost in the system. In the *kula* case an armshell or necklace increases in value as its history increases: an object's value is a function of its original quality, the illustriousness of the hands through which it has passed, and the number of times it has completed the circuit. So, for the total value within the system to approach a steady state, the rate of input of new objects will have to decrease even further.

3. I have not, unfortunately, had the opportunity of first-hand field work research. It may be that, in trying to place some library flesh upon theoretical bones, I have inadvertently distorted the ethnography. While this would be regrettable, it would not invalidate the present argument. The explanation that follows holds so long as the SLS ideology imposes *some* constraints while the Big Man ideology does not.

4. For the statement of the theorem, see Thom (1969). A nontechnical article describing the theorem and some of its implications is Zeeman (1971).

5. It would not be effective, for instance, if its time scale were of the same order as or slower than that of the changes in the values of x and y.

270   MICHAEL THOMPSON

6. Strictly speaking, this is not a convention but a theorem. Unfortunately, a name, once given, is not easily taken away.

7. It should be stressed that the term "catastrophe" (as used, for instance, in geology) refers to sudden, discontinuous change. As such it is value free. It is up to us, in any specific situation, to decide whether this sudden discontinuous change is a good thing or a bad thing. For example, many engineers have fallen into the trap of assuming that catastrophes are intrinsically undesirable. Of course, from an engineer's point of view they often are, but not always. Fluidics, for instance, depends on a cusp catastrophe for its bimodal stable flow patterns (see Chilver 1975).

8. For example, see the review of the published results of the fourth Serbelloni conference on theoretical biology (Anon. 1973) in which an anonymous Anglo-Saxon castigates Thom for going (in his opinion) beyond catastrophe theory and linking biological evolution to generative grammar, and Zeeman for producing untestable models linking Lamarckian evolution and dreaming. Thom and Zeeman should perhaps, like good generals, study the enemy's high command and not play into their hands in this careless way!

9. Nor, strictly speaking, is it valid outside the cusp. However, outside the cusp, transaction theory does give a static, local, and approximate description of a dynamic process that can only be fully accounted for by the global picture provided by catastrophe theory.

REFERENCES

Anon. 1973. Review of C. H. Waddington, ed., *Towards a Theoretical Biology,* Vol. IV. In *Times Literary Supplement,* 18 May
Barth, F. 1966. *Models of Social Organization.* Occasional Papers of the Royal Anthropological Institute, No. 23. London.
Brown, P., and H. C. Brookfield. 1959. Chimbu land and society. *Oceania,* 30: 1–75.
Bulmer, R. 1960. Political aspects of the Moka ceremonial exchange system among the Kyaka People of the Western Highlands of New Guinea. *Oceania,* 31: 1–13.
Bus, G. A. M. 1951. The Te festival of gift exchange in Enga. *Anthropos,* 46: 813–824.
Chilver, H. 1975. Wider implications of catastrophe theory. *Nature,* 254 (5499): 381.
Cohen, P. 1967. Economic analysis and economic man. In R. Firth, ed., *Themes in Economic Anthropology,* pp. 91–118. ASA Monograph No. 6. London: Tavistock.
Dalton, G. 1961. Economic theory and primitive society. *American Anthropologist,* 63: 1–25.
Elkin, A. P. 1953. Delayed exchange in Wabag Sub-District, Central Highlands of New Guinea, with notes on social organisation. *Oceania,* 23: 161–201.
Falkenberg, J. 1962. *Kin and Totem.* Oslo: Oslo University Press.
Frankenberg, R. 1967. Economic anthropology. In R. Firth, ed., *Themes in Economic Anthropology,* pp. 47–89. ASA Monograph No. 6. London: Tavistock.
Gitlow, A. L. 1947. *Economics of the Mount Hagen Tribes, New Guinea.* Monographs of the American Ethnological Society, Vol. 12. New York: J. J. Augustin.

Glasse, R. M. 1959a. Revenge and redress among the Huli. *Mankind,* 5: 273–289.
———. 1959b. The Huli descent system: a preliminary account. *Oceania,* 29: 171–184.
Joy, L. 1967. The relationship between economics and anthropology. In R. Firth, ed., *Themes in Economic Anthropology,* pp. 175–189. ASA Monograph No. 6. London: Tavistock.
Keynes, J. M. 1936. *The General Theory of Employment, Interest and Money.* London: Macmillan.
Langress, L. L. 1964. Some problems in the conceptualization of Highlands Social Structures. *American Anthropologist* (special publication), 66 (4, Part 2): 162–182.
Lepervanche, M. de. 1965. Descent, residence and leadership in the New Guinea Highlands. *Oceania,* 38: 134–189.
Malinowski, B. 1922. *Argonauts of the Western Pacific.* London: Routledge.
Matthews, R. C. O. 1959. *The Trade Cycle.* Cambridge: Cambridge University Press.
Meggitt, M. J. 1957a. The Enga of the New Guinea Highlands: some preliminary observations. *Oceania,* 28: 253–330.
———. 1957b. The Ipili of the Porgera Valley, Western Highlands District, Territory of New Guinea. *Oceania,* 28: 31–55.
———. 1958. Mae-Enga time reckoning and calendar. *Man,* 58 (87): 74–77.
———. 1959. Mae-Enga political organisation. *Mankind,* 5: 133–137.
———. 1965. *The Lineage System of the Mae-Enga.* Edinburgh: Oliver and Boyd.
———. 1967. The pattern of leadership among the Mae-Enga of New Guinea. *Anthropological Forum,* 2 (1): 20–35.
———. 1970. Mae-Enga religion. In P. Lawrence and M. J. Meggitt, eds., *Gods, Ghosts and Men in New Guinea,* pp. 105–131. Melbourne: Oxford University Press.
Newman, P. L. 1965. *Knowing the Gururumba.* New York: Holt. Rinehart and Winston.
Oliver, D. L. 1949. Human relations and language in a Papuan speaking tribe. *Papers of the Peabody Museum,* Vol. 29, No. 2, pp. 1–38. Cambridge, Mass.: Harvard University Press.
———. 1955. *A Solomon Islands Society: Kinship and Leadership among the Siuai of Bougainville.* Cambridge, Mass.: Harvard University Press.
Pospisil, L. 1963. *The Kapauku of West New Guinea.* New York: Holt, Rinehart and Winston.
Pouwer, J. 1961. New Guinea as a field for ethnological study. *Bijdragen tot de taal-, land-, en volkenkunde,* 117: 1–24.
Rappaport, R. A. 1967. *Pigs for the Ancestors: Ritual in the Ecology of a New Guinea People.* New Haven: Yale University Press.
Read, K. E. 1951. The Gahuku-Gama of the Central Highlands. *South Pacific,* 5 (8): 154–164.
———. 1952. Land in Central Highlands, New Guinea. *South Pacific,* 6 (7): 440–449.
———. 1966. *The High Valley.* London: Allen and Unwin.
Reay, M. 1959. *The Kuma: Freedom and Conformity in the New Guinea Highlands.* Melbourne: Melbourne University Press on behalf of the Australian National University.
Ross, W. A. 1936. Ethnological notes on the Mount Hagen Tribes, (Mandated Territory of New Guinea) with special reference to the tribe called Mogei. *Anthropos,* 31: 341–363.

Ryan, D. J. 1955. Clan organisation in the Mendi Valley, Southern Highlands of Papua-New Guinea. *Oceania*, 26: 79–90.
——. 1959. Clan formation in the Mendi Valley. *Oceania*, 29: 257–289.
Salisbury, R. F. 1962. *From Stone to Steel: Economic Consequences of a Technological Change in New Guinea*. Melbourne: Melbourne University Press on behalf of the Australian National University.
Stanner, W. E. H. 1934. Ceremonial economics of the Mulluk Mulluk and Madngella tribes of the Daly River, North Australia, a preliminary paper. *Oceania*, 4: 156–175, 458–471.
Strathern, A. 1966–1967. Ceremonial exchange in the Mount Hagen area. Ph.D. thesis. Cambridge University.
——. 1974. *Onka's Big Moka*. Television film in the series "The Disappearing World." London: Granada Television International.
Thom, R. 1969. Topological models in biology. *Topology*, 8: 313–335.
——. 1972. *Stabilité structurelle et morphogenèse*. Paris: Benjamin.
Thompson, M. 1968. Some problems in the study of exchange structures. B. Litt. thesis. Oxford University.
Waddington, C. H., ed. 1968–1972. *Towards a Theoretical Biology*, Vols. I, II, III, IV. Edinburgh: International Union of Biological Sciences.
Weiner, N. 1948. *Cybernetics*. Cambridge, Mass.: MIT Press.
Williams, F. E. 1937. The natives of Mount Hagen, Papua. *Man*, 37 (114): 90–96.
Wilson, The Rev. John M., ed. n.d. Entry under "Hog" in *The Farmer's Dictionary; or a Cyclopaedia of Agriculture, in All Its Departments, Principles, Methods, Recent Improvements, and Business Affairs, as Taught and Practised by the Most Distinguished British Agriculturalists of the Present Day*. Edinburgh and London: A. Fullarton and Co.
Zeeman, E. C. 1971. The geometry of catastrophe. *Times Literary Supplement*, 10 December.

Notes on Contributors

BUCKLEY, JOAN   Born 1940. M.Phil. (London). At present teaching development studies in Botswana.

CRUMP, S. THOMAS   Born 1929. England. First degree in mathematics, law, and anthropology. Ph.D. (London). Senior Lecturer in Anthropology, University of Amsterdam. Field work among the Maya of Mexico and Guatemala. Author of *Law for Everyman* and *Man and His Kind*.

GARBETT, G. KINGSLEY   Born 1935. England. Ph.D. (Manchester). Reader in Anthropology at the University of Adelaide, South Australia. Field work among the Korekore and Zezuru in Rhodesia and the Sena and Mang'anja in Malawi. Author of papers on social change, labor migration, spirit mediumship, methodology, and mathematical techniques.

GOODY, JACK   Born 1919. England. Ph.D. (Cantab.). William Wyse Professor of Social Anthropology at the University of Cambridge. Field work among the LoDagaba and Gonja of Ghana. Author of several studies of these peoples and of works in comparative sociology and demography. Recent publications include *Production and Reproduction* (1977) and *The Domestication of the Savage Mind* (1978).

INGOLD, TIM   Born 1948. England. Ph.D. (Cantab.). Lecturer in Social Anthropology at the University of Manchester. Field work among the Skolt Lapps in northeast Finland. Author of *The Skolt Lapps Today*.

MITCHELL, HILARY FLEGG   1918–1976. M.A. (Witwatersrand). Formerly Research Associate, Department of Social Preventive Medicine, University of Manchester. Research mainly in the epidemiology of cancer in Lourenco Marques (now Maputo) and Bulawayo. Most recent publication: *Aspects of Urbanisation and Age Structure in Lourenco Marques, 1957* (Lusaka: Institute for African Studies, 1975).

MITCHELL, J. CLYDE   Born 1918. South Africa. D.Phil. (Oxon). Official Fellow. Nuffield College, Oxford. Field work among Yao of Malawi and in towns in Zambia and Rhodesia. Formerly Professor of African Studies, University College of Rhodesia and Nyasaland, and Professor of Urban Sociology, University of Manchester. Publications on urbanism, urbanization, labor circulation, and social networks.

273

ROMNEY, A. KIMBALL   Born 1925. U.S.A. Ph.D. (Harvard). Professor of Anthropology, University of California, Irvine. Field work in Central America. Extensive publications, particularly on cognitive anthropology and methods. Editor, with Roger Shepard and Sara Nerlove, of *Multidimensional Scaling: Theory and Applications in the Behavioral Sciences* (2 vols., 1972).

SPENCER, PAUL   Born 1932. England. First degree in mechanical sciences and anthropology. D.Phil. (Oxon). Lecturer in African Anthropology, School of Oriental and African Studies, London. Formerly staff member at the Institute for Operational Research (Tavistock Institute, London). Field work among the Samburu, Rendille, and Maasai of Kenya. Author of *The Samburu* (1965), *Nomads in Alliance* (1973).

THOMPSON, MICHAEL   Born 1937. England. Ph.D. (London). Visiting Fellow at the International Institute for Environment and Society, Berlin. Field work in Nepal. Author of *Rubbish Theory: The Creation and Destruction of Value* (1979).

Index

1 2 3 4 5 6 7 8 9 10 11 12 13   89 88 87 86 85 84 83 82 81 80